留学中国

Crossing Paths

Living and Learning in China

AN INTERMEDIATE CHINESE COURSE

SIMPLIFIED CHARACTER EDITION

HONG GANG JIN
靳洪刚

DE BAO XU
许德宝

WITH

DER-LIN CHAO
赵德麟

YEA-FEN CHEN
陈雅芬

MIN CHEN
陈旻

Photography by
Laurie A. Wittlinger

Cheng & Tsui Company
Boston • Worcester

Published by

Cheng & Tsui Company
25 West Street
Boston, MA 02111-1213 USA
Fax (617) 426-3669
www.cheng-tsui.com
"Bringing Asia to the World"™

Printed in the U.S.A.

09 08 07 06   10 9 8 7 6 5 4 3 2

Library of Congress Control Number: 2002115107

(Simplified Character Edition)

Book and 2 Audio CDs, ISBN 0-88727-370-X

To our daughter Ingrid

目录

课文
(Texts)

附录
(Appendixes)

Acknowledgments

We would like to express our heartfelt thanks to those people who have been most instrumental to this project. Among them are our special student, Laurie Wittlinger, who took spectacular photographs for the book while she was a project assistant at Hamilton College, and the students of the Associated Colleges in China (Hamilton College's China Program) who appear in the photographs. Without these visually valuable pictures, the book would not be as effective and attractive as it is.

We also deeply appreciate the professors, instructors, and students of Associated Colleges in China (ACC) for their valuable comments and suggestions at the various stages of the project. Among them are Professor Hsin-hsin Liang who offered many valuable suggestions based on her own first-hand teaching experiences and ACC instructors Min Chen, Chunxue Yang, Wenzheng Liu, Fei Wang, Chen Wang, and many others who proof-read early drafts and made comments. Our special thanks also go to our four-year student assistant, Megan Manchester, for her English editing at the initial stage, and our Chinese students Joshua Jenkins and Benjamin Zoll for their time and efforts on this project.

We would also like to acknowledge the people who have assisted us throughout the six years of the project development. Among them are Pei Pei who has been a hard working assistant in collecting authentic materials for us, Dana Hubbard for her kind assistance in picture scanning and editing, and Amy James for her assistance in selecting pictures.

We are especially grateful for Vivian Ling who has done a superb job editing the book and providing the most valuable comments and suggestions.

We would like to thank Jill Cheng for her support for this project and her faith in us, and Sandra Korinchak, Production Manager at Cheng & Tsui, who worked patiently with us to ensure the quality of the book.

前言

　　《留学中国》是为学过两至三个学期以上中文的学生设计的语言文化教科书。这本教科书以语言功能为中心，旨在通过在中国的各种学习、生活实例以及课外活动让学生了解并掌握在国外留学所需的一系列汉语语言结构、表达方法和交流方式。

　　自1997年开始，《留学中国》就在美国部分大学、美国政府机关、北京的ACC汉语中心和其他语言项目进行试用，至今已经修改了五版，实验使用了近五年。《留学中国》主要由课本和配合课本的光盘组成。

一、教学目的与教学设计

　　多年的教学实践和理论研究告诉我们，中级汉语教学的目标应集中在以下三个方面：第一、培养学生在目标语国家进行生活和思想文化交流的基本能力；第二、培养学生有目的地、有效地使用整句或段落来表达思想、进行交流，以作好向篇章过渡的准备；第三，训练学生利用已知信息和已经掌握的语言结构对新的语言信息进行科学推理、猜测的能力，以便在真实语境下进行语言文化交流。除了以上三个方面，我们还认为中级汉语的学习是进入目标语社会、与当地人进行思想文化交流的一个十分关键的阶段；中级汉语的教学目标应放在真情实景的教学上，不仅应该为学生去目标语国家留学或在目标语国家生活和学习作好充分的准备，而且应该让学生能最大限度地利用语言环境进行语言文化方面的学习和交流。基于以上几个方面的教学目的，我们设计了《留学中国》一书。下面是我们在设计全书时遵循的一些原则：

　　（一）在教材的话题选择上，尽量选择与留学生活、学习密切相关的交际情景及交际话题。做到每一课的话题都有一定的真实性、客观性以及实用性，让学生感觉到语言学习是一种有目的的真实交流。

　　（二）在课文文体的选择上，尽量采用叙述、描述与对话相结合的方式，以介绍生活和学习的方式引出交际话题。

　　（三）在教学重点的设计上，打破以前语法重点就是教学重点的旧框框，将教学重点放在以交流为中心的多个语言层次上，不局限于较复杂的语法结构，而是从词汇、语法、语义、语用等多个层次出发决定每课的重点。此外，我们还将课文中出现的语言结构分为两大类：一类是交际价值较高的重点结构，另一类为语法或语义较复杂、容易成为理解障碍的基本结构。第一类是每课练习的重点，要通过不同类型和不同形式的解释与练习让学生掌握并使用自如；第二类是帮助学生预习课文、进行课堂有效交流的必要知识，大都以参考阅读和课文脚注的形式出现。

（四）在教学安排上，坚持以句型串词汇的教学法，即句型领先、词汇辅助的原则。首先帮助学生理解和巩固句型在交流中的作用以及在整句中的基本位置和使用限制，然后帮助学生建立词汇和句型的联系以正确运用词汇。使用这种方法可以避免以词汇为中心的教材常见弊端（例如，学生往往出现语言表达零散、简单，交际不连贯问题等）。

（五）在练习设计上，采用以语言结构为中心和以语言功能为中心的两种练习。首先让学生有重点地练习在交际中必须用到的一些结构和词汇，在此基础上，再让学生将所学结构和词汇运用到与之相应的语言功能上。语言功能的练习突出真实语境下的交流以及对学习策略的培养，如猜测能力，推理能力等等。

（六）在教材的版面设计上，采用各种媒体及图象信息加强语料和练习的真实性及视觉效果。

二、课文内容及设计

《留学中国》共有课文十二篇，话题包括：机场会友、宿舍安排、饭馆点菜、与中国家庭交流、上中文课、去医疗中心看病、骑自行车看北京、去书店买书、给朋友过生日、公共交通、与小贩讨价还价、郊外游览等。围绕每一个主话题，课文均介绍一系列与之相关的交际功能，例如询问、打听、描述、叙述、列举事例、解释、说明等等。此外，这十二个话题集中反映了美国留学生在中国学习和生活的真实情况。每一个情景的素材均为作者与学生在京共同生活时的所经所见。例如"学校附近的饭馆"一课即以真实的语言环境为基础，向学生介绍中国饭馆的情况以及如何在中国饭馆点菜、吃饭等。课文所介绍的饭馆既反映了北京饭馆的特色，又具有其地方的独特之处。

每篇课文一般由三个主要部分组成：课文、语言重点和练习。

（一）每课的课文部分均有三个分项：课文、生词以及课文注释。课文部分一般由两个部分组成，以两种文体呈现主题。第一部分是对主题的介绍，采用第一人称叙述形式；第二部分是与主题有关的对话，采用两个人的对话形式。例如，"外国留学生宿舍"一课的开始先由叙述性的文字介绍宿舍的布局、设备和条件，然后以对话的形式介绍和展现留学生宿舍的真实情景，角色由叙述者和宿舍的服务员两人组成，对话生动真实。每课生词的编纂按出现顺序编号，书后附有全书生词索引，以便于查找和使用。课文注释部分将一些语法较为复杂、容易混淆的词汇以及文化知识进行详细解释、辨析。在排版上，课文注释与有关的词条都有数字编号，同时列出有关例句和解释，以方便学生对比查找。

（二）语言重点着重解释有交际价值的句型，一般每课有八到十二个。每一个重点句型下都附有课文原句，以便于查找学习。句型附有详细的英文解释及相关词语辨析以说明句型使用的规则及限制。在英文解释之下，一般列举两个以上运用目标句型的例句以进一步说明句型使用的上下文及词汇搭配规则等。

（三）练习部分包括两种类型的活动：语言形式练习和语言功能练习。语言形式练习旨在加强学生对语言结构和词汇的掌握，通过回答问题、完成对话、听力练习、翻译和阅读短文等形式使学生在课下有重点地练习和复习课上所学的语言结构及其使用规则。在语言形式练习的基础上，学生进而转入语言功能练习。语言功能练习一般有以下几种形式：

1、不加删改和详细注释的真实情景练习：每课一般附有三个到四个有图片或照片的真实情景由学生通过其语言知识、猜测及推理能力回答问题。例如，学生须看一个广告，然后根据广告描述饭馆的价钱、服务及气氛，并向其他同学推荐饭菜等。

2、讨论：讨论通过不同方面的问题和话题为学生提供自由延伸和扩展语言功能和知识的机会，同时也提供学生与学生、学生与老师之间的进一步交流的机会。

3、作文：通过写作练习来进一步强化本课所学的语言功能与结构。

4、语言实践：通过课外的一系列有目的的活动来进一步加强和巩固课上所学的知识。

5、看图讨论。

我们希望通过教材的新尝试来推动中级汉语教学，使之更上一层楼。

靳洪刚，许德宝
纽约克灵顿小镇
2002年10月

To Students

Welcome to *Crossing Paths: Living and Learning in China.* This set of textbooks uses authentic and multimedia materials to help you acquire the basic communication skills required in daily interaction with Chinese speaking people. Whether you are planning to go to China or you are in China, *Crossing Paths: Living and Learning in China* will help you establish a solid foundation for interaction and communication with Chinese people and to help you move on to the advanced level of language proficiency.

The topics and settings of the lessons in this text all come from the real experiences of hundreds of students who studied abroad in China and from professors who taught and lived with students in China. These topics have been rated as the most important and useful ones for living and learning in China.

In *Crossing Paths: Living and Learning in China* each lesson consists of three important parts: the text, key sentence structures, and exercises. In order to help you use this textbook effectively and master as much material in the lesson as possible, we would like to make the following suggestions:

Text

We suggest that you start your class preparation with the text rather than vocabulary. Before going to your daily Chinese class, read through the text carefully at least two or three times. The first time, read along with the audio CD and try to get the gist of the story, for example, the topic sentence, the main ideas, the characters involved, the setting, etc. The second time, read for more detailed information, for example, the factual information supporting the main topic and the relationship of the setting and characters to the main idea. At the same time, you should mark down unfamiliar words and sentences and check them against the vocabulary list and grammar notes. Each time you read the text, try to comprehend the text by asking yourself questions and answering them according to the text. The questions listed in Item I of Tasks on Language Forms can be used for this purpose. After you have finished reading the text twice, write down any questions you have about the text. It is vitally important that you are familiar with the story before going to class.

Vocabulary

We suggest that you study the vocabulary list in the lesson along with the text. You can take the following three steps to learn the new words. First, while reading the text, highlight unfamiliar words and check them against the vocabulary list for Pinyin and English meaning. Second, read the sentence containing the new word(s) and try to comprehend the meaning of the entire sentence. Finally, go over the text in its entirety with the CD. In this way, you will learn new words in context rather than in isolation.

Notes

In each lesson, notes on the text are provided at the bottom of the text page. You should read them either during or after the second round of text reading. The numbers of the notes correspond to the numbers marked in the text; these numbers will help you understand the context of each note. The notes are not meant to be key structures for you to master and practice during class time. They are, however, very helpful for comprehending the text, reviewing the learnt grammar, distinguishing similar words and structures, and understanding the cultural context.

Key Sentence Patterns

Key sentence patterns are listed after the text in each lesson. Each pattern is accompanied by an original sentence from the text, a detailed grammar and usage explanation in English, and two sentences in Chinese exemplifying the usage of the structures. While studying the sentence patterns, you should pay special attention to the following three elements: (a) the communicative context of the structure; (b) the rules and constraints of the structure; and (c) the examples on the usage of the structure. It is important that you go over the sentence patterns before coming to class so that you can be ready to use the structures to engage in interaction with your instructor and your classmates. We believe conscious use of the patterns in your conversation will help increase the level of sophistication, efficiency, and accuracy in your communication.

Exercises

1. Form-oriented Tasks

A variety of form-oriented tasks are provided at the end of each lesson to help you master the key structures and vocabulary of the lesson and to help improve your ability to listen, read, and discuss in Chinese. The tasks include question-answer, dialogue completion, listening comprehension, reading comprehension, and English to Chinese translation exercises. We suggest that, while working on these exercises, you remind yourself of the new sentence patterns and new vocabulary learned in that lesson and in previous lessons. It is important to make a conscious effort to use these newly acquired structures to express your thoughts and feelings.

2. Function-oriented Tasks

After you are familiar with language forms, you must learn to apply your linguistic and cultural knowledge to real life situations. A variety of function-oriented tasks are provided in the exercises of each lesson to help you use language forms to achieve communicative functions effectively. These tasks include: (a) activities involving authentic situations; (b) discussions of various aspects of the theme of the lesson, such as "birthday celebration in different countries", "traffic and transportation in large cities", "the single-child generation", etc.; (c) language practica, which center on the same theme but are conducted outside of the classroom with Chinese speaking people. These exercises help extend your learning beyond the classroom; (d) essay writing on given topics; and (e) pictocomp, which uses picture sets and your own imagination to encourage creativity with newly acquired language forms and functions.

You should keep in mind that we purposely selected materials that are unedited and authentic for you to read and comprehend, for example, real advertisements, newspaper segments, brochures, and photographs. Because of the nature of these materials, you should expect to encounter unknown words and new structures. While you are working on performance tasks, we suggest that you keep an open mind and try to use your language knowledge, context, and cultural information to make an educated guess about the materials. Ultimately these "risk-taking" activities will prove to be helpful in developing language-learning strategies, such as tolerance of ambiguity and the ability to infer meaning by guessing and using contextual clues.

An Intermediate Chinese Course

第一课 到北京去留学

天安门广场

课文

今天是我最兴奋的一天，因为我要到北京去学中文了。从一年级起我就开始计划⁽¹⁾去北京留学，今天这个理想终于要实现了。尽管我在美国已经学过几个学期的中文，但是说话的时候还是非常紧张。这次去北京，我一定要好好儿⁽²⁾利用这个机会学中文。

我坐的班机是美国西北航空公司直飞北京的。一上飞机就碰到了大学的同学王义。王义的家就在北京，放了暑假正好⁽³⁾回大陆看父母。见到王义，我觉得非常高兴。

王：哎，周玲，你怎么也坐这班飞机？

周：对，我去北京学中文，打算暑假学两个月，秋天三个月。你呢？

王：我回家看父母。

周：是吗？

王：北京是学习中文最理想的地方，学完这几个月后你的中文一定会有很大的进步。

Notes (1) "计划" vs. "打算"：Both words can function as a verb or noun, and both mean "plan to do something"; plan "计划" is more formal than "打算"， and can be used in both written and spoken form, whereas "打算" is used mostly in the spoken language.

(2) "好好儿 V"："好好儿" is an adverb that often precedes a verb to mean "properly" or "well". It can mean different things in different contexts; e.g. "好好儿玩儿" means "to have fun"，"好好儿利用" means "to make good use of"， "好好儿念书" means "to study hard". Sometimes the particle "地" (de in neutral tone) is added, with no difference in meaning, e.g. "好好儿地学习"。

(3) "正好"： Here, this term means "by coincidence, as it happens, happen to", e.g. "他正好经过这里"。(He happened to pass by here.) See more notes and examples in Lesson 9.

周：我希望是这样。

王：这是你第一次去北京吗？

周：不是。五年以前，我和妈妈度假去过三个礼拜。现在的中国跟那个时候一定大不一样了。

王：对啦。中国这几年的变化可⁽⁴⁾大啦，你到北京一看就会知道。下了飞机以后有朋友来接你吗？

周：没有。可是我有去学校的地图。听说学校离机场不远，坐出租汽车或者机场大巴都行。你知道哪个比较方便？

王：要看你的行李多不多。要是不多，坐机场大巴比较便宜，十六块钱就到市中心；要是行李多，倒是坐出租汽车比较方便。

周：那我得换一些人民币。机场有换钱的地方吗？

王：有，一出海关就有。我也需要换一点儿。

周：好极了。到时候⁽⁵⁾我们一块儿去。

生词

1. 留学	liúxué	*VO.*	to study abroad
2. 最	zuì	*Adv.*	most, -est
3. 兴奋	xīngfèn	*Adj.*	excited
4. 计划	jìhuà	*V/N.*	to plan; plan
5. 理想	lǐxiǎng	*N/Adj.*	ideal; ideal dream
6. 终于	zhōngyú	*Adv.*	finally

Notes ⁽⁴⁾ "可" + Adj.: In addition to the meaning of "but" and "however", "可" can also be used for both emphasis and contrast, meaning "really" or "very". At the same time, the speaker is making an assumption: "It was not this way before", e.g. "这种事情现在可多了". (Nowadays such a thing is quite common.) Using "可" here implies that "这种事情以前不多". (This thing wasn't common before.) This usage is mostly used in the colloquial.

⁽⁵⁾ "到时候" is a set phrase that functions as a time expression. It means "when the time comes", "by the time when ...", e.g. "我下个月去中国，到时候我一定去看你". (I am going to China next month. When I get there I will definitely come and see you.)

7. 实现	shíxiàn	*V.*	to realize, to become reality
8. 尽管	jǐnguǎn	*Conj.*	though, even though
9. 学期	xuéqī	*N.*	semester
10. 紧张	jǐnzhāng	*Adj.*	nervous
11. 利用	lìyòng	*V.*	to use, to utilize
12. 机会	jīhuì	*N.*	opportunity
13. 航空公司	hángkōng gōng sī	*NP.*	airline company
14. 班机	bānjī	*N.*	flight
15. 直飞	zhífēi	*VP.*	to fly directly to
16. 碰到	pèngdào	*VP.*	to encounter
17. 王义	Wáng Yì	*Personal N.*	Wang Yi
18. 放暑假	fàngshǔ jià	*VO.*	to have a summer vacation (放假: to have a vacation, 暑: summer)
19. 大陆	dà lù	*Place N.*	mainland China
20. 周玲	Zhōu Líng	*Personal N.*	Zhou Ling
21. 打算	dǎsuàn	*V/N.*	to plan; plan
22. 秋天	qiūtiān	*N.*	autumn
23. 进步	jìnbù	*N/V.*	progress; to make progress
24. 希望	xīwàng	*V/N.*	to hope; hope
25. 度假	dùjià	*VO.*	to spend a vacation
26. 礼拜	lǐ bài	*N.*	week (星期)
27. 变化	biàn huà	*N.*	change
28. 接	jiē	*V.*	to pick up (someone), to receive
29. 地图	dì tú	*N.*	map
30. 听说	tīng shuō	*VP.*	it is said that, (I) heard that
31. 机场	jī chǎng	*N.*	airport
32. 出租汽车	chū zū qì chē	*NP.*	taxi
33. 机场大巴	jī chǎng dà bā	*NP.*	airport bus
34. 比较	bǐ jiào	*Adv/V.*	relatively, quite; to compare
35. 方便	fāng biàn	*Adj.*	convenient
36. 要看	yào kàn	*VP.*	it depends on...
37. 行李	xíng li	*N.*	luggage

38. 市中心	shì zhōng xīn	N.	downtown, city center
39. 换	huàn	V.	to exchange, to change
40. 人民币	rén mín bì	N.	renminbi (RMB) (Chinese currency)
41. 海关	hǎi guān	N.	customs
42. 需要	xū yào	V./N.	to need; need

—◆— 补充词汇 —◆—

43. 留学生	liú xué shēng	NP.	students studying abroad, foreign students
44. 签证	qiānzhèng	N.	visa
45. 照片	zhàopiàn	N.	photo
46. 机票	jīpiào	N.	airplane ticket
47. 联合航空公司	lián hé háng kōng gōng sī	NP.	United Airlines, UA
48. 美国航空公司	měi guó háng kōng gōng sī	NP.	American Airlines, AA
49. 登机	dēng jī	VO.	to board a plane
50. 登机牌	dēng jī pái	NP.	boarding pass
51. 登机门	dēng jī mén	NP.	boarding gate
52. 降落	jiàng luò	V.	to descend, to land
53. 首都	shǒu dū	N.	capital
54. 首都经贸大学	shǒu dū jīng mào dà xué	NP.	Capital University of Business and Economics
55. 申报单	shēn bào dān	NP.	declaration form
56. 关税	guān shuì	NP.	customs duty, tariff
57. 春天	chūn tiān	N.	spring
58. 夏天	xià tiān	N.	summer
59. 冬天	dōng tiān	N.	winter
60. 司机	sī jī	N.	driver
61. 美元	měi yuán	NP.	U.S. dollar
62. 毛	máo	N.	ten cents, dime
63. 分	fēn	N.	cent
64. 手续费	shǒu xù fèi	NP.	service charge, processing fee

句型

一、从……起 (starting from)

> ✍ "从……起" means "starting from". It can be used with a simple time expression of past, present or future, such as "昨天", "今天" and "明天". It can also be used with a noun phrase formed by "……的时候" to indicate "...since then", e.g. "我从学中文的时候起就想去中国". (I have wanted to go to China ever since I started studying Chinese.) For this usage, the adverb "就" is often used in the main clause.

☞ 从一年级起我就开始计划去北京留学。

1、从今天起，我们就只能说中文，不能说英文了。
    Beginning today, we can only speak Chinese; we cannot speak English any more.

2、从下个星期起，这个班机开始直飞北京。
    Starting next week, this flight begins flying directly to Beijing.

二、尽管……但是…… (although..., even though...)

> ✍ "尽管……但是" is a paired adverb meaning "even though". "尽管" appears at the beginning of the first phrase either preceding or following a subject; whereas "但是" or "可是" will appear at the beginning of the second phrase, NEVER after the subject.

☞ 尽管我在美国已经学过几个学期的中文，但是说话的时候还是非常紧张。

1、尽管我从上学期就计划去中国大陆，但是我知道这个理想很难实现。
    Although I've planned to go to mainland China since last semester, I know this dream is very hard to realize.

2、尽管中国这几年的变化很大，可是王义老家的变化并不大。
    Even though China has undergone great changes in the past few years, Wang Yi's hometown has not changed much.

三、 利用 (to make use of, to utilize)

> ✍ "利用" is a verb meaning "to make use of". It is often used with noun phrases which denote a specific time, facility, or opportunity. When it is used with a person, it has the negative condition of taking advantage of someone to reach some goal, e.g. "他利用了我"．(He exploited me.)

☞ 我一定要好好儿利用这个机会学中文。

1、 我要利用暑假去北京学中文。

    I want to use (my) summer vacation to go study Chinese in Beijing.

2、 我一定要好好儿利用这个机会去看看中国的变化。

    I definitely want to make use of this opportunity to go see China's changes.

四、 听说 (it is said that, (I) heard that)

> ✍ "听说" is a very useful verb meaning "it is said that", "(I) heard that", or "(I) was told that". The subject of "听说" does not have to be specified. "听说" often appears at the beginning of a sentence to introduce some information without indicating the source of the information.

☞ 听说学校离机场不远，坐出租汽车或者机场大巴都行。

1、听说坐机场大巴去市中心很方便。

    I heard that taking the airport bus to the downtown area is very convenient.

2、听说北京是学习语言最理想的地方。

    It is said that Beijing is the most ideal place to study the language.

五、 A离B不远/近 (Place A is not far from/near to Place B)

> ✍ "A离B远/近" means "to be far from" or "to be near to". When used in the negative, "不" is placed before "远/近"；e.g. "机场离学校不远"．(The airport is not far from the school.) "这儿离市中心可不近"．(It sure isn't close to downtown from here.)

☞ 听说学校离机场不远，坐出租汽车或者机场大巴都行。

1、 机场离学校不太远，坐20分钟车就可以到。

    The airport is not too far from the school; it only takes 20 minutes by bus.

2、学校离市中心不远是不远，可是坐车不太方便。

Granted the school isn't far from downtown, but taking a bus is not very convenient.

六、 比较Adj. (relatively + Adj.)

> ✍ "比较" has two grammatical functions. One is a verb meaning "to compare A with B". The other function of "比较" is as an adverb to express a comparative degree meaning "relatively". The function and meaning of "比较" in this lesson is the latter. In this latter usage, sometimes a comparison is implied (as in example 1 below), but sometimes it simply means "rather, quite" without implying a comparison (as in example 2 below).

☞ 你知道哪个比较方便？

1、坐出租车去市中心比较方便，可是坐机场大巴比较便宜。

Taking a cab downtown is relatively more convenient, but taking the airport bus is cheaper.

2、我尽管学过几个学期的中文，但是说起话来还是比较紧张。

Although I have studied Chinese for several semesters, I am still rather nervous when I speak.

七、 要看 (it depends on)

> ✍ "要看" (literally "have to see") here is a verb meaning "it depends", and its object is normally an interrogative structure. A "要看" clause may also be preceded or followed by a topical phrase, e.g. "我们去不去机场要看天气怎么样"。(Whether we will go to the airport or not depends on the weather.) In response to a question, the "要看" expression is usually preceded by "这" or "那"。"我们在机场能吃什么？" "吃什么都行，这要看你有多少钱"。(What can we eat at the Airport? We can eat anything, it depends on how much money you have.)

☞ 要看你的行李多不多。

1、A: 你觉得去北京学中文非常理想吗？
   B: 这要看你在哪个学校学中文。

   A: Do you feel that going to Beijing to study Chinese is very ideal?
   B: It depends on the school at which you study Chinese.

2、A: 暑假你要不要去工作？

B: 这要看我有没有时间，还有能不能找到工作。

A: Do you want to work during summer vacation?

B: It depends on whether I have time and whether I can find a job.

八、倒 (on the contrary)

> "倒" is an adverb meaning "on the contrary". It is used to indicate that something is contrary to common assumptions.

☞ 要是行李多，倒是坐出租汽车比较方便。

1、虽然第一次到北京，我倒不觉得很奇怪。

Even though this is my first time in Beijing, oddly it does not feel strange to me.

2、尽管学校离商店不近，可是骑车倒比坐车快一些。

Although the school is not close to the store, riding a bike is actually somewhat faster than taking a taxi.

坐机场大巴比较便宜

语言形式练习
Tasks on Language Forms

一、 读课文回答问题 (Answer questions based on the text)

1、周玲到北京做什么？她打算在北京待多长时间？
2、王义为什么到北京去？
3、周玲是第一次到北京去吗？为什么？
4、从机场怎么到学校去？
5、为什么周玲得换人民币？换钱的地方在哪儿？

二、 完成对话 (Complete the dialogs)

1、A：你什么时候开始计划暑假要做什么？
　　B：
　　（从……起；利用……）

2、A：去北京坐哪家航空公司的飞机好呢？
　　B：
　　（要看……；尽管……但是……）

3、A：为什么去市中心还要坐大巴？
　　B：
　　（离……远/近；比较 Adj.）

10

三、听录音回答问题 (Answer questions while listening to the audio CD)

1、周玲为什么说她有点儿紧张？
2、王义第一次到美国的时候紧张吗？为什么？
3、换钱的时候，周玲说的是英文还是中文？
4、周玲想坐什么车到学校？最后，她坐了什么车，为什么？
5、王义为什么坐出租车回家？
6、为什么王义要给周玲打电话？

四、阅读回答问题 (Answer questions based on the reading passage)

你知道北京的中学生们放暑假的时候会做些什么吗？这要看你是几年级的学生。如果你是高中三年级的学生，大概你的暑假就得在暑期学习班中度过了。因为中国的父母大多认为孩子上一个好大学非常重要，所以他们会让孩子利用暑假的时间好好儿学习，准备下一年的大学考试。尽管对这些孩子们来说在暑假期间学习是一件很难让人兴奋的事情，但是为了能考上大学，实现自己的理想，这点苦也就不算什么了。要是你不是高中三年级的学生，你就可以好好儿计划一下你自己的暑假！去旅行，去看朋友或者打工……想做什么就可以做什么。

问题:
1、北京的学生们放暑假的时候会做什么？
2、为什么高中三年级的学生要在暑假里学习？
3、如果你不是高中三年级的学生，你在暑假的时候可以做什么？
4、美国大学生的暑假都是怎么过的？什么样的暑假对你来说最有意思？

五、翻译 (Translation)

1. I am very excited today because my dream of going to China is finally coming true.

2. Downtown would be the most ideal place to meet new friends. What do you think?

3. A: Excuse me, do you know where I can catch the airport bus?

B: Yes, it is not far from here. I am going there now. Let's go there together.

4. Three months ago, I decided to spend my vacation in Beijing because I wanted to use the opportunity to practice my Chinese.

5. Although I have talked to him a few times, I still feel nervous when (or about) speaking with him.

我们这些刚来北京的留学生

语言使用练习
Tasks on Language Use

一、真实情景活动 (Authentic situations)

（一）上飞机以前，航空公司会给每一个坐飞机的人一张"乘客联系卡"。"乘客"在这儿的意思是坐飞机的人。根据 (according to)你自己的情况把右边的表填 (fill out) 一下。有一些字你可能没有学过，你可以查字典 (look up in the dictionary) 或者猜猜看。

乘 客 联 系 卡

尊敬的乘客，请您协助我们提供以下信息：

1. 乘 客 姓 名：＿＿＿＿＿＿＿

2. 联 系 人 姓 名：＿＿＿＿＿＿＿

（未与您同行乘坐此航班之联系人）

3. 联 系 人 电 话：＿＿＿＿＿＿＿

（包括国家代码、地区代码、联系电话）

4. 您是美国公民吗？　　　是□　　否□

以上信息属绝密，将在我站保留二十四小时，感谢您的合作。

以下信息必须回答：

5. 是否有不相识的人请您帮忙带行李到飞机上？

是□　　否□

6. 您的行李是否是由别人帮您整理，是否离开过您的控制范围？　　是□　　否□

（二）现在中国也有了e-bank，中文叫电子银行。要是你想在这个银行开户 (to open an account) 并且换钱，你就需要把你个人的情况填在下面的表中：

中国银行电子银行服务开销户申请表

根据中国银行电子银行服务协议书条款规定，本人现向贵行申请办理电子银行服务。

开户：（　）／销户：（　）（请划✓）　　　　　　　　　　　　　　　年　月　日

姓　名		住　址		电话	
邮　编		E-MAIL 地址		传真	
证件类型		证件号码		呼机	
借记卡号			活期存折帐号		

经办：　　　　　　经办银行（盖章）：　　　　　　事后监督：　复核：

（三）根据下边的牌子(sign)用你学过的词写出下面词的意思：

● 民航客车 =
● 开往 =
● 售票处 =
● 首发车 =
● 末班车 =

王义需要下午三点半到机场坐五点半的飞机去上海。因为他的钱不多，所以他想坐大巴去机场。他知道坐大巴三十分钟就可以到机场。根据右边的牌子你能不能告诉他票价是多少钱，最好几点去车站等机场大巴？

民航客车开往首都机场
售票处
首发车6:00　末班车19:00　票价16元
每隔30分钟发车

（四）根据下面的表，你知道 HRB-HKG 的航班号是什么？什么时间起飞？每个星期几有一班飞机？

北航天鹅航空公司

航線	航班號	時間	飛行周次	經停
HRB – CAN 哈爾濱—廣州	CJ6261	0840	1－7	
HRB – SZX 哈爾濱—深圳	CJ283	0940	1＼5	CSX 長沙
	CJ6285	0940	2＼3＼6	WNZ 溫州
	CJ6281	0940	4＼7	YNT 煙台
HRB – HKG 哈爾濱—香港	CJ639	1250	4＼6	
HRB – KIJ 哈爾濱—新潟	CJ615	0805	1＼3＼5	
HRB – SEL 哈爾濱—漢城	CJ683	0900	1＼3＼5＼6	
HRB – KHV 哈爾濱—伯力	CJ601	0805	4	

二、讨论 (Discussion)

1、到北京留学得做哪些准备？

2、从美国到北京，你坐的是哪家航空公司的飞机？在飞机上你做了什么？

3、谈谈你到北京的第一天：你觉得怎么样？是怎么从机场到学校的？北京给你的印象 (impression) 怎么样？

4、你计划怎么利用在北京的时间？

5、你为什么学中文？

三、作文 (Composition)

《我是怎么开始学中文的》

四、看图说话 (Picto-discussion)

1

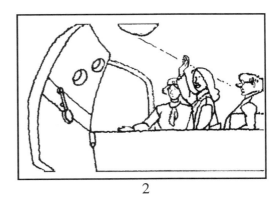

2

3

4

5

An Intermediate Chinese Course

第二课　外国留学生宿舍

总服务台

课文

坐出租车到学校的时候已经是晚上九点了。一进留学生宿舍大厅，前台服务员刘小姐就过来帮我办理登记手续，为我安排房间。刘小姐带我去房间的时候，给我简单地介绍了一下外国留学生宿舍的情况。留学生楼的右边是学生宿舍，楼上是教室，楼下是餐厅和咖啡厅，生活、学习都很方便。到了房间，我用钥匙打开门一看，觉得很吃惊，没想到外国留学生宿舍的条件这么好。房间里的东西整理得干干净净，有电视、电话，还有空调、热水瓶；卫生间里不但有卫生纸，而且有洗澡设备，还24小时供应热水。看到这么好的条件，我心里很高兴。以前在美国常听人说中国还比较落后，可是从这儿的宿舍来看，中国很现代化，一点儿也不落后。这到底是不是真正的中国，我还需要时间去慢慢了解。

我洗了个热水澡以后觉得很渴，就决定去楼下的咖啡厅买一些冷饮喝。在那儿碰到了正在工作的王小姐。

———————————◆———————————

王：你是今天到的吗？

周：对，才到了一个钟头，渴得要命，想喝点冷饮。你们有什么？

王：我们有汽水、矿泉水、啤酒，还有各种冰淇淋。

周：这些冷饮都怎么卖？

王：可乐、雪碧都是五块一瓶，矿泉水三块，果汁六块。

周：要一瓶矿泉水。对了，小姐，跟您打听一下⁽¹⁾，在哪儿可以打国际长途？

王：在一楼电话亭就可以直⁽²⁾拨美国，不过⁽³⁾你得先在前台买磁卡⁽⁴⁾，你也可以用电话卡或者信用卡在你的房间里打。要是你是AT&T的用户，拨10811就可以。要是你用MCI，拨10812就行。

周：那⁽⁵⁾太方便了。我要赶快回房间给我的父母打个电话，告诉他们我已经平安到北京了。

生词

1. 大厅	dà tīng	N.	lobby, hall
2. 前台	qián tái	N.	front desk
3. 服务员	fú wù yuán	N.	attendant, service personnel
4. 过来	guò lai	V.	to come over
5. 办理	bàn lǐ	V.	to handle, to process
6. 登记	dēng jì	V.	to register, to check in
7. 手续	shǒu xù	N.	procedure
8. 安排	ān pái	V./N.	to arrange; arrangement

Notes ⁽¹⁾ "跟您打听一下"：This expression is slightly more formal than "请问". Both are polite ways to say "may I ask". It is often used before a question or inquiry; e.g. "跟您打听一下，电话亭在哪儿"？(May I ask, where is the phone booth?)

⁽²⁾ "直+V"，"直"：Here this term is an adverb meaning "directly". It is often followed by a verb. In that form, it indicates "to do something directly or without stopping", e.g. "直拨" (to dial directly); "直飞" (to fly directly). These phrases are commonly used to modify a noun, e.g. "直拨电话" (direct telephone); "直飞班机" (direct flight); and "直达车" (non-stop train).

⁽³⁾ "不过"：This term has the same meaning as "但是" or "可是". It is often used in conversations or informal settings, but seldom in formal written contexts.

⁽⁴⁾ "磁卡"：This word refers to a magnetic card used in making long distance or local phone calls. The card can be purchased at department stores or local telephone companies at the value of 50 or 100 RMB good for a certain number of minutes. This kind of card is not rechargeable.

⁽⁵⁾ "那"：The particle is often used at the beginning of a sentence meaning "in that case", e.g. "那我就不要了"。(In that case, I don't want it.) In the sentence "那太方便了" in Lesson 2, "那" has the dual function of "in that case" and "that" or "it"; so the sentence means "in that case, it is really convenient".

9. 简单地	jiǎn dān de	*Adv.*	briefly, simply (简单: simple)
10. 介绍	jiè shào	*V/N.*	to introduce; introduction
11. 情况	qíng kuàng	*N.*	condition
12. 楼	lóu	*N.*	building, stairs, floor
13. 餐厅	cān tīng	*N.*	dining hall, restaurant, cafeteria
14. 咖啡厅	kā fēi tīng	*N.*	coffee shop
15. 打开	dǎ kāi	*VP.*	to open
16. 钥匙	yào shi	*N.*	key
17. 吃惊	chī jīng	*VO.*	to be shocked, to be surprised
18. 没想到	méi xiǎng dào	*VP.*	didn't expect
19. 条件	tiáo jiàn	*N.*	(living) conditions
20. 整理	zhěng lǐ	*V.*	to tidy up, to put in order
21. 干干净净	gān gān jìng jìng	*Adj.*	clean
22. 电视	diàn shì	*N.*	TV
23. 电话	diàn huà	*N.*	telephone, phone call
24. 空调	kōng tiáo	*N.*	air conditioning
25. 热水瓶	rè shuǐ píng	*N.*	thermos bottle
26. 卫生间	wèi shēng jiān	*N.*	bathroom (厕所 cè suǒ, restroom)
27. 卫生纸	wèi shēng zhǐ	*N.*	toilet paper
28. 洗澡	xǐ zǎo	*VO.*	to take a bath or shower
29. 设备	shè bèi	*N.*	facilities, equipment
30. 供应	gōng yìng	*V.*	to supply, to furnish
31. 落后	luò hòu	*Adj.*	backward, underdeveloped
32. 现代化	xiàn dài huà	*Adj.*	modernized
33. 到底	dào dǐ	*Adv.*	after all, in the final analysis (conveys emphasis in questions)
34. 了解	liǎo jiě	*V/N.*	to understand; understanding
35. 热水澡	rè shuǐ zǎo	*NP.*	hot bath or shower
36. 渴	kě	*Adj.*	thirsty
37. 决定	jué dìng	*V/N.*	to decide; decision
38. 冷饮	lěng yǐn	*N.*	cold drink
39. 要命	yào mìng	*Adv.*	extremely
40. 矿泉水	kuàng quán shuǐ	*N.*	mineral water
41. 啤酒	pí jiǔ	*N.*	beer

42.	种	zhǒng	*Classifier.*	kind
43.	冰淇淋	bīng qí lín	*N.*	ice cream
44.	可乐	kě lè	*N.*	Coca-Cola
45.	雪碧	xuě bì	*N.*	Sprite
46.	瓶	píng	*Classifier.*	bottle
47.	果汁	guǒ zhī	*N.*	fruit juice
48.	打听	dǎ tīng	*V.*	to check around, to find out
49.	国际	guó jì	*Adj.*	international
50.	长途	cháng tú	*Adj.*	long distance (phone call)
51.	电话亭	diàn huà tíng	*N.*	telephone booth
52.	直拨	zhí bō	*VP.*	to dial directly
53.	磁卡	cí kǎ	*N.*	IC Card
54.	信用卡	xìn yòng kǎ	*N.*	credit card
55.	用户	yòng hù	*N.*	customer, user
56.	拨	bō	*V.*	to dial
57.	赶快	gǎn kuài	*Adv.*	quickly, at once
58.	告诉	gào sù	*V.*	to tell
59.	平安	píng ān	*Adj.*	safe and sound

————◆—— 补充词汇 ——◆————

60.	电灯	diàn dēng	*N.*	light, lamp
61.	台灯	tái dēng	*N.*	desk lamp
62.	开关	kāi guān	*N.*	switch
63.	床	chuáng	*N.*	bed
64.	床单	chuáng dān	*N.*	bed sheet
65.	枕头	zhěn tou	*N.*	pillow
66.	枕头套	zhěn tou tào	*N.*	pillow case
67.	被子	bèi zi	*N.*	quilt
68.	毛巾	máo jīn	*N.*	towel
69.	自来水	zì lái shuǐ	*N.*	running water
70.	牙刷	yá shuā	*N.*	toothbrush
71.	牙膏	yá gāo	*N.*	toothpaste
72.	洗发水儿	xǐ fà shuǐr	*N.*	shampoo (also called 香波 xiāng

				bō)
73. 护发素	hù fà sù	*N.*	hair conditioner
74. 洗衣粉	xǐ yī fěn	*N.*	(powder) detergent
75. 烘干机	hōng gān jī	*N.*	dryer
76. 垃圾桶	lā jī tǒng	*N.*	trash can
77. 洗澡间	xǐ zǎo jiān	*N.*	bathroom
78. 抽水马桶	chōu shuǐ mǎ tǒng	*N.*	flush toilet
79. 蹲	dūn	*V.*	to squat
80. 饮料	yǐn liào	*N.*	drink, beverage
81. 热饮	rè yǐn	*N.*	hot drink
82. 国家代码	guó jiā dài mǎ	*N.*	country code
83. 长途区号	cháng tú qū hào	*NP.*	area code
84. 打不通	dǎ bu tōng	*VP.*	cannot get through (on phone)
85. 想家	xiǎng jiā	*VO.*	to miss home, to be homesick
86. 外办	wài bàn	*N.*	foreign affairs office

没想到外国留学生宿舍的条件这么好

句型

一、为……安排 (to arrange something for...)

> ✍ "安排" is a verb meaning "to make arrangements". "为" is a preposition meaning "for". "为" is followed by a person who receives the arrangement which is performed by the subject. The negative form is "不/没为……安排". The question form is "为不/没为……安排".

☞ 前台服务员刘小姐就跑来帮我办理登记手续，为我安排房间。

1、我的父母为我安排好了暑假的工作，一放假就开始。

My parents arranged a summer job for me, so as soon as summer vacation starts I will begin working.

2、宿舍的服务员早已为我们安排好了房间。

The dormitory's service personnel already arranged a room for us.

二、给……介绍 (to introduce someone/something to)

> ✍ "介绍" "to introduce" is a verb. "给" is a preposition meaning "for". "给", similar to "为", is used to specify the recipient or beneficiary of the action. The difference between "给" and "为" is that "为" is more formal than "给" and "给" indicates "to or for whom" the action is directed, whereas "为" specifically means "for (the sake of)..." The object of "给" may be understood (as in example 1) whereas the object of "为" must be explicit.

☞ 给我简单地介绍了一下外国留学生宿舍的情况。

1、请你给介绍一下学校的设备。

Could you please give a brief introduction about the school's facilities?

2、请你给我们介绍一下怎么用磁卡打长途电话。

Give us a brief introduction on how to use the IC card to make a long distance call.

三、V + 一下 (to do something briefly)

> ✍ The expression "一下" is used to modify verbs meaning an action is performed in a casual and brief manner. "下", if used with a number other than "一" means "a number of strokes or physical movements", e.g. "打两下" (hit twice), "擦三下" (wipe three times).

☞ （刘小姐）给我简单地介绍了一下外国留学生宿舍的情况。

1、请你给我们简单地安排一下。

Please just make some simple arrangements for us.

2、我先去咖啡厅看一下他们的设备怎么样，再去看教室。

I will first go to the cafe to take a look at what the facilities are like, and then I will go look at the classrooms.

四、没想到 (unexpectedly, did not expect)

> ✍ "没想到" is a fixed expression used to express surprise. The subject of "没想到" may be implicit and therefore omitted. The omission often occurs when the subject of the sentence is the first person, e.g. "（我）没想到这儿的出租车这么多". (I did not expect there to be so many taxis here.)

☞ 没想到外国留学生宿舍的条件这么好。

1、真没想到学校为我们安排的生活还不错。

I really did not expect the school to arrange such a good daily life for us.

2、没想到在中国信用卡还真方便。

I did not expect it to be so convenient to use credit cards in China.

五、不但……而且 (not only...but also...)

> ✍ "不但……而且" expresses a progressive relationship. The second clause takes the first one a step further. When the subjects in the two clauses are identical, "不但" should follow the first subject and the second subject is often omitted. When the two subjects are different, "不但" and "而且" should precede them. The adverbs "也" or "还" can be used in the second clause to reinforce "而且", or if the subjects of the two clauses are the same, in lieu of "而且". (cf. example 2)

☞　卫生间里不但有卫生纸，而且有洗澡设备。

1、在中国留学不但很有意思，而且很有意义。

Studying in China is not only interesting, but is also very significant.

2、用磁卡给家里打长途电话不但很贵，（而且）也很不方便。

Using the IC card to make long distance calls home is not only expensive, but also very inconvenient.

3、这种事不但政府不管，而且学校也不管。

The government does not take care of these kinds of things, and neither does the school.

六、从……来看 (looking from, from the perspective of, from the standpoint of)

> ✍ "从……来看" is a prepositional phrase often used at the beginning of a sentence to indicate a topic. It can mean "looking from", "viewing from the perspective of", or "from the standpoint of".

☞　从这儿的宿舍来看，中国很现代化，一点儿也不落后。

1、从学中文来看，北京大概是最理想的地方。

From the standpoint of learning Chinese, Beijing is probably the most ideal place.

2、从市场来看，中国的经济发展还不错。

From the market perspective, China's economic development is fairly good.

七、一点儿也／都不…… (not at all, not the least bit...)

> ✍ "一点也／都" is always used in a negative sentence to modify an adjective or a verb, meaning "not at all".

☞　从这儿的宿舍来看，中国很现代化，一点儿也不落后。

1、厕所的设备一点儿也不落后，非常现代化。

The restroom facilities are not backward at all, they are quite modern.

2、了解这里的情况一点儿也不难，因为服务员都可以告诉你。

Understanding the circumstances here is not hard at all because the service personnel can tell you everything.

八、到底 (after all)

> ✍ "到底" (after all) when used in a question, shows that the speaker is asking for a definite final answer. "到底" is used with "question word" or "choice type" questions, never with "吗" questions. An optional "呢" may be added in the end to soften the question. "到底" in this sense can only be used in a question, and not in responding to a "到底" question.

☞ 这到底是不是真正的中国，我还需要时间去慢慢了解。

1、你的同学到底为什么要给你介绍女朋友？

Why on earth does your classmate want to fix you up with a girlfriend?

2、你能不能给我们介绍一下信用卡到底有什么用？

Can you tell us what is the use of credit cards after all?

九、Adj. + 得要命 (extremely + Adj)

> ✍ "得要命" can be used after an adjective to emphasize the intensity of the adjective. More often than not, the adjective denotes an undesirable state. The adjective must be a positive form, therefore it cannot be modified by "不" or "没". One can say "这个菜难吃得要命" but NOT * "这个菜不好吃得要命".

☞ 渴得要命，想喝点冷饮。

1、刚才我紧张得要命，因为厕所里没有卫生纸。

Just now I was awfully nervous because that restroom did not have any toilet paper in it.

2、我渴得要命，能不能给我来点冷饮？

I am extremely thirsty. Can you bring me a cold drink?

宿舍房间的钥匙

语言形式练习
Tasks on Language Forms

一、读课文回答问题

1、周玲到留学生宿舍的时候，前台服务员刘小姐帮她做了哪些事情？
2、留学生楼的旁边和楼上楼下有什么？
3、外国留学生宿舍的条件怎么样？有什么设备？在美国的时候周玲觉得中国怎么样？现在呢？
4、楼下的咖啡厅有什么冷饮？
5、在哪儿可以打国际长途？怎么打？

二、完成对话

1、A：你怎么认识你的中国爸爸妈妈的？
　　B：
　　　　（为……安排；没想到……）

2、A：你觉得什么样的宿舍比较理想？
　　B：
　　　　（要看……；到底……）

3、A：你真的可以用磁卡打国际长途吗？
　　B：
　　　　（不但……而且……；一点也不……）

4、A：
　　　　（给……介绍一下）
　　B：没想到学校的学习条件还真不错。

三、听录音回答问题

1、小张为什么到了机场大厅以后就不紧张了？
2、刘行为什么来接小张？
3、刘行是一个人到机场去的吗？为什么？
4、老刘想先带小张到哪儿去？为什么？
5、小张的宿舍条件怎么样？
6、小张可以用宿舍的电话给父母报 (tell) 平安吗？为什么？

四、阅读回答问题

　　来北京留学以前，我一直以为中国现在还不够现代化，从中国打国际长途电话会比较困难。可是，到了以后才发现北京打国际长途既便宜又方便。不管你是在街上还是在宿舍里，你都可以买到电话卡。北京的电话卡有两种。一种叫IP卡，另一种叫IC卡。这两种卡用起来都很容易，一点儿也不麻烦。如果你在房间里打长途，用IP卡比较方便。每一张卡的后面都会有很清楚的说明来告诉你怎么用卡。如果你用"网通"公司的IP卡，你要先拨"17920"，再拨卡号和密码，最后拨你家人或者朋友的电话号码就可以接通讲话了。IC卡也很有用，因为在北京市差不多所有的公共电话亭都可以用IC卡打电话。要是你没有手机，出门带一张IC卡是非常方便的。

问题:
1、"我"在北京发现了什么？我以前的什么看法有什么改变？
2、怎么用 IP 卡打长途电话？
3、IP 和 IC 电话卡有什么不同？
4、美国人现在打电话都用什么方法？

五、翻译

1. A: Can you please briefly tell me about your host family (Chinese family)?

　　B: Certainly. My Chinese father teaches at the university and my Chinese mother works at the coffee shop. Their living conditions are quite modern.

A: When you first went to see their house, were you surprised?

B: Yes. Very much. Not only do they have a modern TV and telephone, they also have computers.

2. I did not expect that he would be so excited when he saw the equipment in our bathroom.

3. A: May I ask, if I want to make a long distance phone call, what should I do?

   B: Dial 10810 with your calling card, that's all.

4. I want to tell my parents that we have safely arrived in Beijing and ACC has made dorm arrangements for us.

在楼下的咖啡厅买冷饮喝

语言使用练习
Tasks on Language Use

一、真实情景活动 🎥

（一）下边这张 IP（吉通）卡的价钱是多少？

（二）看了这张 IP 卡上的说明以后，用你自己的话告诉你的同学怎么用这个 IP 卡打电
话：

第一步：

第二步：

第三步：

第四步：

第五步：

（三）下边这个广告(ad)是为谁提供服务的？他们提供什么服务？

（四）猜猜看或者问你的中国朋友什么是"一站式"服务？用英文怎么说"一站式"服
务？

（五）根据下面的广告，北京东方晨光青年旅馆在北京的什么地方？(Circle the correct answer)

　　a. 市中心　　　b. 天安门　　　c. 北京站　　　d. 首都机场

（六）这家旅馆的房间不提供哪一种设备？

　　a. 空调　　　b. 电梯　　　c. 洗澡设备　　d. 电视　　　e. 洗衣机

（七）这家旅馆为客人提供什么服务？(Circle the correct answer)

总服务台　　　　　小卖部　　　　　酒吧　　　　洗衣服
飞机票　　　　　　长途电话　　　　洗照片

北京东方晨光青年旅馆
EASTERN MORNING SUN YOUTH HOSTEL

HOSTELLING INTERNATIONAL

风靡全球的国际青年旅舍联盟 IYHF 在北京又添新店北京东方晨光青年旅馆。

宗旨 安全、卫生、经济。

位置 位于首都的心脏部位——金银街中间，亚洲最大的联体建筑群——东方广场东配楼 B4 层，距天安门、北京站仅一箭地。

条件 中央空调，24 小时新风系统，直达电梯，全新装修，特色自助厨房，自助洗衣房、公共盥洗室及淋浴间，旅馆共有 42 个双人间，5 个三人间，6 个单人间，可容纳 105 人住宿。

旅馆首层设有总服务台及旅馆咨询柜台，可代理预订飞机票及火车票，北京市内及周边游，彩扩，小卖部，客房区设有阅览室、酒吧、保险箱等业务，为您在京的商务及旅游活动提供全面、周到的服务。

价格
单人间：	80 元／间
双人间：A	120 元／间
双人间：B	140 元／间
三人间：	180 元／间

二、讨论

1、谈谈你刚到留学生宿舍的时候，办了哪些手续，做了什么事情？
2、简单地介绍一下你的宿舍：附近有什么？宿舍里有什么设备？跟你在美国的宿舍有什么不同？
3、你给父母打了电话没有？你们谈了什么？你在中国，他们最担心 (worry about) 什么？
4、你觉得外国留学生宿舍和中国大学生宿舍的条件应该不一样吗？为什么？

三、语言实践

　　去中国大学生的宿舍看一看他们房间的条件和设备，请他们谈谈对自己宿舍的看法。比较一下外国留学生宿舍、中国大学生宿舍、和美国大学生宿舍有什么不同。

四、作文

　　《我看到的中国大学生宿舍》

五、看图说话

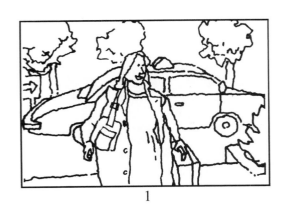

1

2

An Intermediate Chinese Course

第三课　学校附近的饭馆

学校东边的饺子馆

课文

　　我的大学附近有很多饭馆，三步一家，五步一个，所以在校外吃饭根本不⁽¹⁾是一个问题。这些饭馆风味不同，价钱也不一样，有便宜的，有贵的。同学们最喜欢去的饭馆有三家，一个是学校对面的饭馆，那儿的饭菜很简单，可是离学校最近，价钱也很公道，所以学生们都喜欢去。另一家是学校东边的饺子馆，从学校出来往东走，过了十字路口再往前走一、两分钟就到了。很多同学喜欢吃那里的饺子：有鸡肉玉米馅儿的，有猪肉大葱馅儿的，还有素馅儿的等等⁽²⁾。那儿的饭可以说是又经济又实惠。除了这些以外，这家饺子馆还有几个特点：一是气氛轻松，环境很好；二是服务员小姐很客气；三是饭菜上⁽³⁾得很快。所以这家饭馆最受学生的欢迎。第三家是学校北边，商场对面的饭馆，那儿专⁽⁴⁾卖各种炒菜、小吃。大饼、腰果鸡丁、烧茄子、西红柿炒鸡蛋等等都是同学们最常点⁽⁵⁾的。

Notes　⁽¹⁾ "根本不/没…"：When functioning as an adverb to modify a verb, "根本" is mostly used with a negative particle "不" or "没" to mean "not at all" or "simply not", e.g. "他根本不了解这儿的情况"。(He does not understand the situation here at all.) "我根本没有去饺子馆"。(I simply did not go to the dumpling restaurant.)

　　⁽²⁾ "………等等"：This term is commonly used alone or in duplication after a series of nouns or noun-phrases meaning "and so on" or "etc.", e.g. "宿舍有空调、电话等"。(The dorm has air conditioning, telephone, and so on.) "那儿有肉菜、素菜等等"。(There they serve meat dishes, veggie dishes, etc.)

　　⁽³⁾ "上（菜）"："上" in this context means "to serve (the dishes)". It is an idiomatic usage often used in a restaurant setting, e.g. "小姐，请上米饭"。(Miss, please serve the rice.) "那家饭馆小是小，可是饭菜上得很快"。(That restaurant is small all right, but the food is served very quickly.)

　　⁽⁴⁾ "专 V"："专" comes from "专门", meaning "to specialize in something". "专" is an adverb which precedes a verb to specify what one specializes in. Unlike English in which one can say "he specializes in English literature", in Chinese, one must use a verb after "专", e.g. "他专（门）研究英国文学"。A direct translation of this sentence into English would sound awkward because the verb "to specialize" and the verb "to study" would be redundant if contained in the same sentence. See Lesson 6 for more explanation and examples of "专门".

来北京三天以后，我约了一位同学去学校对面的那家饭馆吃饭。

——◆——

服务员：几位？

男学生：两位。

服务员：（带两个同学到一张桌子）请坐，请坐。这是菜单。

（两个同学看菜单）

男学生：你想吃点儿什么？

女学生：我也不知道。我的中文不行，点菜还有困难。你来点吧。

（服务员走过来）

男学生：小姐，请问你们有没有铁板牛肉跟宫爆鸡丁？

服务员：有，有。

男学生：可以不可以请您告诉炒菜的师傅不要太辣。

服务员：好，没问题。还要点儿什么？

男学生：我的这位同学不吃肉，你们这儿有什么素菜？

服务员：素菜有松仁玉米、尖椒土豆丝、拔丝香蕉。

男学生：尖椒土豆丝是什么菜？

服务员：就是青椒炒土豆丝。

男学生：好，来一个[6]。请您不要放味精，我对味精过敏，吃了会有反应。

服务员：要点儿什么饮料？

Notes [5] "点（菜、歌）"："点" is often used for ordering, pointing, or counting things such as dishes, songs, or others, e.g. "点菜" (to order dishes); "点歌" (to ask for a song); "点人" (to count the people); "点东西" (to count things). Instead of "点菜" one can also say "叫菜".

[6] "来一个"："来", "to come", can also be used as a generic verb resembling the generic English verb "to do". "来" is used in lieu of a specific verb, e.g. "来一碗汤" meaning "给我上（拿）一碗汤". (I would like a bowl of soup.) "这次你点菜，下次我来" (This time you order, next time I'll do it) means "下次我点" (next time I'll order).

男学生：饮料是不是冰的？

服务员：是的。都是刚从冰箱里拿出来的。

男学生：好。要一瓶雪碧，一瓶可乐，再要一瓶果汁。

（周和同学吃完了饭）

男学生：小姐，请结账。

服务员：好，就来⁽⁷⁾。

—◆◆◆— 生 词 —◆◆◆—

1. 附近	fù jìn	N/Adj.	vicinity; nearby, neighboring
2. 步	bù	N.	step
3. 校外	xiào wài	N.	off campus
4. 根本	gēn běn	Adv.	(used in negative sentences) simply, fundamentally, (not)...at all
5. 风味	fēng wèi	N.	special flavor (style or region of cuisine)
6. 价钱	jià qián	N.	price
7. 便宜	pián yi	Adj.	cheap, inexpensive
8. 对面	duì miàn	N.	the place across from
9. 公道	gōng dào	Adj.	reasonable
10. 饺子馆	jiǎo zi guǎn	N.	dumpling restaurant
11. 往	wǎng	Prep.	towards
12. 十字路口	shí zì lù kǒu	N.	intersection
13. 鸡肉	jī ròu	N.	chicken
14. 玉米	yù mǐ	N.	corn
15. 馅儿	xiànr	N.	filling, stuffing
16. 猪肉	zhū ròu	N.	pork
17. 大葱	dà cōng	N.	scallion

Notes ⁽⁷⁾ "就来": This is an idiomatic expression meaning "I'll be there in a minute", "I'm coming", or "it is coming", e.g. "先生，你要的米饭就来"。(Sir, the rice you ordered will be coming soon.)

18. 素馅	sù xiàn	NP.	vegetable filling
19. 等等	děng děng		and so on, etc.
20. 经济	jīng jì	Adj/N.	economical; economy
21. 实惠	shí huì	Adj.	substantial, solid
22. 除了……以外	chú le ...yǐ wài	Prep.	except for, in addition to
23. 特点	tè diǎn	N.	characteristic, distinguishing feature
24. 气氛	qì fēn	N.	atmosphere, ambience
25. 轻松	qīng sōng	Adj.	relaxing, relaxed
26. 环境	huán jìng	N.	environment
27. 上	shàng	V.	to serve (food), to bring on (a dish)
28. 受	shòu	V.	to receive (used in passive voice)
29. 欢迎	huān yíng	N/V.	welcome, popularity; to welcome
30. 商场	shāng chǎng	N.	shopping center
31. 专卖	zhuān mài	VP.	to sell something exclusively
32. 炒菜	chǎo cài	VO.	stir-fried dish/vegetable
33. 小吃	xiǎo chī	N.	snacks, light refreshment
34. 大饼	dà bǐng	N.	a kind of large flat bread
35. 腰果鸡丁	yāo guǒ jī dīng	NP.	cashew chicken
36. 烧茄子	shāo qié zi	NP.	stewed eggplant
37. 西红柿	xī hóng shì	N.	tomato
38. 鸡蛋	jī dàn	N.	egg
39. 点	diǎn	V.	to order (food)
40. 约	yuē	V.	to make an appointment or date, to agree to meet
41. 菜单	cài dān	N.	menu
42. 困难	kùn nan	N/Adj.	difficulty; difficult
43. 铁板牛肉	tiě bǎn niú ròu	NP.	beef on an iron plate
44. 宫爆鸡丁	gōng bào jī dīng	NP.	Gong Bao chicken
45. 师傅	shī fu	N.	chef, master worker, general term of address for service personnel
46. 辣	là	Adj.	spicy, hot
47. 素菜	sù cài	N.	vegetable dish
48. 松仁	sōng rén	N.	pine nut
49. 尖椒	jiān jiāo	N.	elongated pepper or hot pepper
50. 土豆丝	tǔ dòu sī	N.	shredded potato

51. 拔丝	bá sī	VO/Adj.	to "pull out floss"; caramel floss (a sweet dish)
52. 香蕉	xiāng jiāo	N.	banana
53. 青椒	qīng jiāo	N.	green pepper
54. 味精	wèi jīng	N.	MSG
55. 过敏	guò mǐn	V.	to be allergic to
56. 反应	fǎn yìng	N.	reaction, response
57. 冰箱	bīng xiāng	N.	refrigerator
58. 结账	jié zhàng	VO.	to settle up, to pay the bill

———◆—— 补充词汇 ——◆———

59. 小菜	xiǎo cài	N.	appetizer, small side dish
60. 馅儿饼	xiànr bǐng	N.	stuffed flat bread
61. 包子	bāo zi	N.	steamed stuffed bun
62. 馒头	mán tou	N.	steamed bun
63. 煎饺	jiān jiǎo	N.	fried dumpling
64. 蒸饺	zhēng jiǎo	N.	steamed dumpling
65. 面条	miàn tiáo	N.	noodle
66. 鱼	yú	N.	fish
67. 麻婆豆腐	má pó dòu fu	NP.	a spicy tofu dish
68. 甜酸肉	tián suān ròu	NP.	sweet and sour pork
69. 酸辣汤	suān là tāng	NP.	hot and sour soup
70. 蛋花汤	dàn huā tāng	NP.	egg drop soup
71. 辣椒酱	là jiāo jiàng	NP.	hot sauce
72. 酱油	jiàng yóu	N.	soy sauce
73. 胡椒	hú jiāo	N.	pepper
74. 盐	yán	N.	salt
75. 酸	suān	Adj.	sour
76. 甜	tián	Adj.	sweet
77. 苦	kǔ	Adj.	bitter
78. 咸	xián	Adj.	salty
79. 花茶	huā chá	N.	jasmine tea (also called 香片 xiāng piàn)

80.	账单	zhàng dān	*N.*	bill, check
81.	小费	xiǎo fèi	*N.*	tip

鸡肉玉米馅儿的饺子

西红柿炒鸡蛋

句型

一、有……的，有……的 (some are..., some are...)

> ✍ "有……的, 有……的" is used to indicate that the topic of conversation has a variety of different forms or manifestations, e.g. "中国点心很多，有甜的，有咸的，有热的，有凉的"。(There are many different kinds of Chinese snacks. There are sweet dishes, salty dishes, hot dishes, and cold dishes.) "我有很多鞋，有白的，有黑的"。 (I have many shoes, white ones and black ones.) "有高的，有矮的" (tall ones, short ones); "有打球的，有跳舞的" (sneakers, dancing shoes) etc. Please note that when this pattern is used, there must be at least two items which belong to the same category. Therefore, "我有很多鞋，有白的" is not a complete sentence. Semantically, "我有很多鞋，有白的，有跳舞的" is also not acceptable since "白的" and "跳舞的" cannot be put into the same category.

☞ 有便宜的，有贵的。

1、那儿的饭菜真不错，有热的，也有凉的，有北方风味的，也有南方风味的。

The dishes there are not bad; some are hot and some are cold. They also have northern and southern cuisines.

2、学校宿舍的设备好象不太一样，有带空调的，也有不带空调的。

The school's dormitory facilities do not appear to all be the same; some have air conditioners and some don't.

二、(Localizers) ……（的）对面，……（的）附近，……（的）东边

> ✍ The words "对面" (across from), "附近" (close by), and "东边" (to the east) are all localizers. The noun, if stated explicitly, MUST precede the localizer, e.g. one uses "学校对面" NOT * "对面学校" (across from the school). (对面的学校 means "the school across from here".)

☞ 一个是学校对面的饭馆，那儿的饭菜很简单……

1、宿舍对面有一家素菜馆，那儿的菜又便宜，又好吃。

There is a vegetarian restaurant across from the dorm. The food there is inexpensive and tastes good.

2、学校对面、商场附近、和小店的西边都有一些经济实惠的饭馆。

Across from the school, near the shopping center, and on the west side of the store, there are restaurants where you can get a good meal inexpensively (or cheaply).

三、往……走 (to go toward)

> ✍ "往" , meaning "towards," can be used with an action verb such as "走, 跑, 骑, 看, 开" , etc. "往" is followed by an expression indicating a direction or location, e.g. "往东边走" (to walk east), "往北京飞" (to fly toward Beijing), "往上边看" (to look up).

☞ 从学校出来往东走，过了十字路口再往前走一、两分钟就到了。

1、你要去的那家饭馆就在学校西边，出了校门往西走，过了马路就是。

The restaurant that you want to go to is on the west side of the school. Once you go out of the school's gate, go west and cross the street, and you are right there.

2、你往前走一点就可以看见那家饺子馆，他们的素馅儿饺子很好吃。

If you walk a little further on, you will see that dumpling restaurant. Their vegetable dumplings taste very good.

四、可以说 (one may say, you can say)

> ✍ "可以说," meaning "it can be said..." or "one can say...," is inserted either at the beginning of a sentence or between a subject and a verb, e.g. "可以说，东京的发展比北京快" (One can say that the development of Tokyo is faster than that of Beijing.) "北京可以说是中国最大的城市之一" . (One can say that Beijing is one of the largest cities in China.) Note that when inserted between a subject and a verb, "可以说" does not require a comma to signal that it is an inserted element.

☞ 那儿的饭可以说是又经济又实惠。

1、刚来北京，最困难的可以说是用菜单点菜。

Having just arrived in Beijing, one could say that the most difficult thing was using a menu

43

to order food.

2、那儿的铁板牛肉、宫爆鸡丁和拔丝苹果可以说是最受同学们欢迎的菜。

You could say that the Iron-Plate beef, Gong Pao Chicken and Basi Apples (pulled caramel apples) there are the dishes most popular with the students.

五、A. 除了……以外，……还/也…… (besides, in addition to)

> ✍ "除了……以外" has two meanings, "in addition to" and "except for." When using either meaning, "以外" can be omitted. When it means "in addition to" it is followed by adverbs such as "也" or "还". When it means "except for," it is followed by the adverb "都". The meaning of "除了……以外" in the lesson text is "in addition to."

☞ 除了这些以外，这家饺子馆儿还有几个特点。

1、除了牛肉馅儿饺子以外，他也喜欢吃鸡肉玉米馅儿的饺子。

Besides beef dumplings, he also likes chicken and corn stuffed dumplings.

2、除了星期天以外，我星期三也很忙。

In addition to Sundays, I am also busy on Wednesdays.

B. 除了……以外，……都…… (except for)

1、除了我以外，其他的人都去过上海。

Except for me, everyone else has been to Shanghai before.

2、除了星期一以外，我每天都很忙。

I am very busy every day except for Monday.

六、有……特点 (to have the characteristics of)

> ✍ "有……特点" can be used to describe what characteristics someone or something has. For example, one may begin a sentence by saying "这本书有很多特点". (This book has many special characteristics.) Then in the second sentence one can further specify what the characteristics are, e.g. "这些特点是A、B、和C". (These special characteristics are A, B, and C.) One may also use a phrase to modify the expression "特点", especially when there is only one, e.g. "这本书有语言简单，容易读的特点". (This book has the characteristics of simple language and being easy to read.)

☞ 除了这些以外，这家饭馆还有几个特点。

A: 学校的餐厅有什么特点？
B: 有这么几个特点：吃饭方便，价钱便宜，环境很干净。
A: 在外边吃饭又有什么特点呢？
B: 在外边吃饭的特点是：很方便，价钱不贵，气氛也不错。

A: What are the characteristics of the school's cafeteria?

B: It has these characteristics: convenient dining, inexpensive prices, and very clean surroundings.

A: What are the characteristics of eating out?

B: The characteristics of eating out are that it is very convenient, the prices aren't expensive, and the atmosphere is pretty good.

七、 一是……二是……三是…… (first...; second...; and third...)

> ✍ This expression is used to specify a number of points that the speaker wants to make about a certain topic， e.g. "这本书有很多特点，一是有生字，二是有句型，三是有练习"。 (This book possesses many different characteristics: one, it has a vocabulary list; two, it has sentence patterns; and three, it has exercises.)

☞ 一是气氛轻松，环境很好；二是服务员小姐很客气；三是饭菜上得很快。

1、我们的宿舍有这么几个特点：一是干净；二是有自己的洗澡设备；三是二十四小时供应热水。

Our dorm has these characteristics: first, it is clean; second, we have our own showering facilities; and third, hot water is supplied 24 hours a day.

2、要是想学好中文，一是要天天说，二是要好好预备功课，三是要每天练习新字。

If you want to learn Chinese well, first, you must speak daily; second, you must prepare your classwork diligently; and third, you must practice the new characters every day.

八、受……的欢迎 (to be welcomed by)

> ✍ "受……的欢迎" means "to be welcomed by" or "popular among". The preposition coupled with "欢迎" must be "受", e.g. "这本书受学生的欢迎". (This book is very well received by students.) When negating the sentence, the negative particle "不" must be placed before "受", NOT before the verb of the sentence, e.g. "这本书不受学生的欢迎". (This book is not popular among the students.)

☞ 所以这家饭馆最受学生的欢迎。

1、这种经济实惠的咖啡厅受到了学生的欢迎。

This economical and practical type of cafe is welcomed by the students.

2、又快又安全的直航班机最受人们的欢迎。

A direct flight that is both quick and safe is most welcomed by the people.

九、约…… (to make an appointment/a date, to agree to meet)

> ✍ "约" is used here to make an appointment with someone to do something together, e.g. "我约他明天去看电影". (I made a date with him to go see a movie tomorrow.) Please note that in the case of making a professional appointment, one would NOT say * "我约医生去看病". but rather "我跟医生约好了明天下午三点去看病". (I have a doctor's appointment at 3 in the afternoon tomorrow.)

☞ 我约了一位同学去学校对面的那家饭馆吃饭。

1、我约老师跟我一块儿去学校对面的饭馆吃饭。

I made a date with a teacher to dine with me at the restaurant across from the school.

2、你要不要我帮你约一个时间跟你的中国父母见面？

Do you want me to help you set up a time to meet your Chinese parents?

十、对……过敏 (to be allergic to)

> ✍ The preposition "对" is used with the expression "过敏" meaning "to be allergic to", e.g. "我对味精过敏". (I am allergic to MSG.) When negating the sentence, the negative particle "不" or "没" is normally placed before the verb, e.g. "我对这种东西倒不过敏".

☞ 我对味精过敏，吃了会有反应。

1、对不起，我对茄子过敏，一吃就觉得不舒服。

Sorry, I am allergic to eggplant. I feel sick as soon as I eat it.

2、因为我对腰果过敏，所以我不能吃腰果鸡丁。

I cannot eat cashew chicken because I am allergic to cashews.

这儿的饭菜可以说是又经济又实惠

语言形式练习
Tasks on Language Forms

一、读课文回答问题

1、为什么学生们喜欢去学校对面的饭馆吃饭？

2、从学校到饺子馆怎么走？

3、学校东边的饺子馆有什么特点？

4、学生们常在学校北边、商场对面的饭馆点什么菜？

5、这两位同学点了什么菜跟饮料？

6、为什么男学生告诉服务员不要放味精？

二、完成对话

1、A：你怎么差不多每天都去那家饭馆呢？

　　B：因为那家的饭菜……

　　（有……特点；有……的，有……的）

2、A：你要不要试试看这儿的铁板牛肉？

　　B：不行。

　　（对……过敏，可以说……）

3、A：你能不能告诉我从国际展览中心怎么去昆仑饭店？

　　B：可以。

　　（见地图）

4、A：你知道为什么人们喜欢吃素吗？

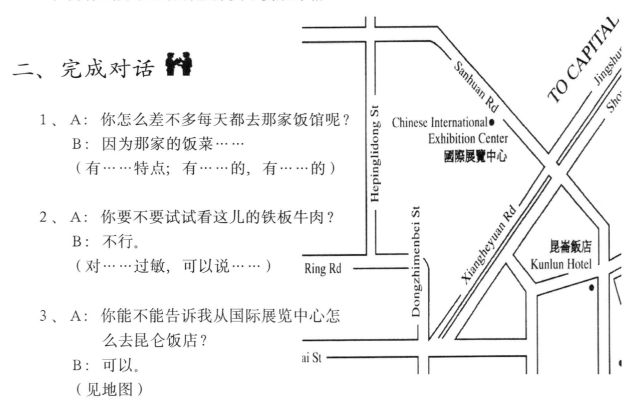

B：

（一是……，二是……，三是……）

三、听录音回答问题

1、那个女同学为什么常到这家饭馆儿吃饭？

2、男同学为什么要他的同学给他介绍饭馆的菜？

3、为什么男同学没点宫爆鸡丁也没点铁板牛肉？

4、为什么他们没叫米饭？

5、女同学点汤了吗？为什么？

6、吃饭以后，他们上哪儿去？为什么？

四、阅读回答问题

　　　　来中国以前就听说麦当劳（McDonald's)和肯德基 (Kentucky Fried Chicken)在中国很受欢迎。在北京住了一个星期以后我发现真是这样！在北京，麦当劳和肯德基不但受到小孩子的欢迎，而且更受到年轻人的欢迎。最让我吃惊的是，多半儿去麦当劳和肯德基的年轻人不是去吃饭，而是在那里会朋友！我问了一个我的中国朋友以后才明白年轻人喜欢在麦当劳和肯德基会朋友是因为他们觉得麦当劳和肯德基的环境好，气氛轻松，而且不必点很多菜就可以坐很长时间。听起来，这种会朋友的办法的确是又经济又现代。

问题:

1、为什么中国的年轻人喜欢去麦当劳和肯德基？

(1) 他们的饭好吃

(2) 环境很好

(3) 是约会的好地方

2、为什么说在麦当劳和肯德基会朋友很经济？

五、翻译

1. A: Do you know which restaurant near our school is relatively good?

   B: It depends on what kinds of food you like to eat. Are you a meat-eater or a vegetarian?

   A: I am a meat eater and I don't like to go too far.

   B: Then I would go to the restaurant right across the street. Their food is economical and practical. You would probably want to (should) order their cashew chicken and green pepper and beef.

2. There are several characteristics about this shop. The atmosphere is relaxing, the place is clean, and their service people are very polite.

3. This small restaurant specializes in Shanghai dishes. Their food is our students' favorite.

4. I made an appointment to see the front desk clerk today (约一个时间跟……见面), because I would like to ask her a few questions about the dorm.

5. My stomach feels very uncomfortable now. I must have had some MSG. Darn. I forgot to tell the waitress that I am allergic to it.

请您告诉炒菜的师傅不要放味精

语言使用练习
Tasks on Language Use

一、真实情景活动

（一）王兰的母亲昨天从美国来看王兰，住在金叶大厦。今天早上她想走路来首都经贸大学的留学生宿舍看王兰。你可以利用这张地图告诉她怎么来宿舍吗？

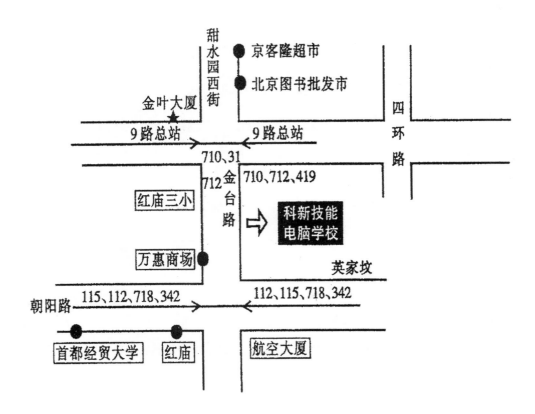

（二）听说枫林小馆 (Maple Restaurant) 是一家最受同学们欢迎的饭馆。下面是这家饭馆
　　　的介绍。请你根据"介绍"回答下面的问题:

1、枫林小馆在北京的什么地方? 小馆的西边、南边、北边都有些什么有名的大楼?

2、枫林小馆主要为客人提供什么风味的饭菜? 最贵的和最便宜的饭菜是多少钱?

3、要是你没时间来枫林小馆吃饭，这家饭馆可以提供什么服务?

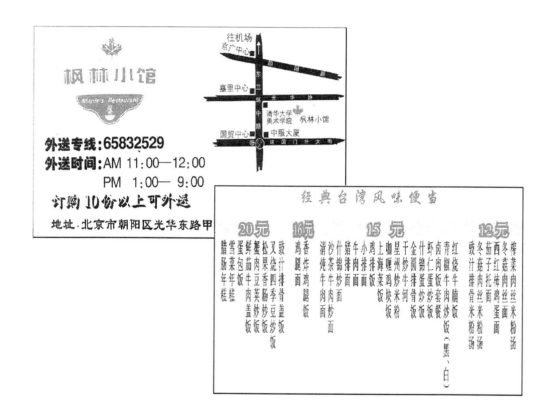

（三）今天我们五个同学要去枫林小馆吃饭。由于我们刚刚到北京，用中文点菜还不
　　　行。你能不能帮我们点几个菜? 我这儿有他们的菜单。我们五个人中，有一个人
　　　吃素，一个人对虾过敏，还有一个人只吃鸡肉不吃牛肉。还有，我们的钱也不
　　　多，一共差不多120块。你看我们应该点什么菜? 点几个菜就够我们吃了? (See the
　　　menus on this page and next page)

枫林小馆点菜单

套餐类	单价	数量	凉菜类	单价	数量	饮品类	单价	数量
卤肉饭	15元		拍黄瓜	5元		酸梅汤	8元	
鸡排饭	15元		香辣海带	5元		蛋蜜汁	15元	
上海菜饭	15元		姜汁松花蛋	5元		鲜桔汁	15元	
干炒牛河	15元		黄瓜凉粉	8元		维C果汁	15元	
星州炒米粉	15元		台湾泡菜	8元		苦中作乐	15元	
什锦蛋炒饭	15元		炝锅青笋	8元		珍珠奶茶	15元	
虾仁蛋炒饭	15元		肉皮冻	8元		芋头沙奶茶	15元	
咖喱鸡块饭	15元		萝卜干毛豆	8元		泡沫咖啡	15元	
红烧牛腩饭	15元		皮蛋豆腐	10元		水果茶	15元	
金圆排骨饭	15元		水果沙拉	16元		台湾高山茶	15元	
青椒牛肉炒饭(黑)	15元		**热炒类**	**单价**	**数量**	紫苏梅汁	15元	
青椒牛肉炒饭(白)	15元		清炒油菜	8元		**凉面类**	**单价**	**数量**
香炸鸡腿饭	18元		醋溜白菜	8元		炸酱凉面	15元	
大排饭	18元		醋溜土豆丝	8元		麻酱凉面	15元	
沙茶丝瓜炒饭	18元		炝炒高丽菜	10元		鸡丝凉面	15元	
沙茶牛肉炒饭	20元		清炒菠菜	10元		牛肉凉面	15元	
咖喱牛肉盖饭	20元		蒜茸菠菜	10元		**冰品类**	**单价**	**数量**
蚝油牛肉盖饭	20元		糖醋茄子	12元		西瓜汁	10元	
鲜茄牛肉盖饭	20元		西红柿炒鸡蛋	12元		红豆牛奶冰	10元	
豉汁排骨盖饭	20元		菜莆蛋	12元		绿豆牛奶冰	10元	
松果香肠炒饭	20元		麻婆豆腐	12元		水果刨冰	12元	
叉烧四季豆炒饭	20元		红烧豆腐	12元		菠萝刨冰	12元	
红烧扣肉饭	20元		开阳白菜	15元		草莓刨冰	12元	
蹄花饭	20元		姜汁芥兰	15元		爱玉刨冰	12元	
蛋包饭	20元		清炒芥兰	15元		麦角葡萄冰	12元	
狮子头盖饭	20元		苦瓜咸蛋	16元		乌梅牛奶冰	12元	
面、米粉类	**单价**	**数量**	清炒丝瓜	16元		红豆沙冰	12元	
茄子托面	12元		蛤蜊蒸蛋	16元		绿豆沙冰	12元	
西红柿鸡蛋面	12元		鱼香肉丝	16元		菠萝沙冰	15元	
冬菇肉丝面(米粉)	15元		天府牛里脊	18元		草莓沙冰	15元	
榨菜肉丝面(米粉)	15元		宫爆鸡丁	18元		乌梅沙冰	15元	
豉汁小排面(米粉)	15元		砂锅鱼头	20元		百香沙冰	15元	
大排面(米粉)	15元		客家小炒	25元		柳橙沙冰	15元	
鸡排面(米粉)	15元		红烧肉	25元		金桔沙冰	15元	
猪排面(米粉)	15元		豉汁排骨	28元		冰镇水果茶	15元	

二、讨论

1、你平常在哪儿吃饭？为什么在那儿吃？

2、现在你最喜欢吃的中国菜是什么？为什么？

3、美国的中国菜跟北京的中国菜有什么不同？（比较一下菜的风味、饭馆儿的服务、气氛、跟付钱 (pay) 的方法。）

三、语言实践

选 (select) 北京市的一个小饭馆跟一个大饭馆去采访 (interview)。比较一下这两家饭馆的风味、服务、跟气氛，并告诉别的学生怎么去这两家饭馆。

四、作文

《我常去的两家饭馆》

五、看图说话

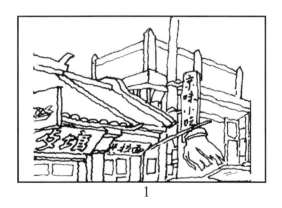

1

2

3

4

5

6

我的大学附近有很多饭馆，三步一家，五步一个

An Intermediate Chinese Course

第四课　中国家庭

我们的中国母亲

课文

　　我来中国以前以为在中国交朋友很容易，其实并不容易。虽然到处都是中国人，但是一方面因为我们的汉语⁽¹⁾水平还不够高，一方面因为留学生宿舍里住的都是外国人⁽²⁾，除了我们的老师以外，没有合适的机会认识其他的中国人。为了解决这个问题，我们学校为我们安排了中国家庭，使我们在留学期间能了解一些中国家庭的生活情况，也使我们在北京的生活不至于太寂寞、无聊。我的中国家庭人口很少，只有父母和女儿婷婷。我的中国父母都是大学教授，女儿在一所公立学校上初中三年级，明年就要考高中了，所以功课很紧张。

　　我的中国父母对我非常关心，常常打电话邀请⁽³⁾我去他们家吃饭。他们住在学校的职工宿舍，两室一厅⁽⁴⁾。听说这样的住房条件在北京算是非常好的。中国人很好客⁽⁵⁾，每次都准备一桌子的菜，让我

Notes (1) "汉语" vs. "中文": "汉语" literally means "the language of Han Nationality". It is the term used mainly in Mainland China to refer to Mandarin Chinese. "中文", however, is used outside of Mainland China to generally refer to the Chinese language. This is controversial because what really constitutes the Chinese language is debatable. (For more information on these two terms, read Chapter 10, <u>Chinese</u> by Jerry Norman, 1988.)

(2) "住的都是外国人": "住的" here is a typical Chinese modifying clause with the modified element omitted because it is clear in the context and therefore need not be mentioned explicitly. Its full form is "住的人" which means "those who live there". Other examples of this structure include "在这儿吃饭的都是学生"。(Those who are eating here are all students.) "他手里拿的都是钱"。(What he is holding in his hand is money.)

(3) "邀请" vs. "请": "邀请" and "请" both mean "to invite". "邀请" is commonly used in formal and written settings, e.g. "中国家庭常常邀请他们的美国孩子们来家中作客"。(The Chinese families often [formally] invite their American children to their home); "请", however, is used more often in spoken language for casual or sometimes formal invitations, e.g. "他请我去那家饭馆吃晚饭" (He invited me to that restaurant to have dinner.) "请" in this sentence indicates an informal invitation. In addition, "请" also has the meaning of "treating someone to something", e.g. "我请你吃龙虾，好吗"? (I will treat you to lobster, OK?) In face-to-face conversations, one rarely uses "邀请" to invite someone, unless it is an official or formal invitation.

非常不好意思。所以每次去拜访(6)他们的时候，我也带一些小礼物送给他们。

———————◆———————

（吃完饭以后，大家在客厅聊天）

学生： 爸爸，妈妈，这些是我从美国带来的风景明信片，有纽约的世界贸易中心和自由神像，希望你们喜欢。

爸： 谢谢，谢谢。纽约是美国第一大城，两年前我去过一次。

婷： 姐姐，纽约是不是真的很可怕，每天都有抢劫、偷窃、杀人的事情？

学生： 其实任何一个大城市都有社会治安问题，纽约当然也不例外。

妈： 最近几年，北京的治安也有问题了，晚上最好不要一个人出去。离开房间得锁门，贵重的东西，像护照、现金什么的(7)要收好，锁在保险柜里，或者交给前台保管，免得发生意外。

学生： 我觉得您的这些建议非常好。

Notes (4) "两室一厅" : This expression really refers to the typical two-bedroom apartment in China. One must remember most Chinese people's concept of "两室一厅" is quite different from the one in the US. "厅" to most Mainland Chinese is an area which makes up the center of the apartment. It often has the multiple functions of living room, dining room, family room, and sometimes bedroom.

(5) "好客" : "好" can also mean "like or love to do something". In this case, it is pronounced with a fourth tone and is a verb often used with a noun or a verb to form an idiomatic expression, e.g. "好客" (hospitable); "好名" (nameseeking); "好学" (love to learn); "好动" (very active).

(6) "拜访" vs. "看" : "拜访" and "看" both can mean "to pay a visit". "拜访" often carries a respectful tone and is normally used to refer to a formal visit to a respected person, or a person senior by generation, age, or rank. In this lesson, "拜访" is appropriate for the speaker to use to express his respect for his Chinese parents. "看" , on the other hand, is often used in spoken language for an informal visit. It does not necessarily carry the formal tone of "拜访" , e.g. "今天下午你的父母来看我，下个星期我也得去拜访他们" 。 (Your parents came to see me this afternoon. I will have to pay a [formal] visit to them next week.)

(7) "什么的" vs. "等等" : Both "什么的" and "等等" have the meaning of "and so on" or "so on and so forth". "什么的" is often used in informal spoken settings, e.g. "你为什么常常带你的书、本子、什么的去咖啡厅" ？ (Why do you always bring your books, notebook, and so on to the Coffee House?) "等等" can be used in both formal or informal situations， e.g. "你为什么常常带你的书、本子、等等去咖啡厅" ？ or "我们今天上课要讨论的问题跟中国的社会、文化、经济等等有关系" 。 (The questions we will discuss today in class relate to Chinese society, culture, economics, etc.)

说到这儿，我一看表，已经九点了，我大吃一惊，因为我还得预备明天的课呢，所以我就告辞⁽⁸⁾回家了。

—— 生词 ——

1. 家庭	jiā tíng	*N.*	family
2. 交朋友	jiāo péng you	*VO.*	to make friends
3. 其实	qí shí	*Adv.*	actually
4. 到处	dào chù	*Adv.*	everywhere
5. 汉语	hàn yǔ	*N.*	Mandarin Chinese
6. 水平	shuǐ píng	*N.*	proficiency, standard
7. 一方面	yì fāng miàn	*Adv.*	on one hand
8. 合适	hé shì	*Adj.*	suitable, appropriate
9. 其他	qí tā	*Adj.*	other, else
10. 为了	wèi le	*Prep.*	in order to
11. 解决	jiě jué	*V.*	to solve, to resolve
12. 为	wèi	*Prep.*	for
13. 使	shǐ	*V.*	to let, to cause
14. 期间	qī jiān	*N.*	time period, duration
15. 不至于	bú zhì yú	*Adv.*	cannot go so far as..., not reach the point of...
16. 寂寞	jì mò	*Adj.*	lonely
17. 无聊	wú liáo	*Adj.*	boring, bored
18. 人口	rén kǒu	*N.*	the number of people in a family, population
19. 女儿	nǚ ér	*N.*	daughter

Notes ⁽⁸⁾ "告辞" vs. "再见"："告辞" and "再见" are used in different contexts and for different purposes. "告辞" is normally used in a descriptive context meaning "to take leave", "to bid farewell", or "to say good-bye", e.g. "我是九点告辞的" (I took off at 9:00). One CANNOT say ＊"我是九点再见的"。 "再见", on the other hand, is a parting expression used at the end of any conversation, whether it be on the street or over the phone. One can say "再见" to end a conversation or to bid farewell but not "告辞". On rare occasions, "告辞了" is used for "再见". This usage, however, sounds rather bookish and showy.

20. 婷婷	tíng ting	*Personal N.*	Tingting
21. 教授	jiào shòu	*N.*	professor
22. 所	suǒ	*Classifier.*	classifier for schools and other institutions
23. 公立	gōng lì	*Adj.*	public, established/operated by government
24. 初中	chū zhōng	*N.*	junior high school
25. 高中	gāo zhōng	*N.*	senior high school
26. 功课	gōng kè	*N.*	schoolwork
27. 关心	guān xīn	*V.*	to be concerned, to care about
28. 邀请	yāo qǐng	*V.*	to invite
29. 职工	zhí gōng	*Abbrev.*	staff, employees
30. 两室一厅	liǎng shì yì tīng	*Abbrev.*	two rooms and one living room
31. 住房	zhù fáng	*N.*	housing, lodging
32. 算	suàn	*V.*	to regard as, to be considered
33. 好客	hào kè	*Adj.*	hospitable, sociable
34. 准备	zhǔn bèi	*V.*	to prepare
35. 一桌子	yì zhuō zi	*N.*	a tableful
36. 让	ràng	*V.*	to let, to cause
37. 不好意思	bù hǎo yì si	*Adj.*	embarrassed
38. 拜访	bài fǎng	*V.*	to visit (someone)
39. 礼物	lǐ wù	*N.*	present, gift
40. 送	sòng	*V.*	to give something as a gift
41. 客厅	kè tīng	*N.*	living room
42. 聊天	liáo tiān	*VO.*	to chat
43. 风景	fēng jǐng	*N.*	scenery
44. 明信片	míng xìn piàn	*N.*	postcard
45. 纽约	niǔ yuē	*Place N.*	New York
46. 世界贸易中心	shì jiè mào yì zhōng xīn	*Place N.*	World Trade Center
47. 自由神像	zì yóu shén xiàng	*N.*	Statue of Liberty
48. 城	chéng	*N.*	city
49. 可怕	kě pà	*Adj.*	terrible, terrifying
50. 抢劫	qiǎng jié	*N\V.*	robbery; to rob

51. 偷窃	tōu qiè	N/V.	theft, to steal
52. 杀人	shā rén	VO.	to kill people
53. 任何	rèn hé	Adj.	any
54. 城市	chéng shì	N.	city
55. 社会	shè huì	N.	society
56. 治安	zhì ān	N.	safety, security
57. 例外	lì wài	Adj/N.	exceptional; exception
58. 最近	zuì jìn	Adv.	recently
59. 最好	zuì hǎo	Adv.	had better
60. 离开	lí kāi	V.	to leave
61. 锁门	suǒ mén	VO.	to lock door
62. 贵重	guì zhòng	Adj.	precious, valuable
63. 护照	hù zhào	N.	passport
64. 现金	xiàn jīn	N.	cash
65. 收	shōu	V.	to store, to put away, to collect
66. 保险柜	bǎo xiǎn guì	N.	safe
67. 交	jiāo	V.	to turn in, to hand over
68. 保管	bǎo guǎn	V.	to take care of, to keep safely
69. 免得	miǎn dé	Adv.	so as not to, so as to avoid
70. 发生	fā shēng	V.	to happen, to occur
71. 意外	yì wài	N/Adj.	accident, mishap; unexpected
72. 建议	jiàn yì	N/V.	suggestion; to suggest
73. 大吃一惊	dà chī yì jīng	VO.	to be greatly shocked or startled (cf. 吃惊, Lesson 1)
74. 预备	yù bèi	V.	to prepare
75. 告辞	gào cí	V.	to take leave (of one's host)

———◆——— 补充词汇 ———◆———

76. 儿子	ér zi	N.	son
77. 孙子	sūn zi	N.	grandson
78. 爷爷	yé ye	N.	paternal grandfather

79.	奶奶	nǎi nai	N.	paternal grandmother
80.	姥爷	lǎo ye	N.	maternal grandfather
81.	姥姥	lǎo lao	N.	maternal grandmother
82.	伯伯	bó bo	N.	father's older brother
83.	伯母	bó mǔ	N.	wife of father's older brother
84.	叔叔	shū shu	N.	father's younger brother
85.	舅舅	jiù jiu	N.	mother's brother
86.	阿姨	ā yí	N.	mother's sister, auntie
87.	单位	dān wèi	N.	work unit
88.	高考	gāo kǎo	N.	college entrance examination
89.	饭厅	fàn tīng	N.	dining room
90.	洗碗	xǐ wǎn	VO.	to do dishes
91.	地下室	dì xià shì	N.	basement
92.	纪念品	jì niàn pǐn	N.	souvenir
93.	华盛顿	huá shèng dùn	Place N.	Washington
94.	费城	fèi chéng	Place N.	Philadelphia
95.	芝加哥	zhī jiā gē	Place N.	Chicago
96.	洛杉矶	luò shān jī	Place N.	Los Angeles
97.	旧金山	jiù jīn shān	Place N.	San Francisco
98.	吸毒	xī dú	VO.	to "inhale" drugs, to take drugs
99.	犯罪	fàn zuì	VO.	to commit crimes
100.	印象	yìn xiàng	N.	impression

句型

一、 到处都······ (to be everywhere)

> ✍ "到处都" is normally used in a topic comment structure meaning "everywhere" or "anywhere". It is placed immediately before a verb, e.g. "到处都是"; "到处都有"; "到处都能买到". Depending on the emphasis of the sentence, "到处都" can be preceded by elements functioning as subject, object, place word, or time word of the sentence, e.g. "修车的人到处都去". (A bike/car repairman will go anywhere.) "这种车到处都有". (This kind of vehicle can be seen everywhere.) "北京到处是人". (People are everywhere in Beijing.) "现在到处都卖这种东西". (Such a thing is sold everywhere these days.) In the four examples above, although the elements preceding "到处都" have different grammatical functions, that is "修车的人" is an subject, "这种车" is an object, "北京" is a place adverb, and "现在" is a time adverb, these elements all function as the topic of the sentence. When negating the sentence with "到处都", the negative particle is placed immediately before the verb, e.g. "到处都没有," "到处都不卖".

☞ 到处都是中国人······

1、 在北京到处都是出租汽车。
Beijing is filled with taxis.

2、 学校的附近到处都是饭馆，非常方便。
There are restaurants everywhere around the school; it is very convenient.

二、 一方面······一方面······ (on the one hand...; on the other hand...)

> ✍ "一方面······一方面······" is used to connect two related cases or two aspects of one topic. It can be used to express two abstract situations occurring at the same time; while "一边······一边" is used to connect two concrete actions, e.g. "他一边吃饭一边看报". (He eats while reading the paper.) In this sentence, "一边······一边······" cannot be replaced by "一方面······一方面". The adverb "另" can be used before the second "一方面······".

☞ 一方面因为我们的汉语水平还不够高，一方面因为留学生宿舍里住的都是外国人，除了我们的老师以外，没有合适的机会认识其他的中国人。

1、我到北京来一方面是因为北京是中国的首都，一方面也是因为北京是学中文最理想的地方。

I came to Beijing because, on the one hand, it is the capital of China, and on the other hand, it is the most ideal place to study Chinese.

2、这家饭馆一方面气氛很好，一方面离学校很近，所以很受学生的欢迎。

On the one hand the atmosphere at this restaurant is very good, and on the other it is very close to the school. Therefore, it is popular with students.

三、为了 (in order to)

> ✍ "为了" is used in a sentence to introduce the purpose of an action. "为了" normally appears at the beginning of a sentence indicating the purpose. The usage of "为了" is somewhat different from "因为", e.g. in the sentence "因为我有空所以我去看电影". (Because I have free time, I'm going to see a movie.) "因为" cannot be replaced by "为了".

☞ 为了解决这个问题，我们学校为我们安排了中国家庭，使我们在留学期间能了解一些中国家庭的生活情况。

1、为了坐出租汽车，我一出海关就去换了些人民币。

In order to take a cab, I changed some money to RMB as soon as I came out of customs.

2、为了打国际长途电话，我买了一张电话磁卡。

In order to make an international phone call, I bought an IC card.

四、使 (to make, to cause)

> ✍ "使" meaning "to make, to cause", is used more frequently in a written context than in a spoken context. The object of 使 is always a situation expressed by a sentence and not by a noun phrase or adjective; e.g. one CANNOT say * "他使许多错误的看法"; but CAN say "他使学生有许多错误的看法". (He causes the students to hold many erroneous viewpoints.)

☞ 使我们在留学期间能了解一些中国家庭的生活情况。

1、我们的中文水平提高得很快，使老师们非常高兴。

Our Chinese level has risen rapidly, which makes our teachers very happy.

2、他送了我一个很贵重的礼物，使我不知道怎么办好。

I did not know what to do when he gave me a very expensive gift.

五、 在……期间 (during the period of)

> "期间" refers to a period of time. "……的时候" oftentimes means "when". (It can also mean "during" depending on the context). "在……期间" is more formal than "……的时候" and is often used with a time expression denoting a relatively long time-period.

☞ 使我们在留学期间能了解一些中国家庭的生活情况。

1、在北京期间，我有机会了解很多不同的中国人。

During my time in Beijing I had the opportunity to get to know many different Chinese people.

2、在学校期间，学生们可以说每天都要学习五个钟头。

While at school, it can be said that students will have to study for five hours every day.

六、 不至于 (cannot go as far as, not reach the point of)

> The expression "不至于" is used to indicate that even though the situation is not favorable, it is unlikely that it will go to the extreme case suggested after "不至于". Please note that this expression is usually used in negative form. "我很累，可是不至于不能上课"。(I am tired all right, but not to the degree that I can't go to class.)

☞ 使我们在北京的生活不至于太寂寞，无聊。

1、我们的功课虽然多，可是不至于太难。

Although we have a lot of homework, it is not so hard.

2、那家馆子虽然有名，可是并不至于太贵。

Although that restaurant is very famous, it hasn't reached the point of being too expensive.

3、我很忙，可是不至于忙得连睡觉的时间都没有。

I am very busy, but not to the extent that I don't even have time to sleep.

七、算（是）(to be considered as)

> ✎ "算 (是)" means "to consider", "to regard as". "算" may be followed directly by an adjective indicating one's conclusion about the topic. "算" cannot be followed by a direct object. One CANNOT say * "我算餐厅不远". The CORRECT way of saying it would either be "餐厅不算远". or "我想餐厅不算远". (I don't think that the cafeteria is far.) The original meaning of "算" is "to count". This usage of "算" is derived from the idea of "to be counted/reckoned as..."

☞ 听说这样的住房条件在北京算是非常好的。

1、 这家的冰淇淋和啤酒都算是最好的。
This restaurant's ice cream and beer are considered to be the best.

2、 学校为我们安排的饭菜算是非常经济实惠的。
The dishes the school arranged for us are considered to be very inexpensive and the portions are generous.

八、任何 (any)

> ✎ "任何" is a noun modifier meaning "any N" or "every N". When used with a negative verb (不 or 没), it means "none". Thus "任何" indicates all-inclusiveness, or all-exclusiveness when used with a negative verb. "任何" can occur either before or after the main verb in a sentence. When it occurs before the main verb, the idea of all-inclusiveness or all-exclusiveness is always reinforced by the adverb "都"; e.g. "任何人都可以来", (Anyone can come.) "他可以说没有任何问题". (One could say that he does not have any problems.)

☞ 任何一个大城市都有社会治安问题。

1、 要是你有问题，任何时间都可以去问老师。
If you have a problem you can go ask a teacher any time.

2、 他对任何人都很关心。
He cares about everyone.

九、免得 (so as to avoid)

> ✍ "免得" is a transitive verb meaning "to avoid". The object of "免得" is usually not a simple noun or adjective, but an expression by a sentence indicating a condition, a piece of advice, or a statement.

☞ 免得发生意外。

1、你要是不能回家，一定得打电话给父母，免得他们担心。

  If you are unable to return home, you must call your parents so they won't worry about you.

2、你多带些钱，免得买东西的时候钱不够。

  Bring more money so as to avoid running out of money when you are shopping.

我的中国父母常常邀请我出去玩

语言形式练习
Tasks on Language Forms

一、 读课文回答问题

1、 为什么这个美国学生觉得在中国交朋友并不容易？

2、 这个美国学生的中国家庭里有些什么人？他们都做什么工作？

3、 为什么这个美国学生每次去拜访中国家庭的时候，都带些小礼物？

4、 婷婷对纽约的印象怎么样？

5、 中国妈妈给了这个美国学生什么？

二、 完成对话

1、 A： 他为什么不想住在纽约？

　　 B：

　　 （一方面……一方面……）

2、 A： 在留学生宿舍里住的都是外国人吗？

　　 B：

　　 （除了……以外，……都……）

3、 A： 为什么学校为我们安排到长城去参观？

　　 B：

　　 （使）

4、 A： 这几年北京的社会治安越来越坏吗？

　　 B：

　　 （不至于）

5、A：王先生，我们什么时候可以来拜访您？

B：

（任何）

6、A：为什么不可以喝生水？

B：

（免得）

三、听录音回答问题

1、小李来美国以前觉得美国的治安怎么样？
2、小李为什么觉得他住的地方治安比北京好？
3、小李的英文听力进步了吗？为什么？
4、小李的英文水平为什么没有太大的进步？
5、为什么小李的美国朋友不多？

中国人很好客，每次都准备一桌子的菜

四、阅读回答问题

爸爸妈妈：

我来纽约大学也差不多一个星期了，很想念你们。这几天大学还没有开学，我就跟几个同学约好了一起去纽约市中心和其它地方看看。前天我们还去了一趟世界贸易中心。虽然，贸易中心的大楼已经没有了，但是还有很多人去那儿参观。"九一一"以后，这块没有大楼的空地也变成了一个有历史意义的地方。尽管纽约是一个大城市，但是并不像人们说的那么可怕，我觉得社会治安和交通治安都还不错。

我跟我的其他几个同学住在一个三室一厅的房子里。这里的住房条件很好，就是离别的住家都很远。所以，到现在，我们还没有很多机会认识一些美国朋友，有机会用英语跟他

You're unforgettably nice!

们交流。现在我们的生活还真有一点儿寂寞无聊。也许，开学以后就会好得多。

好了，先写到这儿。

祝

好！

儿：王义

问题：

1、王义在哪里上大学？

2、开学前他去过什么地方参观？他觉得那个地方怎么样？

3、王义觉得那个地方的治安怎么样？

4、说说王义的住房情况。

5、你建议王义应该怎么找机会跟美国人交朋友或者交流？

五、翻译

1. Society's security is getting worse and worse nowadays. You should keep your valuables in a safe place.

2. The living conditions in Beijing are not good. In many families, four to five people crowd

into a one-bedroom apartment. They don't even have their own private bath facilities.

3. In order to have more opportunities to practice Chinese, I often spend time with my Chinese family. They care very much for me. They often give me some useful suggestions for living in Beijing.

4. Two years ago, I went to New York. I visited the World Trade Center and the Statue of Liberty there.

5. Mr. Wang called to invite me to have dinner at his house yesterday. Every time I go to visit them, I always bring a gift. This time, I am going to give them some fruit.

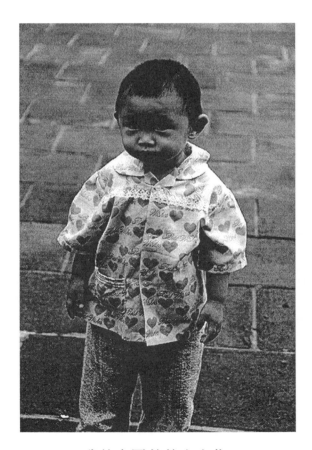

我的中国弟弟小小儿

语言使用练习
Tasks on Language Use

一、真实情景活动 📹

（一）在中国到处都可以看到下边这样的广告，你知道广告上写的是什么吗？用英文写出这个广告的意思。

（二）下边这个广告写的是什么？用你自己的话把这个广告的意思说一说。

刘先生

客厅 (living room)

卧室 (bedroom)

（三）刘先生十年前就是一所公立学校的职工，住的是一室一厅的单位宿舍，十年后孩子
们都大了，刘先生还住在这套房子里。虽然屋子大小没有变化，可是家里的东西比
以前多多了。这是我去年看见的他的家，请你根据上边这几张照片(photos)说一说
他家的住房情况。

（四）今年六月，我又在北京见到了刘先生。他说他刚买了新房，在北京的东边，离市中心差不多四十分钟。下边是他家新房的平面图 (lay-out)。请你给他一些建议，告诉他这几间屋子应该怎么安排，他家的东西应该怎么放。

卧室 (wò shì)=bedroom

厨房 (chú fáng)=kichen

卫生间 (wèi shēng jiān)=bathroom

餐厅 (cān tīng)=dining room

客厅 (kè tīng)=living room

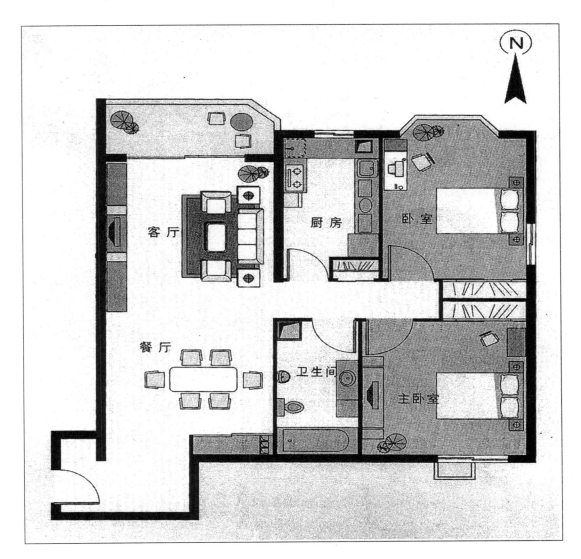

刘先生家新房平面图

（五）看了刘先生的新房后，我问他为什么买房买到这么远的地方，他说了下面的一段话。后来他的话让卖房子的人拿去作卖房广告了。

> 刘先生（退休职工）：早就厌倦了每天的噪音和污浊空气，可真要住到郊区去，又害怕生活不方便，华馨园算是解决了这一难题，各种生活设施非常齐全，最主要是价格还非常便宜，一套二居才14万多，周末全家都可以住得下，现在我可以放心享受郊区的青山绿水和清新空气了。

（六）根据刘先生的话，回答下面的问题：

1、刘先生买新房是为了什么时候去住？。
2、为什么他喜欢那里的房子？
3、他喜欢城里的什么？讨厌城里的什么？

二、讨论

1、你觉得交中国朋友容易吗？为什么？
2、在北京你的生活寂寞吗？你怎么安排下课以后的时间？
3、请你介绍一下你的中国家庭。
4、你跟你的中国家庭多久见一次面？你们常一块儿做什么？
5、你的中国家庭对美国的文化感兴趣吗？他们常问你什么问题？你怎么回答这些问题？
6、你喜欢学校为你安排中国家庭吗？为什么？

三、语言实践

1、请你问问你的中国家庭，他们为什么愿意作美国学生的中国父母？
2、访问大学的学生，问问他们愿意不愿意和外国留学生交朋友？为什么？
3、访问附近的居民，问问他们对北京社会治安的看法。

四、作文

《我的中国家庭》

五、看图说话

没想到我的中国家庭的生活条件还真不错

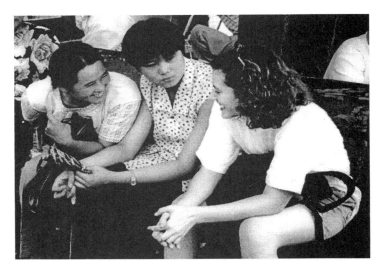

我的中国家庭让我在北京的生活一点儿都不寂寞

An Intermediate Chinese Course

第五课　我的中文课

大班课

对话课

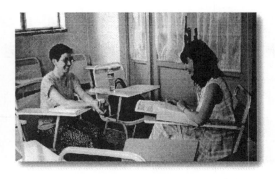

单班课

课文

爸爸、妈妈：

　　你们好！离上课还有半个钟头，我想利用这点时间给你们写封信，告诉你们我这几天生活和学习的情况。从到这里的第一天起，我们就开始执行语言誓约：只说中文不说英文。到现在已经三天了，我还没说过一句英文。看到我能三天一句英文也不说，我心里非常高兴。我觉得我们都应该遵守这个誓约，这对我们是有好处的。

　　这里的中文课可真不简单。每天学生都要上四堂课，课上[1]要求也很严。我们的课分四种类型：大班、小班、对话课和单班课。大班是老师讲课文和语法，小班是五位学生和一位老师一块儿练习生词和句型。课上以练习为主，有时候也有讨论。对话课通常是一个老师帮助两个学生进行对话和讨论。单班课是一个学生一个老师，学生不但可以问老师问题，而且有大量[2]的机会跟老师练习，让老师改正错误。单班课是我最喜欢的课。

　　这些不同的课对我来说非常理想，因为我可以直接[3]跟中国老师和同学用中文交流。我的单班课老师是一个研究生，上课的时候我们

Notes [1] "课上"："上" here has the meaning of "within/during a certain event". "课上" thus means "during class". "会上" means "during the meeting". "书上" means "in the book".

[2] "大量"：This expression literally means "a large quantity of". It is mostly used with "的" to modify noncountable or uncounted nouns, e.g. "大量的钱" (a large amount of money); "大量的时间" (a great deal of time); "大量的人力" (a great deal of manpower).

[3] "直接"：This word, meaning "directly", can be an adverb preceding the verb in a sentence, e.g. "直接去图书馆" (to go to the library directly), or an adjective preceding a noun, e.g. "直接的关系" (direct relationship).

讨论的问题都非常有意思。比方说，中国的独生子女问题、妇女问题等等。以前，我在大学里选过很多中国政治、历史和社会学方面的课，现在我能把这些知识用到我的讨论中，让我非常高兴。

不多写了，要去上单班课了。

祝

好！

女儿：小星

年　月　日

———◆———

（小星和刘老师在教室里）

星：刘老师，您觉得我应该怎么准备每天的课呢？

刘：我觉得最重要的是课前要准备好新课的生词、语法和句型。最好的办法就是先听录音带，看录像带，然后看生词和课文。

星：预备生词时应该不应该知道一个词的词性？

刘：应该注意词性。比方说，一个词是动词、名词、形容词，还是副词？

星：怎么预备课文呢？

刘：看课文时，要一边看一边理解课文的内容。如果有问题要记下来，第二天可以在上课时问老师。

星：您的办法听起来很有效，我一定试试看。

—◆— 生词 —◆—

1. 封	fēng	*Classifier.*	classifier for letter
2. 执行	zhí xíng	*V.*	to carry out
3. 语言誓约	yǔ yán shì yuē	*NP.*	language pledge
4. 到现在	dào xiàn zài	*PrepP.*	up till now
5. 只	zhǐ	*Adv.*	only
6. 遵守	zūn shǒu	*V.*	to obey, to abide by
7. 好处	hǎo chù	*N.*	advantage, benefit
8. 堂	táng	*Classifier.*	classifier for class period
9. 要求	yāo qiú	*N/V.*	request; to demand
10. 严	yán	*Adj.*	strict
11. 分	fēn	*V.*	to divide, to classify
12. 类型	lèi xíng	*N.*	type
13. 对话课	duì huà kè	*N.*	conversation class
14. 单班课	dān bān kè	*N.*	One-on-one class
15. 讲	jiǎng	*V.*	to lecture, to tell (about)
16. 语法	yǔ fǎ	*N.*	grammar
17. 练习	liàn´ xí	*N.*	exercise
18. 生词	shēng cí	*N.*	vocabulary
19. 句型	jù xíng	*N.*	sentence pattern
20. 以……为主	yǐ...wéi zhǔ	*VP.*	to focus on, to be primarily
21. 讨论	tǎo lùn	*N/V.*	discussion; to discuss
22. 通常	tōng cháng	*Adv.*	generally, usually
23. 大量	dà liàng	*Quan.*	large (amount/quantity)
24. 改正	gǎi zhèng	*V.*	to correct
25. 错误	cuò wù	*N.*	mistake, error
26. 直接	zhí jiē	*Adv/Adj.*	directly; direct
27. 交流	jiāo liú	*V/N.*	to exchange; interchange
28. 研究生	yán jiū shēng	*N.*	graduate student
29. 比方说	bǐ fāng shuō	*Idiom.*	for example
30. 独生子女	dú shēng zǐ nǚ	*NP.*	single child
31. 妇女	fù nǚ	*N.*	woman
32. 选	xuǎn	*V.*	to choose

33. 政治	zhèng zhì	*N.*	politics
34. 历史	lì shǐ	*N.*	history
35. 社会学	shè huì xué	*N.*	sociology
36. 方面	fāng miàn	*N.*	aspect
37. 知识	zhī shi	*N.*	knowledge
38. 用	yòng	*V.*	to use
39. 重要	zhòng yào	*Adj.*	important
40. 录音带	lù yīn dài	*N.*	audio tape
41. 录像带	lù xiàng dài	*N.*	video tape
42. 课文	kè wén	*N.*	text
43. 词性	cí xìng	*N.*	part of speech
44. 动词	dòng cí	*N.*	verb
45. 名词	míng cí	*N.*	noun
46. 形容词	xíng róng cí	*N.*	adjective
47. 副词	fù cí	*N.*	adverb
48. 一边……一边	yì biān...yì biān	*Adv.*	while..., at the same time (cf. Lesson 4, Sentence Pattern 2)
49. 理解	lǐ jiě	*V/N.*	to comprehend, to understand; comprehension
50. 内容	nèi róng	*N.*	content
51. 记	jì	*V.*	to write down, to record
52. 有效	yǒu xiào	*Adj.*	effective

——◆—— 补充词汇 ——◆——

53. 拼音	pīn yīn	*N.*	Pinyin, Romanization
54. 简体字	jiǎn tǐ zì	*N.*	simplified character
55. 繁体字	fán tǐ zì	*N.*	complex (traditional) character
56. 学分	xué fēn	*N.*	course credit
57. 选课	xuǎn kè	*VO.*	to select courses
58. 四声	sì shēng	*N.*	the four tones (in Chinese)
59. 偏旁	piān páng	*N.*	character component
60. 听力	tīng lì	*N.*	listening ability
61. 阅读	yuè dú	*N/V.*	reading; to read

62. 写作	xiě zuò	*N.*	writing, composition
63. 笔记本	bǐ jì běn	*N.*	notebook
64. 作笔记	zuò bǐ jì	*VO.*	to take notes
65. 字典	zì diǎn	*N.*	dictionary
66. 一门课	yì mén kè	*NP.*	one course (门 : classifier for courses)
67. 间接	jiàn jiē	*Adv/Adj.*	indirectly; indirect
68. 地理	dì lǐ	*N.*	geography

我的两个中文老师

句型

一、离……还有 (there is/are still... before...)

> ✍ We have introduced "离" in Lesson 1 in the context of "A 离 B 远/近" meaning "place A is far or close to place B". Here "离" is used with a scheduled event or activity. A time duration expression is used after "还有" indicating how long it is from the present to the designated event, e.g. "离新年还有两个月". (There are still two months before the New Year.)

☞ 离上课还有半个钟头。

1、离开学还有两个星期, 我要好好玩一玩。

I still have two weeks before school starts, I want to have some fun.

2、离飞机起飞还有一个钟头, 我想我们还可以吃饭。

There is still an hour before the flight, I think we can eat.

二、一句 (classifier) N 也 (都) 不 V (not at all)

> ✍ This structure means "not even one, not at all". "连" can be omitted. The noun, if understood, can also be omitted. Please note that it is necessary to use either "也" or "都". This structure, which must be distinguished from the structure "连 N 都……", only appears in negative form. For example, it is grammatically INCORRECT to say: * "我连一条蛇都有". (I even have a snake.) The CORRECT form is: "我连蛇都有". This sentence implies that the speaker has a variety of pets, not only the more common ones such as dogs and cats but even snakes. "我有狗, 我有猫, 我连蛇都有". (I have dogs, cats, and I even have snakes.)

☞ 可是看到我能三天一句英文也不说, 我心里非常高兴。

1、刚到中国的时候, 我紧张得一句话都不会说。

When I first arrived in China, I was so nervous I could not speak at all.

2、我的中文课对我很有帮助, 我一堂课也没有误过。

My Chinese class is very helpful to me. I have never missed a single class.

85

三、分……类型 (to be classified as/into ...types)

> ✍ This expression means something can be further categorized into A, B, and C, etc. The measure word "种" is used, e.g. "学校附近的饭馆分好几种类型：北方菜、南方菜、四川菜"。(In the vicinity of the school there are a variety of different restaurants: those serving northern food, southern food, and Sichuanese food.) The word "类型" is optional. Using it makes the sentence somewhat more formal.

☞ 我们的课分四种类型。

1、我们的学生分为两种类型：一种是大学生，一种是研究生。
   Our students can be classified into two types; one type is college students, the other is graduate students.

2、我们的老师也分为两种类型：一种是专业的老师，一种是研究生。
   Our teachers are also classified into two types; one type is professional teachers, the other is graduate students.

四、以……为主 (to focus on, to be primarily)

> ✍ "以" here is a co-verb or preposition meaning "to take", "为" in literary Chinese means "to be", and "主" means "the primary, the most important". "我们的课以练习为主"。(Our class focuses on practice.) The negative form is "不以……为主". If the sentence is a question, the words "什么" and "谁" are often used, e.g. "你们的课以什么为主"？

☞ 课上以练习为主，有时候也有讨论。

1、这所大学的学生以学经济的为主。
   The students at this college are primarily those who study economics.

2、我们的单班课是以讨论和练习为主。
   Our one-on-one class focuses on discussion and practice.

五、对……来说 (as for ..., from the point of view of...)

> ✍ "对……来说" is a common expression meaning "as for ..., from the point of view of..." It is normally used at the beginning of a sentence to introduce a topic which often is a person or an institution, e.g. "对我来说" (as for me); "对国家来说" (as for the country); "对学校来说" (as for the school).

☞ 这些不同的课对我来说非常理想……

1、对一个刚来中国的学生来说，遵守语言誓约非常重要。

For a student who recently arrived in China, observing the language pledge is very important.

2、对中国人来说，这里的住宿条件已经非常好了。

From the point of view of the Chinese, the dorm conditions here are already good enough.

六、用……交流 (to communicate in/by)

✍ "用……交流" here is a set pattern meaning "to communicate in a certain language or by a certain means". "用" is a preposition which introduces the language or means to be used in communication. The negative form is "不用……交流". The question form is "用不用……交流"? or "用什么交流"?

☞ 因为我可以直接跟中国老师和同学用中文交流。

1、你能不能用简单的中文和中国人交流？

Can you use simple Chinese to communicate with Chinese people?

2、用中文跟中国人交流可以学到很多中国历史和文化方面的知识。

Communicating with Chinese people in Chinese enables me to learn a lot about the history and the culture.

七、比方说 (for example)

✍ "比方说" is normally used at the beginning of one or more examples. Unlike English, it cannot be inserted after the subject.

☞ 比方说，中国的独生子女问题、妇女问题等等。

1、上课之前一定要好好准备功课。比方说，听录音、看课文、准备生词。

Before class one must prepare one's homework well. For example, listen to the tapes, read the text, and prepare the vocabulary.

2、用中文交流的好处很多。比方说，你可以练习学过的句型，也可以了解中国文化。

There are many advantages to communicating in Chinese. For example, you can practice the sentence patterns you learned and you can also come to understand Chinese culture.

八、把……用到……中 (to put something in use in...)

> ✍ "中" is a literary word meaning "in". The colloquial equivalent is "里". With this structure, the "把" construction is used to introduce the thing that is being put into use in some way. Please note that the verb complement "到" or "在" after the verb "用" is necessary, e.g. "我把生字用在讨论里". (I use new vocabulary in discussions.)

☞ 现在我能把这些知识用到我的讨论中，让我非常高兴。

1、我每天都跟中国人用中文谈话，总是把学到的句型用到交流中。

I talk with Chinese people in Chinese everyday. In this way, I always use the sentence patterns that I have learned in my interactions.

2、对话课上的讨论非常有用，我可以把讨论的问题直接用到作文中。

Discussions in Conversation Class are very useful, so I can use the topics discussed directly in my essay.

九、一边……一边…… (while..., at the same time)

> ✍ "一边……一边……" can be used to mean "do one thing while doing another" or "do two things simultaneously".

☞ 要一边看一边理解课文的内容。

1、一边听录音，一边看课文是非常有效的学中文的方法。

Listening to the tape while reading the text is a very effective method for studying Chinese.

2、一边吃饭一边看书是好习惯吗？

Is reading while eating a good habit?

十、VV看(to try to V)

> ✍ "VV 看" is a fixed expression meaning "try to do something (and see)" or "give something a try". Unlike the English "try", one can only use "VV 看", and NOT * "试 + V", to express the idea of "try to do something", e.g. "吃吃看" (to give it a try and taste it); "练练看" (to try to practice); "试试看" (try it and see).

☞ 我一定试试看。

1、张老师介绍的学习方法很有效，你们可以试试看。
The study method that Professor Zhang introduced is very effective. You can give it a try.

2、妈妈，你猜猜看，今天我的听写得了多少分？
Mom, guess what grade I got on my dictation today.

除了上课以外我还有大量的机会学习中国文化

89

语言形式练习
Tasks on Language Forms

一、读课文回答问题

1、为什么到现在为止 (up until)，小星一句英文还没说过？
2、这里的中文课大致 (approximately) 分为哪四种类型？
3、大班课和小班课有什么不同？
4、小星最喜欢什么课？为什么？
5、为什么小星喜欢她的中文课？
6、刘老师觉得学生应该不应该准备每天的课？
7、刘老师告诉小星她应该怎么预备课文？

二、完成对话

1、A：你打算假期去哪儿？
　　B：我还没想好。因为……
　　（离……还远；一边……一边……）

2、A：你对中文誓约有什么看法？
　　B：
　　（对……来说；比方说……）

3、A：你能给我介绍一下首都经贸大学学生的情况吗？
　　B：好吧。
　　（……分为……类型；以……为主）

4、A：你觉得学中文最要紧的是什么？

90

B：

（用……交流；把……用到……中）

三、听录音回答问题

1、小张和小王是不是老朋友？你是怎么知道的？
2、小张到北京多长时间了？
3、小张为什么认为他的中文有了进步？
4、小张可以说英文吗？为什么？
5、小张每天上几堂中文课？他觉得累吗？为什么？
6、小王在学校上英文课的时候练习的机会多不多？为什么？
7、小王是怎么提高他的英文水平的？

四、阅读回答问题

　　最近，听说很多大学改变了上英语课的方式。传统的方法是以老师讲课文为主，学生只要听就行了。这种教法的好处是学生可以比较好地理解语法和课文的内容，但坏处也不少，就是学生没有机会利用英语跟别人直接交流。因为没有大量练习的机会，所以传统办法教出来的学生差不多一个句子都说不出来。很多教育学家已经注意到了这个问题，并且正在试着改变这种情况。比方说，在我们参观过的一所中学里，他们的英文课是以学生说话为主。老师鼓励学生把新学习的生词和句型用到课上的讨论中。学生和学生之间，学生和老师之间都用英文交流。现在，很多大学还专门请了一些母语是英文的外国教师来给学生上课，这些老师特别受到学生的欢迎。来自美国的大伟是一个很好的例子，他从研究所毕业以后就来中国教英文了。到现在，他已经在人民大学教了两年英语了。他说，在这两年中他不但交了很多中国朋友，而且也了解了很多中国社会的情况。

问题：

　　1、传统英文课的教法有什么好处？什么坏处？

　　2、我们参观的中学英文课有什么特点？

　　　　(1) 老师用英文问问题，学生用中文回答

　　　　(2) 以老师讲课为主

　　　　(3) 老师和学生之间用英文交流

　　　　(4) 学生用以前学过的生词和句型讨论问题

　　3、请你用今天新学习的生词和句型给你的老师或者中国朋友介绍你在大学里的一门课。

五、翻译

1. A: Can you tell me what you mainly study here in China?

   B: I mainly study Chinese language and history.

   A: Do you usually communicate with your teacher in Chinese or English?

   B: I use Chinese because I want to use what I learn in class in everyday life.

2. Although local Chinese people divide these restaurants into three different types [use the "ba" construction], they are all the same to us.

3. This type of course is very useful for students because it provides a great deal [in large quantity] of opportunities for them to practice. For example, our one-on-one session is a class with one teacher and one student. All we do in that class is practice sentence patterns and discuss issues about China.

4. I think the best way to learn Chinese is to live together with a Chinese friend and try to communicate with him in Chinese everyday.

语言使用练习
Tasks on Language Use

一、真实情景活动

中国现在人人都在学英语，在报纸上你会常常看到下面的广告。

怎样安排一个充实的假期？中学生英语"听说"能力训练

你参加过这样的英语培训班吗？

☞ 听力训练——让学生全面适应英语环境
☞ 口语训练——让每个学生都开口讲英语
☞ 互动式教学——让学生在轻松的活动中培养英语学习兴趣
☞ 以能力带动分数——提高英语应用能力，带动考试分数提高

广告一

（一）看广告一，回答问题：

1、这个英语培训班是一个为什么人提供的班？他们的课以练习什么能力为主？

2、这个班有几种类型的课？每一种课都有什么特点？

3、你知道不知道什么是以"能力带动分数"？用你的话说明一下。

4、用你学中文的经验给中国学生写一些学英文的建议。

（二）看广告二回答下边的问题：

欢迎邮购"小学生语言练习实用丛书"

《新编小学生组词词典》，以字为条目，在编字注音、释义的基础上分义项组词。每本定价12.00元。

《新编小学生同义词、反义词词典》，所收同义词、反义词以双音节词为主，适当收入一些成语和常用短语。每本定价11.00元。

广告二

1、查字典找出下面词的意思：
同义词 =
反义词 =
成语 =
常用短语 =

2、新编小学生《同义词、反义词词典》有什么特点？这个广告认为这本词典对什么样的学生比较合适？

3、你认为让小学生学习同义词和反义词对提高他们的语言水平有没有好处？为什么？

（三）看右边的报纸回答
下面的问题:

1、吉池是谁？她跟作
者是什么关系？

2、说说吉池的课有什
么特点？这些特点
对学生有什么好
处？

3、找出文章中的三个
句子说明作者其实
很喜欢他的老师。

4、你喜欢吉池的教课
方法吗？请你说说
你的老师教课有什
么特点？

东 京 记

田 川 著

吉池老师

吉池是我们语言学校的老
师,我们语言学校的老师又恰好都
是女的。

不得不承认,吉池是学校里讲
课最好的老师。她的讲课方式很独
特,能想出很多种方法调动学生反
复地练习口语。听完她的课,所有
内容就会自动地记住。我喜欢上她
的课,还因为喜欢看她的手势,她
在黑板上画图来讲解语法关系的
时候,那些圆圈和直线敏感而到
位。当她叙述一件事的时候,你感
觉像在看一部卡通电影,又可爱又
清晰。身体语言也非常放松,使人
愉快。

选自《作家文摘》

95

二、讨论

1、介绍一下你的老师？
2、你最喜欢什么课？为什么？
3、你每天怎么预备功课？
4、你的中文课跟你的别的课比有什么不同？
5、你对中文誓约有什么看法？要遵守难不难？

三、语言实践

去听一堂大学的外语课，看看外语课的类型、教课方法跟讨论的题目，并跟课堂上的学生谈谈他们学外语的情况。

四、作文

《中国的学生是怎么学英文的？》
《我们大学的语言课》

五、看图说话

1

2

3

4

5

6

我想给你们写封信，告诉你们我这几天生活和学习的情况

我们有很多机会可以跟中国老师和同学用中文交流

An Intermediate Chinese Course

第六课　我生病了

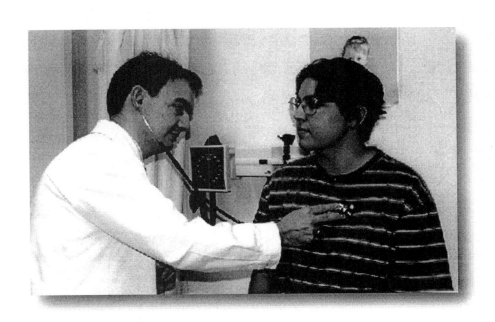

在国际医疗中心看病

课文

我今天一大早起来就觉得不舒服。头昏，肚子疼，全身没力气，不到半个钟头就去了五次厕所。我对自己说："真糟糕，一定是生病了"。我给老师打了一个电话请假⁽¹⁾，然后就又躺到床上去了。我觉得身上一会儿热，一会儿冷，简直不知道怎么办才好。到了中午，我的同屋回来了，我请她拿来温度计给我试体温⁽²⁾，结果发现我已经烧到100度了。我的同屋说："不行，你得赶快⁽³⁾去医院看病"。

去哪个医院比较好呢？

听老师介绍，北京有三、四家中外合资的医院和诊所，专门为外国人服务。收费比一般医院高一点儿，可是医生的医疗水平都比较高，医疗设备也很现代化。还有⁽⁴⁾，这些医院和诊所二十四小时都有医生看病，对病人来说很方便。离学校比较近的是中德诊所，就在长城饭店的旁边，挂号看病都很容易。还有一家是国际医疗中心，也离学校不远，坐车十分钟就到。那儿收费比中德诊所高一点儿，但是医生和医疗条件都很好。

我比较了一下，决定去国际医疗中心。

Notes ⁽¹⁾ "请假": In addition to the meaning of "invite", "请" can mean "to request". "假", meaning "leave" or "vacation", can be preceded by a modifier, e.g. "请病假" "to ask for a sick leave" or "请事假" "to ask for a personal leave".

⁽²⁾ "试体温": The verb used with the noun "体温" to mean "measure one's temperature" is either "试" (test or try) or "量" (measure).

⁽³⁾ "赶快": This expression, literally "make a dash" or "quickly", is used as an adverb immediately preceding a verb, e.g. "赶快回家去" (to rush home).

⁽⁴⁾ "还有": This expression is an adverb meaning "in addition, furthermore". It is used informally in conversation, and is followed by a brief pause, e.g. "还有，那儿的设备也很不错"。(In addition, the facilities there are not bad either.) The more formal way of saying " in addition" is "此外".

（丁新到了<u>国际医疗中心</u>）

丁：　　小姐，请问在哪儿登记挂号[5]？

护士：就在这儿。你是第一次来吗？

丁：　　对。

护士：请把这个表填一下，填完后在那儿稍等[6]。

（丁新填表，等候）

医生：丁新？

丁：　　是我。

医生：你哪儿不舒服？

丁：　　我今天早上起来就头疼，肚子也疼，到现在已经上了七次厕所了，刚才还吐了。

医生：吐了几次？

丁：　　只吐了一次。

医生：发烧不发烧？来，我给你试一下体温。

丁：　　来以前试过，差不多100度。大夫，100度是摄氏多少度？

医生：差不多是38度。昨天你吃过什么东西？

Notes [5] "挂号"，"登记"，"注册"：By now you have probably encountered "挂号，" "登记，" "注册，" all of which have the English translation of "register". They are, however, used in different contexts for different purposes. "挂号" normally refers to registration or signing in a hospital or clinic, e.g. "到医院得先挂号才能看病" (In a hospital, one has to sign in before being treated.) It can also be used with "信" to form "挂号信" for "registered mail". "登记" means "to register" or "to check in" in order to fulfill the procedural requirements or to observe rules or regulations of particular institutions, e.g. "旅馆登记" (to check in at a hotel), "结婚登记" (marriage registration); "进去要先登记"。 (Registration is necessary for entrance.) "注册" refers to the formal registration for a class, a school, or a trademark, e.g. "去学校注册" (to register at school), "注册商标" (trademark registration); "跟政府申请商业注册" (to apply to the government for trade registration).

[6] "稍"：This word, meaning "a little bit" or "slightly", is an adverb used before a verb or an adjective. In a sentence with "稍", the verb is usually followed by "一点" or "一会儿", or words indicating briefness of the action, e.g. "稍吃一点" (just eat a little bit)，"稍看一下" (take a quick look at)， "稍等一会儿" (just wait for a second), etc. The exceptions to this rule are idiomatic and fixed expressions, e.g. "请稍等"

101

丁：　昨天好象没吃什么，就去饭馆吃了些米饭、炒菜，晚上就开始不舒服了。

医生：可能是吃得不干净。来，我给你听听心脏。

丁：　好。

医生：张开嘴，让我看看。好，你得去化验一下大便和小便。估计⁽⁷⁾是急性肠炎。

丁：　大夫，我的病是不是很严重？要不要打针、吃药？

医生：不用太担心，我给你开点儿药。只要按时吃药⁽⁸⁾，好好休息，过几天就会好的。以后吃东西要注意些。

——◆◆◆—— 生 词 ——◆◆◆——

1.一大早	yí dà zǎo	NP.	very early in the morning
2.头昏	tóu hūn	Adj.	dizzy
3.肚子	dù zi	N.	belly, abdomen
4.疼	téng	V.	to hurt
5.全身	quán shēn	N.	the whole body
6.力气	lì qi	N.	strength, energy
7.自己	zì jǐ	N.	oneself
8.糟糕	zāo gāo	Intj.	terrible, awful
9.请假	qǐng jià	VO.	to ask for leave of absence, to

Notes ⁽⁷⁾ "估计" : This word, meaning "to estimate" or " to surmise", is a verb which can be used with or without a subject, e.g. "他估计明天会下雨"。(He guessed that it is going to rain tomorrow.) "估计那儿的人都来不了"。(It is surmised that people there will not come.) When the subject of the sentence is a first person or an unspecified noun, the subject is often omitted, e.g. "估计他明天到"。(I guess he will arrive tomorrow.) "估计我们已经没有机会了"。(It is surmised that we do not have a chance.)

⁽⁸⁾ "按时" : This expression, meaning "on time" or "on schedule", is an adverb normally used before a verb, e.g. "按时吃药" (to take the medicine according to schedule); "按时上课" (to come to class on time). When negating such a sentence, the negative particle "不" or "没" is often placed before "按时", e.g. "他没有按时上课"。(He did not start the class on time.)

				request to be absent
10.	然后	rán hòu	*Adv.*	then
11.	躺	tǎng	*V.*	to lie (down) on one's back
12.	一会儿	yì huǐr	*NP.*	a little while
13.	简直	jiǎn zhí	*Adv.*	simply
14.	温度计	wēn dù jì	*N.*	thermometer
15.	试	shì	*V.*	to test, to measure
16.	体温	tǐ wēn	*N.*	(body) temperature
17.	结果	jié guǒ	*Conj/N.*	as a result; result
18.	发现	fā xiàn	*V/N.*	to discover; discovery
19.	烧到	shāo dào	*VP.*	(fever) reach to (a certain degree)
20.	度	dù	*N.*	degree
21.	医院	yī yuàn	*N.*	hospital, clinic
22.	看病	kàn bìng	*VO.*	to see a doctor
23.	中外	zhōng wài	*Adj/N.*	Chinese and foreign; China and foreign countries
24.	合资	hé zī	*NP.*	joint venture
25.	诊所	zhěn suǒ	*N.*	clinic
26.	专门	zhuān mén	*Adj/Adv.*	special, specialized; especially
27.	服务	fú wù	*V/N.*	to serve; service
28.	收费	shōu fèi	*VO/N.*	to charge a fee; fee
29.	一般	yì bān	*Adj.*	ordinary, general
30.	医疗	yī liáo	*N.*	medical treatment
31.	中德诊所	zhōng dé zhěn suǒ	*Place N.*	Sino-German Clinic
32.	长城饭店	cháng chéng fàn diàn	*Place N.*	Great Wall Hotel (Sheraton Hotel in Beijing)
33.	挂号	guà hào	*VO.*	to register (at a hospital)
34.	国际医疗中心	guó jì yī liáo zhōng xīn	*Place N.*	International Medical Center
35.	坐车	zuò chē	*VO.*	to go by car
36.	护士	hù shì	*N.*	nurse
37.	表	biǎo	*N.*	form
38.	填	tián	*V.*	to fill out

39.稍等	shāo děng	V.	to wait a moment
40.等候	děng hòu	V.	to wait
41.吐	tù	V.	to vomit
42.发烧	fā shāo	V.	to have a fever
43.摄氏	shè shì	N.	Celsius
44.好象	hǎo xiàng	Aux/V.	it seems
45.米饭	mǐ fàn	N.	cooked rice
46.开始	kāi shǐ	V.	to start
47.心脏	xīn zàng	N.	heart
48.张开	zhāng kāi	VP.	to open (mouth, eye, etc.)
49.化验	huà yàn	V.	to have a laboratory test
50.大便	dà biàn	V/N.	to have a bowel movement; feces
51.小便	xiǎo biàn	V/N.	to urinate; urine
52.估计	gū jì	V.	to estimate, to surmise
53.急性肠炎	jí xìng cháng yán	N.	acute enteritis
54.严重	yán zhòng	Adj.	serious, severe
55.打针	dǎ zhēn	VO.	to give or have an injection
56.吃药	chī yào	VO.	to take medicine
57.休息	xiū xi	V/N.	to rest; rest
58.担心	dān xīn	V.	to worry
59.开药	kāi yào	VO.	to prescribe medicine, to give prescription
60.按时	àn shí	Adv.	on schedule
61.注意	zhù yì	V.	to pay attention

——◆—— 补充词汇 ——◆——

62.免费	miǎn fèi	Adj.	free (of charge)
63.病假	bìng jià	N.	sick leave
64.感冒	gǎn mào	V/N.	to catch a cold; cold
65.咳嗽	ké sòu	VO/N.	to cough; cough
66.流鼻涕	liú bí tì	VO.	to have a runny nose
67.打喷嚏	dǎ pēn tì	VO.	to sneeze

68.拉肚子	lā dù zi	*VO.*	to suffer from diarrhea
69.胃疼	wèi téng	*VP/N.*	to have a stomach-ache; stomach-ache
70.救护车	jiù hù chē	*N.*	ambulance
71.药水	yào shuǐ	*N.*	liquid medicine
72.药片	yào piàn	*N.*	tablet
73.药店	yào diàn	*N.*	drugstore, pharmacy
74.华氏	huá shì	*N.*	Fahrenheit
75.慢性	màn xìng	*Adj.*	chronic
76.针灸	zhēn jiǔ	*N.*	acupuncture
77.健康保险	jiàn kāng bǎo xiǎn	*NP.*	health insurance

北京国际医疗中心是一家中外合资的诊所

105

句型

一、不到……就 (in less than...)

> ✍ "不到"，when used with the adverb "就"，indicates faster or sooner than expected. "了" is necessary when referring to a completed action.

☞ 不到半个钟头就去了五次厕所。

1、不知道为什么他来了不到一个月就回去了。
   I do not know why he went back after staying for less than a month.

2、去中外合资的诊所看病很方便，坐出租车不到十分钟就可以到。
   Going to the Chinese and foreign joint venture clinic to see a doctor is very convenient. It will take less than ten minutes to get there by taxi.

二、一会儿……一会儿…… (now..., now...)

> ✍ "一会儿" is a time expression meaning "for a little while." When used two or three times in succession, it indicates that the situation changes both unpredictably and rapidly.

☞ 我觉得自己身上一会儿热，一会儿冷，简直不知道怎么办才好。

1、你一会儿要量体温，一会儿要吃药，你到底怎么了？
   You want to take your temperature one minute and then take medicine the next. What exactly is wrong with you?

2、今天早上我一起来就觉得一会儿头疼，一会儿肚子疼，真糟糕，看来又要请假了。
   This morning as soon as I got up, I had a headache for a while and then a stomach ache. Drats! Looks like I will have to ask for another leave of absence.

三、给⋯⋯试体温/开药 (to measure the temperature for/to prescribe medication for)

> ✍ Here the preposition "给" is used with the verbs "试体温" and "开药", meaning "to take the temperature of someone" and "to prescribe medication for someone" respectively. When negating the sentence, the negative particle "不" or "没" must precede "给".

☞ 我请她拿来温度计给我试体温。

1、登记挂号后，护士要给你试体温。
   After registering, the nurse will take your temperature.
2、大夫，你能不能给我开一点药，让我的肚子疼好一点。
   Doctor, can you give me some medicine to make my stomach feel a little bit better?

四、结果 (as a result, consequently)

> ✍ "结果," as a noun, means "result". Here "结果" is used as an adverb to introduce the consequence of a situation. In this sense, "结果" usually appears at the beginning of the sentence or immediately after the subject.

☞ 结果发现我已经烧到100度了。

1、我以为只要休息一天就能去上课，不用去看病，结果我病得越来越厉害。
   I mistakenly believed that I only needed to rest for a day, and then I could attend class and not need to see a doctor. As a result, my illness became more and more serious.
2、我们都要求现在的医生比较专业化，医疗设备也比较现代化，结果我们的医疗费也变得很高。
   We all demanded that doctors nowadays be more professionally trained, and medical facilities be more modern. As a result, our medical fees also rose greatly.

五、听……介绍 (as is introduced by, according to)

> ✍ This is a useful verb phrase to indicate the source of one's information. Please note that in Chinese, the passive voice is not used. The implicit subject of the verb "听" is "我", but it is understood and therefore omitted.

☞ 听老师介绍，北京有三、四家中外合资的医院和诊所，专门为外国人服务。

1、听我的中国父母介绍，这里的设备还不算现代化。
　　According to my Chinese parents, the facilities here are still not considered modern.

2、听国际医疗中心的人介绍，中外合资的医院越来越多。
　　According to people at the International Medical Center, there are more and more Chinese and foreign joint venture hospitals.

六、专门 V (to specialize in)

> ✍ "专门" or "专" is an adverb meaning "specially", e.g. "这家医院专门看小孩子的病"。(This hospital specializes in treating children's diseases.) "这条路是专门给自行车走的"。(This route is specially designated for bikes.) Please note that in English, the object of "specialize in" is a noun, e.g. "he specializes in English literature"; but in Chinese one must use a verb after "专门", e.g. "他专 (门) 研究英国文学"。Due to this grammatical difference between English and Chinese, a sentence containing the phrase "专门 V" cannot be translated literally into English. (Also see Note 4 in Lesson 3.)

☞ 专门为外国人服务。

1、这种运动设备是专门为学生准备的，这样学生下课以后就可以运动运动了。
　　This type of exercise facility was specially set up for students. This way the students can exercise after class.

2、因为我今天不太舒服，我的同学专门为我做了一点儿美国饭。
　　Because I was sick today, my classmates prepared American food especially for me.

七、为……服务 (to provide service for)

> "为" is a preposition, meaning "for". It can be used with verbs such as "服务" meaning "to provide service for". The negative form and question form are "不为……服务" (NOT * "为……不服务") and "为不为……服务" (NOT * "为……不为服务"), respectively.

☞ 专门为外国人服务。

1、前台的服务员小姐是专门为宿舍学生服务的。

The front desk attendant specifically provides services for the students in the dorm.

2、这家饭馆是为吃素的人服务的，所以不供应肉菜。

This restaurant only serves vegetarians, so it does not supply meat dishes.

中德诊所离学校比较近

语言形式练习
Tasks on Language Forms

一、读课文回答问题 📖

1、丁新今天觉得哪里不舒服？

2、为什么丁新的同屋说她得赶快去看病？

3、跟一般医院比，中外合资的医院和诊所怎么样？

4、为什么丁新决定到国际医疗中心去看病？

5、医生说丁新得的是什么病？

二、完成对话

1、A：怎么回事？快七点了，你还不起来？

　　B：我觉得……

　　　　（一会儿……一会儿……；跟……请假）

2、A：你觉得对吃素的人来说，在哪儿吃饭最方便？

　　B：

　　　　（听……介绍；专门为……服务）

3、A：你觉得哪儿不舒服？

　　B：我的肚子不舒服。

　　　　（不到……就；还有……）

三、听录音回答问题

1、小李哪儿不舒服？

2、小刘觉得小李是什么病？严重吗？

3、小李为什么没去看大夫？

4、小刘建议小李到哪儿去看大夫？

5、为什么小刘要小李给老师打电话？

6、你想小李为什么今天晚上要请小刘到他家吃饭？

7、小刘去吗？为什么？

四、阅读回答问题

最近我奶奶上了老年大学，老年大学就是专门为老年人办的大学。那儿开的都是一些受老年人欢迎的课，比方说书法、画画、外语等等。听我奶奶介绍，他们大学老师的水平可高了。这些老师都是一些很有名的教授、书法家、画家等等，退休以后在老年大学教书。大学的设备也很现代化，他们有专门的画室，音乐教室和电脑房。但是收费却并不高。对一般的老年人来说根本不算什么。自从我奶奶上了老年大学以后，她成了我们家最忙的人，不是去学画画，就是去学英语。为了让奶奶每次都能按时上课，我们家的墙上贴了一个大大的课表，每次上课以前都有一个人专门负责送她去学校。所以，奶奶从来没迟到过。你还别说，我奶奶的进步可大了！不到一个学期，她就学会了画报中国画，也学会了说一些简单的英语。不知为什么，奶奶的身体也越来越好了，以前的病现在也都没有了，连医生都吃惊地说她越活越年轻了！

问题：

1、请选择正确的说法：

(1) 老年大学的老师都是很有名的教授

(2) 老年大学的学费很贵

(3) 老年大学的教授收入很高

(4) 老年大学的设备非常好

2、为什么奶奶上课从来没迟到过？

3、上了老年大学以后，奶奶有什么变化？

4、请你给老师或朋友介绍一位你认识的老人。

五、翻译

1. A: I think I have to see a doctor. Do you know of a clinic that is close to our school?

   B: Yes. I do. What is the matter? Are you not feeling well?

   A: Yes. I am fine. I just need to have the doctor prescribe some allergy medicine for me.

   B: Then I think you should go to the International Medical Center near the school.

2. As was introduced by our professor, this university's facilities are modern and the professors' teaching ability/level is very high. Furthermore, their services to students are the best.

3. I think he has to take a sick leave for a day because he has a fever of 100 degrees. What's more, there is a possibility that he has to stay in bed for a few days.

4. The fees at this medical center are the lowest and their facilities are the best in Beijing. You should definitely take advantage of this medical center while you are here.

请把这个表填一下

语言使用练习
Tasks on Language Use

一、真实情景活动

（一）你刚在"SOS急救中心"看过病，你觉得那儿的服务还不错，要把这个中心介绍给你的美国朋友。因为他看不懂中文，所以他请你把右边关于中心的中文材料翻译成英文。

Beijing International SOS is part of a global network of clinics and 24hr alarm centers

在北京国际救援中心，国际化的专业护理将为您提供最高质量的医疗服务。

通过本救援中心的**"流动医生"**服务，医生将立即为您上门服务，一周七天，全天侯工作制。

您只需要做的是：
1. 拿起电话
2. 拨打 SOS24 小时求助电话：
   (010)6462 9100
3. 要求接通**"流动医生"**
4. 医生将安排具体时间上门就诊

我们所提供的专业服务：
- 在您的房间提供舒适的诊断
- 国际标准的医疗照顾
- 多种语言服务
- 齐全的药品

（二）请把下边北京国际医疗中心广告的主要意思翻译成英文。

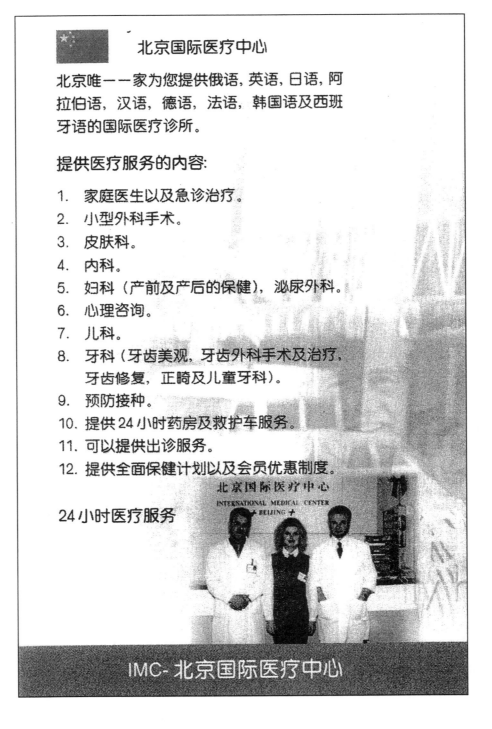

北京国际医疗中心

北京唯一一家为您提供俄语，英语，日语，阿拉伯语，汉语，德语，法语，韩国语及西班牙语的国际医疗诊所。

提供医疗服务的内容:

1. 家庭医生以及急诊治疗。
2. 小型外科手术。
3. 皮肤科。
4. 内科。
5. 妇科（产前及产后的保健），泌尿外科。
6. 心理咨询。
7. 儿科。
8. 牙科（牙齿美观，牙齿外科手术及治疗，牙齿修复，正畸及儿童牙科）。
9. 预防接种。
10. 提供24小时药房及救护车服务。
11. 可以提供出诊服务。
12. 提供全面保健计划以及会员优惠制度。

24小时医疗服务

IMC-北京国际医疗中心

（三）下边这篇文章谈的是一个老农民 (an old peasant) 看病难的故事。请回答下面的问题，然后你就会知道为什么在中国农民看病很难。

1、这个老农民在医院住了多长时间？

2、这次住院他要付多少钱？

2、这个老农民每年的收入是多少？

3、一般的农民有没有医疗保险 (insurance)？

农民看病难

在中国的总人口中，农民占绝大多数，他们的身体健康关系到中华民族的整体身体素质。然而，长期以来，农村医疗保险没有得到普及，农民生了病不能得到很好的治疗。

在中国，尤其是在农村，上医院看病可能是让人陷入贫困的最快途径。在中国现有的医疗保健制度下，最负担不起医疗费用的人恰恰被迫负担最大部分的医疗费用。

宁夏回族自治区65岁的老人杨征善（音译）在省会银川附近的一家医院住了三个星期，医生给他拍了4张X光照片，做了一个核磁共振成像（MRI），诊断为中风。医生开了大量的口服药、针剂并给予按摩治疗。通过治疗，杨征善康复了。但他收到的账单相当于1350美元。在杨征善的家乡，平均年收入只有220美元。所有的医疗费用都是他自己出，像90%的中国农民一样，他没有医疗保险。

在过去20多年中，中国成功地使2.1亿人摆脱了贫困，但由于能享受公费医疗保险的人不断减少，而收入的增加又远远跟不上医药价格的上升，中国脱贫的成绩正在被抵消。

选自《作家文摘》

（四）张老师是一个要求很严的老师，他非常不喜欢学生不来上课。今天你生病了，不能去上课。为了不让张老师觉得你是一个坏学生，你要给张老师写一个条子请假。你应该请清楚楚地告诉他你生病的情况，比方说，肚子怎么样，头怎么样，医生说什么，还有你可能什么时候回来上课等等。

张老师：

　　您好！今天我 _____

_____

_____

_____

_____

_____

_____

_____

　　　　　　　　　　　　　　　学生：

二、讨论

1、到了中国以后，你生过病吗？生病以后怎么办？去了哪家医院或诊所？医生跟护士都很专业化吗？
2、你觉得北京的医院和诊所的医疗设备怎么样？
3、在北京看病和在美国看病有没有什么不一样的地方？
4、到离学校最近的医院怎么走？

三、语言实践

去学校的医疗中心了解他们的设备和收费情况。采访两位医生或者护士和两个病人，问问他们对学校医疗条件的看法。

四、作文

《我们学校的医疗中心》

五、看图说话

1

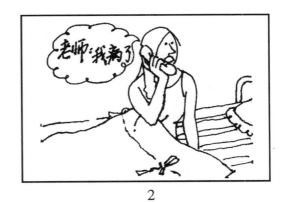
2

3

4

5

An Intermediate Chinese Course

第七课　我的自行车

最方便的交通工具

课文

　　在北京最方便、最经济的交通工具要算自行车了。尤其在北京市内，出去游览也好，办事也好，买东西也好，骑车可以说是又快又方便。比方说，去美国大使馆办登记手续，从学校骑车去只要十多分钟就到了，不用花钱，又把事办了。所以，一般来说，在北京留学的外国学生都要买一辆自行车。有的学生愿意花几百块人民币买新车，有的学生不愿意多花钱，就到旧车市场买旧车。无论是新车还是旧车，有了自行车就可以跑遍北京市。

　　可是，买自行车听起来是件小事，里头的学问可不小。买不好，就会上当受骗。另外，要是牌子没挑对，自行车的质量也可能回有问题，买了以后就会麻烦不断。不过，在中国有什么问题，就有解决什么问题的办法。自行车坏了没关系，修车的小摊儿到处都是。什么时候车坏了或者需要打气，找个小摊儿停下来，三、五分钟就能解决问题，花的钱也不多。下面是周大明车子坏了以后的经历[1]。

———◆———

（下午五点半）

周：　　师傅，对不起，下班了吗？还修车吗？

师傅：还没下班呢。怎么，要修车吗？

✎ **Notes** [1] "经历" vs. "经验"："经历" and "经验" can both be translated as "experience" in English, but have different nuances in Chinese. "经历" refers to the experience of going through a process or event, and often includes the emotions which accompany it, e.g. "去中国的经历"；"旅行的经历"；"找工作的经历"."经验", however, refers to one's cumulative experience in some area of endeavor, e.g. "教书的经验"；"学语言的经验".

周： 对，我的车不知道为什么总是刹不住[2]。

师傅： 来，我看看。啊，是闸松了，紧一紧就行了。

周： 是吗？我这车才买了一星期，已经修了四回了。您说这是为什么？

师傅： 唉，现在买东西得会买，要买信得过的牌子，不然质量没法保证。

周： 这是为什么？

师傅： 改革开放以后，政策活了[3]，可是也有很多人觉得机会来了，看市场上什么赚钱就做什么，根本都不管产品的质量，结果产品常常不合要求[4]。

周： 这不是对老百姓很不好吗？

师傅： 是啊，可是这种现象倒给我们退休和下岗的人一条出路，不然我退休以后什么事都不做，待在家里很难受。

周： 是吗？您已经退休了？那以前您做什么呢？

师傅： 我以前在一家国营汽车厂上班，修车这种事对我来说很容易。好，车好了，你试试看。

周： （试车）行，很好。多少钱？

✎ **Notes** [2] "刹不住" : Here, this expression means "can not put a stop on" or "(the bike's brake) cannot stop". "住" in this structure functions as a complement to indicate the result of an action. It has the meaning of "firmly" or "tightly". It can be combined with many other verbs such as "记住" (to remember firmly); "夹住" (to clench tightly); "拿住" (to hold tightly), etc. These verb complement structures can all be conjugated to the "potential" complement form to indicate the capability, e.g. "记不住" (cannot remember); "夹得住" (can clench); "拿不住" (cannot hold).

[3] "活" : In addition to the meaning of " to live", "活" can also mean "flexible" or "loosen up", e.g. "他的脑子很活"。(His way of thinking is very flexible.) or "现在的经济政策可活了不少"。(Recently the economic policy has loosened up a great deal.)

[4] "合/不合" : In this lesson, "合/不合" means "to fit" or "to suit" (the standard, requirement, procedure, or rules), e.g. "合法" (legal); "合格" (to meet standards); "不合要求" (not meeting the requirement); "很合手续" (following the procedural requirements); "合不合规定" ? (Does it meet the regulation?), etc. "合" is a shortened form of "符合" (to accord with; tally with; conform to).

师傅： 五块钱。

周： 给您。谢谢您，师傅。

生词

1. 交通	jiāo tōng	*N.*	transportation, traffic
2. 工具	gōng jù	*N.*	tool
3. 自行车	zì xíng chē	*N.*	bicycle
4. 尤其	yóu qí	*Adv.*	especially
5. 市内	shì nèi	*N.*	inside the city
6. 游览	yóu lǎn	*V.*	to tour
7. 办事	bàn shì	*VO.*	to handle affairs, to run errands
8. 骑车	qí chē	*VO.*	to ride a bike (or a motorcycle)
9. 大使馆	dà shǐ guǎn	*N.*	embassy
10. 花钱	huā qián	*VO.*	to spend money
11. 一般来说	yì bān lái shuō	*Idiom.*	generally speaking
12. 辆	liàng	*Classifier.*	classifier for vehicle
13. 愿意	yuàn yì	*Aux/V.*	to be willing to
14. 旧车市场	jiù chē shì chǎng	*NP.*	used bike market
15. 无论	wú lùn	*Adv.*	no matter
16. 跑遍	pǎo biàn	*VP.*	to go everywhere
17. 里头	lǐ tou	*N.*	inside
18. 学问	xué wèn	*N.*	learning, knowledge
19. 上当	shàng dàng	*VO.*	to be cheated
20. 受骗	shòu piàn	*VO.*	to be fooled, to be deceived, to be cheated
21. 另外	lìng wài	*Adv/Adj.*	besides; another
22. 牌子	pái zi	*N.*	brand
23. 挑	tiāo	*V.*	to select
24. 质量	zhì liàng	*N.*	quality
25. 麻烦	má fan	*N/Adj.*	trouble; troublesome
26. 不断	bú duàn	*Adj.*	unceasing, continuous, constant

27.	不过	bú guò	Conj.	but
28.	办法	bàn fǎ	N.	way, means
29.	修车	xiū chē	VO.	to fix the vehicle
30.	小摊儿	xiǎo tānr	N.	street stall
31.	打气	dǎ qì	VO.	to inflate, to pump up (a tire)
32.	停	tíng	V.	to stop
33.	经历	jīng lì	N/V.	experience; to experience
34.	刹不住	shā bú zhù	VP.	cannot brake
35.	闸	zhá	N.	brake
36.	松	sōng	V/Adj.	to loosen; loose
37.	紧	jǐn	V/Adj.	to tighten; tight
38.	回	huí	Classifier.	occurrence, times
39.	唉	āi	Intj.	alas (expressing sorrow or regret)
40.	信得过	xìn de guò	Adj.	trustworthy, reliable
41.	不然	bù rán	Conj.	otherwise
42.	没法	méi fǎ	VO.	there is no way
43.	保证	bǎo zhèng	V/N.	to guarantee; guarantee
44.	改革	gǎi gé	V/N.	to reform; reform
45.	开放	kāi fàng	V/Adj.	to open up; open
46.	政策	zhèng cè	N.	policy
47.	活	huó	Adj.	flexible, lively, active
48.	市场	shì chǎng	N.	marketplace, market
49.	赚钱	zhuàn qián	VO.	to earn money
50.	不管	bù guǎn	VP.	do not care, not pay attention
51.	产品	chǎn pǐn	N.	product
52.	不合	bù hé	VP.	do not meet/fit (requirement)
53.	老百姓	lǎo bǎi xìng	N.	common people, the general public
54.	现象	xiàn xiàng	N.	phenomenon
55.	倒	dào	Adv.	on the contrary
56.	退休	tuì xiū	V.	to retire
57.	下岗	xià gǎng	VO.	to be laid off
58.	条	tiáo	Classifier.	classifier for road, river, rope,

			etc.
59. 出路	chū lù	*N.*	way out, outlet
60. 待	dāi	*V.*	to stay (**等待** děng dài to wait, to await)
61. 难受	nán shòu	*V.*	to feel unhappy, to feel unwell
62. 国营	guó yíng	*Adj.*	government-operated, state-owned
63. 汽车厂	qì chē chǎng	*N.*	automobile factory
64. 上班	shàng bān	*VO.*	to go to work

————————— 补充词汇 —————————

65. 火车	huǒ chē	*N.*	train
66. 摩托车	mó tuō chē	*N.*	motorcycle
67. 轮胎	lún tāi	*N.*	tire
68. 车把	chē bǎ	*N.*	handlebar (of a bicycle, motor cycle)
69. 车牌	chē pái	*N.*	license plate
70. 驾驶执照	jià shǐ zhí zhào	*N.*	driver's license
71. 锁	suǒ	*N/V.*	lock, to lock

句型

一、尤其 (especially)

> ✍ "尤其" is an adverb meaning "especially". It is used to introduce a special case within the scope of the topic in the first clause. Unlike English, in which "especially" can be followed by a noun (e.g. "I don't like cold water, especially ice water"), "尤其" must be followed by a verb construction, e.g. "我不喜欢凉水，尤其是冰水". Without "不喜欢" or "是", the sentence would be grammatically incorrect.

> ☞ 尤其在北京市内，出去游览也好，办事也好，买东西也好，骑车可以说是又快又方便。

1、在北京骑自行车尤其要小心，一不小心就有可能出问题。

One must be especially careful while riding a bike in Beijing. A second of carelessness can cause an accident.

2、到中国留学的好处很多，尤其是语言环境好，随时都有老师或者中国人和你练习中文。

There are many advantages to studying in China. In particular, the language environment is good. You can always practice your Chinese with your Chinese teachers and the local people.

二、A也好，B也好……(either A or B, or...)

> ✍ "也好", repeated two or more times, indicates that in either case, the result remains unchanged. The adverb "都" is often used in the second clause.

> ☞ 出去游览也好，办事也好，买东西也好，骑车可以说是又快又方便。

1、上大班课也好，上小班课也好，你不准备就没法上好课。

If you do not prepare, it doesn't matter whether it is a group class or an individual session, you would not be able to have a good class.

2、在中国，在国营单位工作也好，当个体户摆小摊也好，医疗费都是一个问题。

In China, medical expenses are always a problem (no matter) whether you work in a state-operated units or run a stall as a private entrepreneur.

三、 一般来说 (generally speaking)

> ✍ "一般来说"，"generally speaking"，is used only at the beginning of a sentence or a paragraph to introduce a topic.

☞ 一般来说，在北京留学的外国学生都要买一辆自行车。

1、一般来说，中国的工作可以分为三种类型：一种是国营单位的工作，一种是当个体户，还有一种是中外合资企业的工作。

Generally speaking, jobs in China can be divided into three types: the first is working in state-units, the second is as a private entrepreneur, and the third is in a Sino-foreign joint venture.

2、一般来说，退休后最好的出路就是当个体户。

Generally speaking, to be a private entrepreneur is the best outlet after retirement.

四、 无论……都（就）…… (no matter + question)

> ✍ "无论" means that the situation remains the same no matter what condition is given. "无论" must be followed by an interrogative structure indicating the condition. Either adverb "都" or "也" is normally necessary in the second clause to indicate the same result. The less formal forms for "无论" are "不管" and "不论".

☞ 无论是新车还是旧车，有了自行车就可以跑遍北京市。

1、无论上课还是下课，有机会就应该说中文。

Whether in class or out, one should speak Chinese whenever one has the opportunity.

2、无论医院多贵，有病就得去看。

No matter how expensive a clinic is, one must visit it if he/she is sick.

五、 V遍 (everywhere)

> ✍ "遍" here functions as a verb complement, meaning "do something thoroughly", e.g. "我的书不见了，我每个地方都找遍了还是没找到"。 (I can't find my book. I've checked everywhere thoroughly and I still can't find it.) The negation for "V遍" is never "不" but always "没有".

☞ 有了自行车就可以跑遍北京市。

1、 我跑遍了北京城也没找到要买的东西。
> I have gone everywhere in Beijing, but I still haven't found what I wanted to buy.

2、 他看遍了美国的医生也没看好他的心脏病。
> He has seen all the American doctors, but no one can cure his heart disease.

六、 不然or要不然 (otherwise)

> ✍ "不然" or "要不然" functions as a conjunction connecting two clauses with the meaning of "otherwise", "or else", and "if not, then..." It is usually used at the beginning of a sentence.

☞ 要买信得过的牌子，不然质量没法保证。

1、 退休以后，他还得出去摆小摊，不然生活会有问题。
> He still has to set up a stall after retirement, otherwise he'd have problems (e.g. he won't be able to support himself).

2、 买车时一定要看牌子，不然就回麻烦不断。
> You have to pay attention to the brand when buying a bicycle, otherwise you will have constant troubles.

语言形式练习
Tasks on Language Forms

一、读课文回答问题

1、在北京，什么是最方便、最经济的交通工具？为什么？

2、买自行车的时候要注意什么？

3、自行车坏了的时候怎么办？

4、周大明的自行车有什么问题？

5、师傅说为什么现在的产品常常不合要求？

6、师傅为什么说产品的质量不好倒给退休的人一条出路？

二、完成对话

1、A：在美国最方便、最经济的交通工具是什么？

　　B：

　　　　（一般来说；　V遍）

2、A：在小摊儿上买衣服会不会上当受骗？

　　B：当然会。

　　　　（无论……都；　不过）

3、A：在国营汽车厂工作好还是在小摊儿上修车好？

　　B：

　　　　（A也好，　B也好）

三、听录音回答问题

1、小林的自行车是在哪儿买的？

2、小林为什么要买自行车？

3、小林的自行车怎么样？有过什么问题？

4、小林开车上学吗？为什么？

5、小林做什么事的时候才开车？

四、阅读回答问题

昨天是我来北京以后最倒霉的一天，因为我新买的自行车被偷了。下课以后王老师带我到警察（police）那儿去报案 (to file a report)。警察了解了情况以后告诉我，丢车在北京是一个很普遍的事情。无论是给车上两把锁也好，买旧自行车也好，都有可能被偷。无论什么办法都不能完全保证车子不会丢。他建议我以后出门坐公共汽车或者坐出租汽车！最后，警察让我填了一张表，并且告诉我他们一找到车就会打电话通知我。在回学校的路上，王老师告诉我，一般来说，我是不会再见到我的自行车了。可是几天以后在学校附近，我又看到了我的自行车！一个中国人正骑着它！当那个人停下来给自行车打气的时候，我追上去问："请问，这是你的自行车吗"？他很奇怪地看着我说："当然是我的自行车，前天我刚刚在旧车市场买的！怎么了"？我跟他说了我丢车的经历，还告诉他我丢的车就是他现在骑的这辆车。这个中国人不但不相信我说的话，反而推起车就走，根本就不听我说什么。越来越多的中国人围上来盯着我看，让我觉得很害怕，只好走了。那次的经历真可以说是我在中国最不好的一次！

问题：

1、为什么说"昨天是我最倒霉的一天"？我做了什么？

2、什么办法可以保证在北京不丢自行车？警察给我什么建议？

3、"我"有没有找到我的自行车？

4、你能不能给我们讲讲你的一次最不好的经历？

五、翻译

1. A: Can you tell me about your life since the economic reform?

   B: The reform is a good thing for us. Since (the government's) policy has loosened up, our economy has become flexible.

   A: Really?

   B: Take my job for example, I used to work in a state-owned factory. After retirement, because the economic has reformed, I was able to open up my own bike repair shop.

2. Buying brand-name products is a way of finding reliable products. In China especially, there are products which are poorly made and break down easily. If you want to buy things, you'd better look for brand-name products.

3. After he told us about his experience on the flying to Beijing, we were all shocked.

4. Generally speaking, it is impossible for this service center to guarantee the quality of their services. They cannot even improve the environment.

修车的小摊儿到处都是

语言使用练习
Tasks on Language Use

一、真实情景活动 🎥

（一）下边这张意见卡要了解客人的什么情况？

（二）这家公司为什么让顾客填这张意见卡？用意见卡上的话说是为了什么？

（三）在你看来，交通工具和这个公司的服务有什么关系？他们为什么要问顾客使用的交通工具？

顾客意见卡
喜乐迪KTV

进场时间＿＿＿＿＿＿＿＿＿＿

亲爱的贵宾：
　　感谢您的光临与支持，喜乐迪KTV为了提供您的更优质的服务，并坚持诚信理念以完善的观念延续服务，请您提供宝贵意见。

姓名：＿＿＿＿＿＿ 年龄：＿＿＿＿ 性别：＿＿＿＿ 联络电话：＿＿＿＿＿＿＿＿

服务态度：　　＿＿＿＿满意　　　＿＿＿＿尚可　　　＿＿＿＿不佳
音响效果：　　＿＿＿＿满意　　　＿＿＿＿尚可　　　＿＿＿＿不佳
超市种类：　　＿＿＿＿满意　　　＿＿＿＿尚可　　　＿＿＿＿不佳
影碟质量：　　＿＿＿＿满意　　　＿＿＿＿尚可　　　＿＿＿＿不佳
环境清洁：　　＿＿＿＿满意　　　＿＿＿＿尚可　　　＿＿＿＿不佳
歌曲质量：　　＿＿＿＿满意　　　＿＿＿＿尚可　　　＿＿＿＿不佳

推荐歌曲＿＿＿＿＿＿　推荐歌手＿＿＿＿＿＿　推荐餐饮＿＿＿＿＿＿

请问您从事的职业：＿＿＿＿ 上班族＿＿＿＿ 学生＿＿＿＿ 旅客＿＿＿＿ 其他

请问您搭乘的交通工具：＿＿＿＿＿＿＿＿＿＿＿＿＿＿＿＿＿＿＿＿

请问您从哪里知道喜乐迪的：＿＿＿＿＿＿＿＿＿＿＿＿＿＿＿＿＿＿

顾客意见：＿＿＿＿＿＿＿＿＿＿＿＿＿＿＿＿＿＿＿＿＿＿＿＿＿＿

包厢号码：＿＿＿＿＿＿＿＿

定位热线：(010)65131111　65133333　65137777

（四）从下边这个广告来看，这家公司的产品是什么？多数家庭在什么时候和在房子的什么地方使用这种产品？

（五）这家公司产品的最大特点是什么？

（六）看右边的报纸回答问题

1、2005年北京人还可以不可以买电动自行车？为什么？

2、根据这篇文章，人们认为在大城市里应该发展什么样的交通工具，而不应该发展什么交通工具？

3、除了交通方面的问题以外，电动自行车的使用还会造成什么问题？

4、你认为北京的电动自行车政策合理不合理？为什么？

污染环境妨碍交通

3年后 电动自行车 将告别北京

本报讯(记者王远　通讯员杨国平)电动自行车究竟能不能取得合法身份，这个争论已久的问题今天终于有了答案。记者从北京市公安交通管理局了解到，本市将从8月5日到8月31日，对本市已有的电动自行车核发临时号牌和行驶证，逾期不再补领，临时牌证的有效期截止到2005年12月31日。

据了解，作为人口密集的大城市，本市的交通发展战略是大力发展公共交通，因此不适宜发展电动自行车。但考虑到目前的实际情况，市政府批准对本市范围内已有的电动自行车核发临时牌证。一位曾骑过电动自行车的朋友告诉记者，目前大部分电动自行车的时速绝对高于每小时20公里，行驶在慢行道中对自行车极具威胁。

选自《北京晚报》

二、讨论

1、你最常用的交通工具是什么？为什么？
2、你觉得在北京骑自行车安全吗？为什么？
3、你有没有自行车？是新的还是旧的？谈谈你买车的经验。

133

4、你的自行车坏过没有？谈谈你修车的经验。

5、你觉得中国产品的质量怎么样？为什么？

6、你跟小摊儿上的人谈过话吗？他们对改革开放有什么看法？

7、中国退休工人的生活跟美国的有什么不同？

三、语言实践

1、采访一个退休工人，问问他以前和现在的工作和生活情况。

2、去北京的旧车市场看看买卖旧车的情况。采访一个卖车人和一个买车的人。

四、作文

《北京的修车摊儿》

《在北京的旧车市场买车》

《买旧车》

五、看图说话

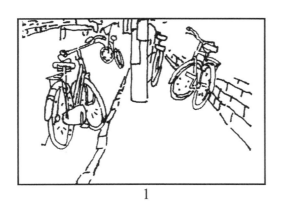

1

2

3

4

5

我退休以后什么事都不做，待在家里很难受

修车也算是一条出路吧

An Intermediate Chinese Course

第八课 去书店买书

书店的书还真不少

课文

在美国的时候，我常听老师说在中国，书的价钱比美国的便宜得多，所以我决定周末的时候骑自行车到书店去逛逛[1]。在北京的市中心和学校附近都有书店，最有名的几家是新华书店、中国书店、三联书店、西单图书大厦和海淀图书城。现在多半的书店都把书放在架子上，桌子上，买书的人可以随便[2]翻看，很方便。不象从前那样把书都收在柜子里，要看书得由售货员替你拿。书的种类非常多，分文史、社会、财经、语言、计算机、教育等类。价钱便宜是便宜，可是有的装订和印刷的质量都不算高。我看来看去，最后总算[3]决定买一本《汉英词典》和一套《鲁迅全集》。这本词典查起来很方便，有拼音和部首的索引，同时收的词很丰富，解释不但详细，而且每个用法都有例句，比我现在用的那本好得多。鲁迅是中国有名的文学家，我看过很多他的小说，可惜都是英文翻译的。我希望中文水平提高以

Notes [1] "逛逛": This is a verb meaning "wander around" for shopping or sight-seeing purposes, e.g. "我们去城里逛逛", (Let's take a walk downtown.) The "wandering around" is assumed to be relaxing and fun, and one usually intends to buy or see something while wandering around. Sometimes it also refers to window shopping. While one can "去公园逛逛," it would be inappropriate to "去机场逛逛," because the latter is not a relaxing activity.

[2] "随便": This expression has two grammatical functions and two meanings. The first one is an adverb meaning "do as one pleases". It is normally used as an adverb preceding a verb, e.g. "随便吃" (eat whatever you like); "随便看" (feel free to look around), etc. The second function of "随便" is an adjective meaning "casual", e.g. "这里的人穿衣服很随便". (People here dress casually.)

[3] "总算" vs. "最后": "总算" and "最后", although sharing a similar meaning, carry different nuances. "总算" often carries an anxious or impatient tone and indicates "at long last", or "after a long period of waiting, something finally has taken place or is completed". "最后" refers to "in the end", "at last", or "the last one". Compare examples A: "他总算吃完了". B: "他最后吃完了". and C: "他最后总算吃完了". Example A indicates that the speaker feels that he/she has waited a long time for the person described to finish eating; Example B means simply that in the end the person described did finish eating; Example C indicates that the speaker waited for a long time for the person to finish eating at the end.

后，能看原文。我决定了以后，就拿着词典和书到柜台去。

（在柜台）

学生：

　　　　小姐，我要买这本词典和这套《鲁迅全集》。

服务员：把书给我。这是交款单，到那边交款。

（在交款处）

服：　一共三百五十五，这儿是四百，你有没有零的[4]？

学：　没有，我只有一百的。请你开一张发票[5]。

服：　找你四十五。

学：　谢谢。

（回到柜台）

学：　小姐，要是我发现书有毛病能不能拿来换？

服：　换是可以，但是不能退。你最好现在查一下。

学：　词典我已经查过了，可是《鲁迅全集》一共有十二本，查起来
　　　太费时间了[6]。

服：　这样吧[7]。要是有问题，三天之内来换，超过三天我们就不负责
　　　了。

Notes [4] "零的" vs "零钱"：Both mean "small change", and can be used interchangeably. In "零的," there is an implicit "钱" after the "的."

[5] "开", in addition to meaning "open", can also mean "to write out". It is often combined with nouns meaning "list, receipt, prescription, etc.", e.g. "开发票" (to write a receipt); "开药方" (to write a prescription); "开一个书单子" (to make a book list).

[6] "费 N"：Used as a verb, "费" can take various noun objects to mean "waste something", e.g. "费钱" (waste money); "费时间" (waste time); "费力" (waste energy), etc. "费" can also be used as a noun to mean "fee", e.g. "费用" (expenses); "收费" (to collect fee); "学费" (tuition).

[7] "这样吧"：This expression means "let's do it this way", "how about this way..." The phrase is often used at the beginning or conclusion of a sentence to add a suggestive tone, e.g. "这样吧，我来看菜单，你来点菜"。(Let's do it like this, I'll look at the menu and you can order.)

学： 好吧。

服： 请你等一下，我替你把书包起来。

学： 这一本词典不必打包了，我现在就用得着。

------ ◆ ------ 生词 ------ ◆ ------

1. 周末	zhōu mò	*N.*	weekend
2. 逛逛	guàng guang	*V.*	to roam around
3. 新华书店	xīn huá shū diàn	*Place N.*	New China Bookstore
4. 中国书店	zhōng guó shū diàn	*Place N.*	China Bookstore
5. 三联书店	sān lián shū diàn	*Place N.*	San Lian Bookstore
6. 西单图书大厦	xī dān tú shū dà shà	*Place N.*	Xi Dan Book Center
7. 海淀图书城	hǎi diàn tú shū chéng	*Place N.*	Hai Dian Book City
8. 架子	jià zi	*N.*	shelf
9. 随便	suí biàn	*Adv/Adj.*	do as one pleases; casual
10. 翻看	fān kàn	*V.*	to browse, to look over (books)
11. 却	què	*Adv.*	on the contrary
12. 柜子	guì zi	*N.*	cabinet
13. 由	yóu	*Prep.*	by, from
14. 售货员	shòu huò yuán	*N.*	shop attendant, salesclerk
15. 替	tì	*Prep.*	for
16. 种类	zhǒng lèi	*N.*	kind, type, variety
17. 文史	wén shǐ	*Abbrev.*	literature and history
18. 财经	cái jīng	*Abbrev.*	finance and economy
19. 计算机	jì suàn jī	*N.*	computer
20. 教育	jiào yù	*N.*	education
21. 装订	zhuāng dìng	*V/N.*	to bind; binding, bookbinding
22. 印刷	yìn shuā	*V/N.*	to print; printing
23. 最后	zuì hòu	*Adv.*	at last, finally

24. 总算	zǒng suàn	*Adv.*	at long last, finally
25. 汉英	hàn yīng	*Adj.*	Chinese-English
26. 词典	cí diǎn	*N.*	dictionary
27. 套	tào	*Classifier.*	set
28. 鲁迅	lǔ xùn	*Personal N.*	Lu Xun, a famous writer
29. 全集	quán jí	*N.*	complete works
30. 查	chá	*V.*	to look up (in a dictionary), to examine, to investigate
31. 拼音	pīn yīn	*N/VO.*	Pinyin; to combine sounds into syllables
32. 索引	suǒ yǐn	*N.*	index
33. 同时	tóng shí	*Adv.*	at the same time
34. 收	shōu	*V.*	to collect
35. 丰富	fēng fù	*Adj/V.*	rich, abundant; to enrich
36. 解释	jiě shì	*N/V.*	explanation; to explain
37. 详细	xiáng xì	*Adj.*	detailed
38. 用法	yòng fǎ	*N.*	usage
39. 例句	lì jù	*N.*	example sentences
40. 文学家	wén xué jiā	*N.*	writer, man of letters
41. 小说	xiǎo shuō	*N.*	novel, fiction
42. 可惜	kě xī	*Adv.*	it's a pity, it's too bad
43. 翻译	fān yì	*N/V.*	translation; to translate
44. 提高	tí gāo	*V.*	to raise
45. 原文	yuán wén	*N.*	original text
46. 柜台	guì tái	*N.*	service counter
47. 交款单	jiāo kuǎn dān	*N.*	payment slip
48. 处	chù	*N.*	(bound form) place
49. 零的	líng de	*N.*	small change
50. 开	kāi	*V.*	to make out, to write
51. 发票	fā piào	*N.*	receipt
52. 找	zhǎo	*V.*	to give change, to search for
53. 毛病	máo bìng	*N.*	defect
54. 退	tuì	*V.*	to return merchandise (and get refund)

55. 费	fèi	*V/N.*	to waste; fee
56. 这样吧	zhè yàng ba	*Idiom.*	Let's do this.
57. ……之内	zhī nèi	*Prep.*	within...
58. 超过	chāo guò	*V.*	to exceed
59. 负责	fù zé	*VO.*	to be responsible, to be in charge of
60. 包	bāo	*V.*	to wrap
61. 不必	bú bì	*VP.*	do not have to, no need
62. 打包	dǎ bāo	*V.*	to wrap
63. 用得着	yòng de zháo	*VP.*	to have use for something

───◆─── 补充词汇 ───◆───

64. 杂志	zá zhì	*N.*	magazine
65. 画报	huà bào	*N.*	pictorial magazine or newspaper
66. 文具	wén jù	*N.*	stationery
67. 信纸	xìn zhǐ	*N.*	letter paper
68. 信封	xìn fēng	*N.*	envelope
69. 明信片	míng xìn piàn	*N.*	postcard
70. 铅笔	qiān bǐ	*N.*	pencil
71. 圆珠笔	yuán zhū bǐ	*N.*	ball-point pen
72. 毛笔	máo bǐ	*N.*	writing brush
73. 尺	chǐ	*N.*	ruler
74. 包装纸	bāo zhuāng zhǐ	*N.*	wrapping paper
75. 记事本	jì shì běn	*N.*	memo book, pocket calendar
76. 日记本	rì jì běn	*N.*	diary (volume)

句型

一、 听……说 (I was told, it is said)

> ✍ "听……说" literally means "hear...say". This expression is used to indicate the information source. The subject "我" is often omitted. For example, "(我)听小李说小王买了一辆新的自行车". (Li told me that Wang bought a new bike.) Sometimes the source of information is unstated, in which case the phrase becomes just "听说". "听说北京的书店很多". "It is said that there are many bookstores in Beijing".

☞ 我常听老师说在中国，书的价格比美国的便宜得多。

1、 听有的北京人说旧车市场的车不一定便宜。
   It is said by some Beijing people that the bikes in the used-bike market are not always inexpensive.

2、 听他说这儿的计算机的质量都不算高。
   I heard him say that the quality of the computers here is not considered high.

二、 却 (on the contrary, however)

> ✍ "却" is an adverb meaning "however," "but". Although "却" shares the same meaning with "但是" or "可是", "却" is different from them in three ways. First, it is mostly used in written form, whereas "但是" or "可是" can be used in both spoken and written forms. Second, it always occurs immediately before a verb, whereas "但是" or "可是" usually occurs at the beginning of a sentence. Third, the meaning of "却" is not as strong as "但是" or "可是".

☞ 有些书店的书却都收在柜子里，要看书得由店员替你拿，比较不方便。

1、 你说你没有时间写作业，却有时间逛书店。
   You said that you did not have time to finish your assignment, yet you still had time to go

windowshop at bookstores.

2、他花了很多钱修车，却没修好。他的闸还是刹不住。

He spent a lot of money repairing his bike. However, the bike is not fixed and the brakes still do not work.

三、 由 (by)

> ✍ "由" is a preposition, used to introduce the agent who is in a position or has the power or prerogative to do something. In contrast to "由", "被" carries a passive voice. "由" cannot be followed by a resultative verb construction, e.g. one CANNOT say * "我由他吵醒了", but rather "我被他吵醒了". (I was awakened by him.)

☞ 不象从前那样把书都收在柜子里，要看书得由售货员替你拿。

1、这些钱都是你的，你想怎么花完全由你自己决定。

This money is all yours. How you want to spend it is entirely up to you to decide.

2、这次的考试时间由学生选，上午下午都行。

The time for this exam will be chosen by the students. The afternoon or the morning are both fine.

四、 替 (for, in so-and-so's stead)

> ✍ "替" meaning "for" is used to indicate that someone is performing an action in place of someone else. For example, "我今天很忙，不能去邮局。请你替我寄一封信". (I am busy today, I can't go to the post office. Please mail this letter for me.)

☞ 要看书得由店员替你拿……

1、你可不可以替我寄这封信?

Can you mail this letter for me?

2、要是你明天有事不能去买东西，我可以替你买。

If you have things to do and cannot go shopping tomorrow, I can buy the things for you.

五、 可惜 (it is a pity that, it is too bad that)

> ✍ "可惜" as an adverb, means "it is a pity that..." or "it is too bad that..." It is placed mostly at the beginning of a sentence but sometimes between a subject and a verb. "可惜" can also be used in the exclamation of "真可惜" following a statement about an unfortunate situation. "我没见到他，真可惜"！("It is really a pity I didn't see him".)

☞ 我看过很多他的小说，可惜都是英文翻译的。

1、很可惜我今天不能跟你骑车去天安门。

It is too bad that I cannot ride my bicycle with you to Tiananmen.

2、这是一本好书，可惜装订和印刷的质量都太差。

This is a good book. It is a pity that both the binding and printing quality are extremely poor.

六、 分……（等）类 (to be categorized into)

> ✍ The expression "分……(等)类" means "to divide into such and such categories". "等" is used to indicate that there is more than one category and it may be replaced by another way of summing up the categories (as exemplified by example 1). For example, "我们的书分语言、历史、文学等类". or "我门的书分语言、历史、文学这三类". (Our books are categorized into language, history and literature.)

☞ 书的种类非常多，分文史、社会、财经、语言、计算机、教育等类。

1、我们的课型分大班、小班、对话课和单班课四大类。

Our classes are divided into four types: large class, small class, conversation class, and one-on-one class.

2、中国的火车票分硬座(hard seat)、软座，和硬卧(hard sleeper)、软卧等类。

China's train tickets are categorized into hard seats, soft seats, hard sleepers, and soft sleepers.

七、 V来V去 (to V back and forth)

> ✍ "V 来 V 去" is a verb complement structure meaning "to do something back and forth", "to do something here and there", or " to do something repeatedly", e.g. "跑来跑去" (to run back and forth); "做来做去" (to do something many times); "听来听去" (to listen to it over and over again); "猜来猜去" (to guess all the things one can think of).

☞ 我看来看去，最后总算决定买一本《汉英词典》和一套《鲁迅全集》。

1、他挑来挑去都没挑到喜欢的衣服。

He could not find any clothes which he liked after going through them so many times.

2、我查来查去都查不到那个字。

I tried and tried to look up that word (in the dictionary) everywhere but I could not find it.

八、 V起来 (when it comes to V, V+up/away, begin to V)

> ✍ "起来," literally "up", takes on several different figurative meanings when used as a verb complement: 1) "when it comes to...", e.g. "这把椅子坐起来很舒服". (This chair is comfortable [when sitting on it]); 2) "V+up/away", e.g. "把门－起来" (lock up the door); 3) "begin to V", e.g. "下起雨来了". (It's begun to rain).

☞ 这本词典查起来很方便。

1、这辆自行车修好以后骑起来象新的一样。

Since repairing the bike, it seems like new when I ride it.

2、你的宿舍又有空调，又有洗澡设备，住起来一定很舒服。

Your dorm has air conditioning and also has bathing facilities; it must be a very comfortable place to live.

3、一大早就下起雨来了。

It's begun to rain in the very early morning.

☞ 我替你把书包起来。 (V + up or away)

1、你帮我把这些东西装起来，放在这个纸盒子里。

Help me put these things away. Put them in this paper box.

2、把护照好好收起来，别丢(lose)了。

Put the passport away. Do not lose it.

九、(在)……之内 (within)

> ✍ "在……之内" is normally used at the beginning of a sentence or between the subject and the verb meaning "within a certain period of time or distance". "在" is optional, e.g. "在五天之内" or "五天之内" (within five days).

☞ 要是有问题，(在)三天之内来换。

1、我得在三天之内把语言实践课的报告交给老师。

Within three days, I have to give the teacher my language practicum report.

2、在这十年之内，北京已经变成了一个很现代化的都市。

Within ten years, Beijing has become a modern metropolis.

十、V得着

> ✍ "着" is a verb complement meaning "successfully achieve a certain result through doing something", e.g. "买着" (to have bought); "找着" (found); "看着" (saw), etc. "着" can also be used interchangeably with "到". "V得着" is a potential complement form meaning "it is possible that". Its negative form is "V不着" and the question form is "V得着V不着". Sometimes the meaning of "successfully achieving an intended result" is muted, so the "V得着" phrase just means "can V", e.g. "用得着". A synonym of "用得着" is "用得上".

☞ 我现在就用得着。

1、住在北京的时候用得着用不着美金？

When living in Beijing, does one have use for American money?

2、在北京吃得着地道的中国饭。

One can eat typical Chinese food in Beijing.

> ✍ 用不着 V = 不必 V (no need; not necessary)

1、明天没有考试，所以今天用不着念书。=明天没有考试，所以今天不必念书。

There is not going to be a test tomorrow. Therefore, there is no need to study today.

2、这种东西学校附近的商场就有，用不着去秀水市场。=这种东西学校附近的商场就有，不必去秀水市场。

The market near the school has these things, there is no need for you to go to the Silk Alley.

北京最大的书店之一：王府井书店

语言形式练习
Tasks on Language Forms

一、读课文回答问题

1、在北京的书店里，书都放在架子上让人随便翻看吗？

2、在中国书的价格和质量跟在美国的比起来怎么样？

3、这位同学买的汉英词典怎么样？

4、为什么这位同学要买一套《鲁迅全集》？

5、买书以后，应该怎么交款？

6、这位学生买的书可以退吗？要是想换书，得什么时候来换？

二、完成对话

1、A：我想买一辆自行车。

B：

（听……说；用不着）

2、A：这个星期谁负责整理房间？

B：

（由；V不着）

3、A：糟糕，我明天有事，不能去机场接我妹妹。你明天忙吗？

B：对不起，

（可惜；替）

4、A：这个宿舍有哪几种房间？

B：

（分……等类）

5、A：我想买一套《鲁迅全集》。

B：

（不必；替）

三、听录音回答问题

1、今天是星期几？为什么小张有空到城里去？
2、这家店给小张的印象怎么样？
3、客人需要售货员替他们拿磁带才能听吗？为什么？
4、为什么很多人来这家店买磁带？
5、小张买到了他要的磁带了吗？为什么？
6、小张想买一本什么样的词典？为什么？

四、阅读回答问题

采访个体书店老板 (boss)

记者：您什么时候开的这家书店？都卖些什么书呢？

老板：去年我开了这家书店。店虽然不大，但是书的种类非常多，文史也好，财经也好，语言也好，生活常识也好，只要你是能想到的书，我这儿都能找到。

记者：您这儿的书可以随便翻看吗？

老板：原来是可以的，可是很多人利用这个条件不买书，只看书！尤其是放暑假的时候，很多学生在我这里一看就是一天，而且天天来看。我这个小书店可受不了。所以，从去年开始我们规定凡是不买书的人，只可以在书店里待一个钟头。您想想，我的书店本来就不大，要是每个人都一待一天，只看不买，我怎么受得了呀！

记者：确实是。可是您也把很多想学习，但是没有钱的孩子挡在了门外。

老板：我也想帮助那些没钱的孩子。这不，我和同事们想来想去，打算从明年起，凡是期末考试成绩在90分以上的学生，来我这儿买书都可以有八折优惠。假期的时候，学生们来我这儿交一些钱还可以借书。

记者：听起来这些办法都很好。希望您的书店越办越好！

问题:

1、下面的哪一种说法跟书店里的情况和做法不一样:
(1) 书店的书的种类非常多
(2) 书店的书原来可以随便翻看

150

(3) 只要是学生来书店买书就可以有八折的优惠

(4) 学生可以来书店交一些钱后借书

2、从去年开始书店有什么新规定？为什么？

3、为了帮助没有钱买书的学生，书店采取了什么措施？

4、请你给老师或者朋友介绍一个你喜欢的书店（名字、地址、特点、为什么喜欢等等）

五、 翻译

1. I went to visit some bookstores yesterday. Since I can't understand the original Chinese, I bought the English version of Lu Xun's novel.

2. Even though this book is expensive, the quality of printing and binding is not good. Besides, there are many typos. I think you'd better spend less money and buy an inexpensive one.

3. Looking up words in a dictionary is beneficial to my Chinese, but it is too time consuming. Fortunately, this dictionary has indexes for both Pinyin and radicals.

4. In China you might neither return nor exchange something after you had bought it. You could not get refunds either. You had to make sure that the thing you bought was in good condition before you paid the money.

5. I asked you to return this television within three days if you found any problems with it. Now it has been more than three days, so of course we are not responsible for any problems.

买书的人可以随便翻看

语言使用练习
Tasks on Language Use

一、真实情景活动 🎥

（一）查字典写英文：

1、初等教育 =

2、学生工具书 =

3、成人考试用书 =

4、少儿读物 =

（二）问问中国人下面的
词有什么意思：

1、数理化

2、科普

王府井书店二层

（三）看右边的广告回答问题：

1、《作家文摘》是什么？每
个星期可以看到几次？

　a.书　　b.报纸　　c.杂志

　a.三次　b.五次　　c.两次

2、你可以在什么地方订到？
你可以用哪两种方法订
阅？有哪几种订阅价钱？

3、查字典看看什么是"热
线"、"发行部"？

欢迎订阅 作家文摘

◆全年均可到当地邮局订阅

◆《作家文摘》邮发代号 1—190
　每周两期　月价 8.15 元　季价 24.45 元
　半年价 48.90 元。

◆北京市读者可拨打电话订阅热线
　185—2 键。

◆您没订全的 2002 年报纸可与本报
　发行部联系：[010]65518026
　　　　　　　65518025

（四）根据右边的报纸回答下面的问题:

1、什么是新书书目？

2、《"玩"的教育在美国》是描写什么人的情况？

3、什么是"玩"？在书中，作者对"玩"有什么特别的看法？

4、根据这个广告，这本书对中国的什么方面有参考价值 (valuable resource)？

作家出版社
新书书目

"玩"的教育在美国

黄全愈著 定价:19.00元

本书以详尽的材料、细致的分析，跨越不同的文化背景,呈现出美国孩子的生活与学习状况。在现今大力提倡素质教育的整体大背景下,有着极好的参考价值。在书中,作者认为"玩"在孩子的成长中起着非常重要的作用,结合美国教育的实际情况并针对中国教育理念进行了探索性的思考。

二、讨论

1、美国书贵还是中国书贵？

2、什么地方有书店？你去过北京的书店吗？

3、你去过的书店是什么样的？可以随便翻看书吗？

4、买了书以后在哪里交款？这个法子跟美国的有什么不一样？

5、你现在用词典吗？你用的词典查起来方便不方便？

6、选词典的时候，你注意什么？解释、例句、还是其它？

三、语言实践

请你去北京一家大书店跟一家小书店，（1）访问在那里买书的人为什么他们在那里买书？他们认为中国的书贵不贵？装订、印刷怎么样？（2）访问卖书的人问问他们通常什么人来他们书店买书？哪一类人买书最多？哪一类书卖得最好？买了书以后可不可以换？等等。

四、作文

《中国的书店》

五、看图说话

1

2

3

4

5

书的种类非常多，分文史、社会、财经、语言、计算机、教育等类

第九课 打 "的" (1)

打 "夏利" 最实惠

✎ **Notes** (1) "打 '的'": Like many verbs in Chinese, "打" has different meanings when combined with different objects. The following is a list of common idiomatic expressions of "打" with different objects: "打针" (to get an injection); "打气" (to pump air); "打球" (to play ball); "打人" (to beat up someone); "打包" (to pack up); "打的" (to take a taxi); "打电话" (to make a phone call). The "打" in "打的" means "to take" or "to ride on". "的" is short for "的士," originally a Cantonese transliteration of "taxi". "打的" became a common term in Mainland China in the late 1980s when Hong Kong and Taiwanese culture started making inroads in Mainland China.

课文

　　这个星期的语言实践报告是关于北京的出租汽车。一下课，周玲就决定打"的"去天安门。一方面去看看天安门，一方面也顺便⁽²⁾跟出租汽车司机聊聊天，正好准备明天的功课。

　　从聊天中，周玲了解到北京这几年发展得非常快。才几年的时间，市里就修建⁽³⁾了好几条环城公路，有二环、三环、还有四环。尽管有了这么多的环城公路，北京的交通还是十分拥挤。尤其是上下班时间，自行车、汽车、出租汽车等都在马路上行驶，人多车多，交通常常阻塞。

　　北京的公共交通工具这十几年也有了很大的变化。除了公共汽车、地铁以外，现在又有了空调大巴、小公共和出租汽车，其中出租汽车最受欢迎。因为它既灵活又方便，北京人管坐出租汽车叫打"的"或者打"车"。根据价钱和车的好坏，北京的出租汽车大致可以分下面几种类型：一块二的、一块六的跟两块钱的。最便宜的是一种叫"夏利"的四门小型⁽⁴⁾轿车，一公里一块二；最贵的是一种"豪

Notes ⁽²⁾ "顺便"：This expression, meaning "conveniently, along the way, in passing", is normally used before a verb. There is no exact equivalent of "顺便" in English. It is thus translated differently in different contexts, e.g. "去买菜的路上，我顺便去买了一些水果"。(On my way to the market, I also bought some fruit.) "请你顺便把这本书带给老师"。(Please bring this book with you and give it to our teacher.) "这个问题现在顺便说一下，以后还会讲到"。(I mention this problem in passing and shall refer to it again later.)

　　⁽³⁾ "修建" vs. "建立"："修建" and "建立" both mean "to build", "to establish". However, the objects of these two verbs are quite different in terms of their categories. "修建" is used for building physical and concrete constructions, e.g. "修建公路" (to build highways)；"修建铁路" (to build railroads)；"修建房子" (to build houses)。"建立" is used for building or establishing an institution, e.g. "建立工厂" (to start a factory)；"建立学校" (to set up a school)；"建立医院" (to establish a hospital). If one says "修建学校", it refers to building the physical structure of the school.

　　⁽⁴⁾ "型"：Here, 型" means "scale", "style", or "type". It normally follows an adjective to form a phrase, e.g. "大型" (large-scaled)；"中型" (mid-sized)；"小型" (small-scaled)；"新型" (new type)；老型 (old type), etc.

华型"的四门轿车，两块钱一公里。一般打"夏利"最实惠，不但便宜，速度也不慢；另外多数的出租汽车司机都来自北京本地或郊区，跟他们聊起天来很有意思，能练习口语，也能了解北京的经济和文化动态。

———◆———

（周招手打的）（一辆"夏利"停下来）

周： 去天安门，师傅。

张师傅：好，快上车。走二环还是走三环？

周： 走二环吧！现在不是上下班时间，也许不会塞车。

张： 那好，听你的了[5]。

周： 师傅，您这车听声音还真不错。哪年的车？

张： 96年的，刚买了一年。

周： 这是您自己的车还是公司的？

张： 自己的，本钱还没还完呢，车是自己出钱买的，

周： 您觉得当出租个体户容易吗？

张： 不容易。现在跑出租[6]的人越来越多，竞争激烈得很。我从早上六点就出来，现在快五点了还没拉多少活儿[7]，要不然早回家了。有时候一天得干十几个钟头。

🖊 Notes [5] "听你的了": This is an idiomatic expression often used in conversation to mean "I will do whatever you say" or "whatever you say".

[6] "跑出租": When "跑", "to run around", is followed by an object, it is an idiomatic usage referring to running all over the place in order to achieve or do something, e.g. "跑火车" (to work on the train); "跑买卖" (to travel for business purposes). "出租" is short for "出租汽车".

[7] "拉活": The verb "拉" is used here to refer to pulling or driving a vehicle which transports people or objects, e.g. "拉人", "拉东西". "活" here means "business" or "work". "拉活" refers to driving around looking for work or business. This is a colloquial expression used in North China.

周：那您一定赚了不少钱。

张：哪里？虽然跑得时间长，但是不一定能赚多少钱，一天最多三四百块钱。北京现在的交通是越来越拥挤，一堵车就是两、三个钟头，哪儿都去不成，怎么能赚钱呢？

周：看来跑出租也不容易。

张：是啊。

周：跑出租这么辛苦，您为什么还要干呢？

张：辛苦是辛苦，可是有一定的自由，能靠自己的本事吃饭。到天安门了。

周：这么快就到了！真不错，今天没塞车。多少钱？

张：十五块二。

周：请您给我开个票。

———◆———— 生 词 ————◆———

1. 实践	shí jiàn	*N/V.*	practicum, practice, to put into practice
2. 报告	bào gào	*N/V.*	report; to report
3. 关于	guān yú	*Prep.*	regarding, concerning
4. 天安门	tiān ān mén	*Place N.*	Tiananmen
5. 顺便	shùn biàn	*Adv.*	conveniently, to do something along the way
6. 司机	sī jī	*N.*	driver
7. 正好	zhèng hǎo	*Adv.*	as it happens, fortuitously, by coincidence
8. 发展	fā zhǎn	*V/N.*	to develop; development
9. 修建	xiū jiàn	*V.*	to build, to construct
10. 环城	huán chéng	*VO/Adj.*	to encircle the city; around

				the city
11.	公路	gōng lù	*N.*	highway
12.	三环	sān huán	*Abbrev.*	The Third Ring Road (三环路)
13.	拥挤	yōng jǐ	*Adj.*	crowded
14.	上下班	shàng xià bān	*VO.*	to go to and get off work
15.	马路	mǎ lù	*N.*	road, street
16.	行驶	xíng shǐ	*V.*	(vehicles) to run along (roads)
17.	阻塞	zǔ sè	*V.*	to block, to clog
18.	公共	gōng gòng	*Adj.*	public
19.	公共汽车	gōng gòng qì chē	*NP.*	public bus
20.	地铁	dì tiě	*N.*	subway
21.	小公共	xiǎo gōng gòng	*NP.*	mini bus (used for public transportation)
22.	其中	qí zhōng	*PrepP.*	among which
23.	灵活	líng huó	*Adj.*	flexible, agile
24.	管……叫	guǎn...jiào	*VP.*	to call something or somebody (by the name of...)
25.	根据	gēn jù	*Prep.*	according to
26.	大致	dà zhì	*Adv.*	roughly, approximately
27.	下面	xià miàn	*Adj.*	following, next
28.	夏利	xià lì	*N.*	a brand of small sedan
29.	小型	xiǎo xíng	*N.*	small size
30.	轿车	jiào chē	*N.*	sedan
31.	公里	gōng lǐ	*N/Classifier.*	kilometer
32.	豪华型	háo huá xíng	*N.*	deluxe model
33.	速度	sù dù	*N.*	speed
34.	来自	lái zì	*V.*	to come from
35.	本地	běn dì	*N.*	local area
36.	郊区	jiāo qū	*N.*	suburb
37.	有意思	yǒu yì si	*Adj.*	interesting
38.	口语	kǒu yǔ	*N.*	spoken language
39.	文化	wén huà	*N.*	culture
40.	动态	dòng tài	*N.*	trends

41. 招手	zhāo shǒu	VO.	to wave, to beckon
42. 公司	gōng sī	N.	company
43. 出钱	chū qián	VO.	to pay
44. 本钱	běn qián	N.	capital
45. 还	huán	V.	to pay back, to return
46. 堵车	dǔ chē	VO/N.	to have a traffic jam; traffic jam
47. 声音	shēng yīn	N.	sound
48. 当	dāng	V.	to be, to become
49. 个体户	gè tǐ hù	N.	self-employed people, independent entrepreneur
50. 竞争	jìng zhēng	N/V.	competition; to compete
51. 激烈	jī liè	Adj.	fierce, intense
52. 拉	lā	V.	to draw in, to pull
53. 活儿	huór	N.	business, work
54. 要不然	yào bu rán	Conj.	otherwise (cf. Lesson 7, Sentence Pattern 6)
55. 干	gàn	V.	(colloquial) to work, to do
56. 哪里	nǎ lǐ	Adv.	"nah" (used to negate what the other just said)
57. 辛苦	xīn kǔ	Adj.	hard, laborious
58. 一定的	yí dìng de	Adj.	fixed, certain
59. 自由	zì yóu	N/Adj.	freedom; free
60. 靠	kào	V.	to rely on
61. 本事	běn shì	N.	capability, ability
62. 票	piào	N.	receipt (abbreviated form for 票, cf. Lesson 8), ticket

—◆— 补充词汇 —◆—

63. 乘客	chéng kè	N.	passenger
64. 红绿灯	hóng lǜ dēng	N.	traffic light
65. 行人	xíng rén	N.	pedestrian
66. 英里	yīng lǐ	N/Classifier.	mile

67. 英尺	yīng chǐ	*N/Classifier.*	foot
68. 寸	cùn	*N/Classifier.*	inch
69. 米	mǐ	*N/Classifier.*	meter
70. 公分	gōng fēn	*N/Classifier.*	centimeter
71. 绕路	rào lù	*VO.*	to make a detour, to take the long route
72. 上下班时间	shàng xià bān shí jiān	*NP.*	rush hour
73. 存钱	cún qián	*VO.*	to deposit money, to save money
74. 借钱	jiè qián	*VO.*	to borrow money

打"的"去天安门

句型

一、 ……是关于……(to be about)

> ✍ "关于" meaning "concerning, about" is often used with "是" or "是……的" construction to introduce the content of a topic. The topic, in the form of a noun-phrase, is usually something like a book, a movie, a lesson, a piece of news, etc.

☞ 这个星期的语言实践报告是关于北京的出租汽车。

1、 这一课是关于周玲 "打的" 的经历。

This lesson is about Zhou Ling's experience taking a taxi.

2、 我们在北京学到的知识都是关于中国语言和文化的。

All the knowledge we acquired in Beijing is about Chinese language and culture.

二、 正好V (as it happens)

> ✍ "正好" meaning "as it happens" is an adverb. It is used before a verb to describe a fortuitous happenstance or coincidence. (See also Note 3 in Lesson 1).

☞ 正好准备明天的功课。

1、 今天一出校门正好碰到来找我的老同学。

As it happens, as soon as I stepped outside the school's gate today, I ran into my old classmate coming to look for me.

2、 今天下雨哪儿也去不了，正好在宿舍写作业。

Today we cannot go anywhere because it is raining. It is just as well that we do our school work in the dorm.

164

三、才……年（天、个月、个星期）的时间 (only for as short as...[year, month, day])

> ✍ "才" is an adverb. Here, it is used BEFORE a time word indicating "only for as short as..." "才" conveying the sense that time lapse is shorter than expected.

☞ 才几年的时间，市里就修建了好几条环城公路……

1、才几个星期的时间，我的中文已经有了很大的进步。

In only a few weeks, my Chinese has already greatly improved.

2、离开北京才一年的时间，这里已经发生了很大的变化，真让人吃惊。

I have only been gone from Beijing for a year and there have already been great changes here. It's really astonishing!

四、好几+Classifier (quite a few)

> ✍ "好几" meaning "quite a few" or "a good number of" is always followed by a classifier or measure word, and may be used to modify a noun. It is normally used in spoken and informal settings.

☞ 市里就修建了好几条环城公路，有二环、三环、还有四环。

1、尽管现在北京已经有了好几条环城公路，可是交通还是非常拥挤。

Although Beijing has quite a few ring roads now, its traffic is still extremely congested.

2、跑出租虽然很辛苦，但是一天能赚好几百块钱，辛苦也就算不了什么了。

Although driving a taxi is laborious, one can earn several hundred dollars a day so the "hardship" doesn't matter much.

五、根据 (according to)

> ✍ "根据" is used here as a preposition meaning "according to". The "根据" phrase normally proceeds the main clause and is rarely used after "不".

☞ 根据价钱和车的好坏，北京的出租汽车大致可以分下面几种类型。

1、我们会根据交通的情况决定去还是不去天安门。

Depending on traffic conditions, we will decide whether we are going to Tiananmen.

2、根据学生的语言实践题目，我们把学生分成三组。

According to the topics of the students' language practicum, we divided the students into three groups.

六、 管……叫……(to call someone/something as...)

> "管……叫" is a colloquial way of saying "to call someone or something..." In Chinese, one can either say "我叫他小李"。or "我管他叫小李"。(I call him Xiao Li.) The two forms are used interchangeably.

☞ 北京人管坐出租汽车叫打"的"或者打"车"。

1、北京人管外国人叫"老外"。

The people of Beijing call foreigners "Lao Wai".

2、人们都管这个修车的老师傅叫"老热心"。

Everyone calls that old master bike repairman "Old Warm-hearted".

七、 来自……(place) (to come from)

> "来自" meaning "coming from" is a more formal way to state the origin of someone or something than "是从……来的"。 "他来自美国"。is the same as "他是从美国来的"。(He is from the United States).

☞ 多数的出租汽车司机都来自北京本地或郊区。

1、我觉得这种竞争激烈的文化来自国外。

I believe that this culture of fierce competition comes from abroad.

2、首都经贸大学的学生大多数来自北京本地和郊区.

Students at the Capital University of Economics and Business, for the most part, come from the local areas of Beijing and its suburbs.

八、 了解……的动态 (to know and understand the development of)

> ✍ "动态" means "trend" or "development". "了解……的动态" means "to know and understand the development of". This pattern is commonly used in written or formal settings.

☞ 也能了解北京的经济和文化动态。

1、 我们的老师要常常了解学生的学习和思想动态。
Our teachers frequently need to know about the learning situation and mental state of their students.

2、 来北京学习的最大好处是能直接了解中国的经济和文化动态。
The greatest advantage of studying in Beijing is being able to directly observe China's economic and cultural development.

九、 靠……吃饭 (to rely on... "to eat")

> ✍ "靠……吃饭" means "to rely on...for one's living". For example, one may say "我的教授靠教书吃饭"。(My professor relies on teaching to maintain his standard of living.) The negative particle is always placed before "靠" instead of the main verb of the sentence.

☞ 能靠自己的本事吃饭。

1、 在国营单位和当个体户的最大的不同就是个体户靠自己的本事吃饭。
The greatest difference between working in a state-owned factory and working as a private entrepreneur is that the latter has to rely on himself for everything.

2、 在美国，大学一毕业就不能再靠父母，要靠自己的本事吃饭了。
In the U.S., once you graduate from college, you can no longer rely on your parents and have to rely on your own abilities "to make a living".

语言形式练习
Tasks on Language Forms

一、读课文回答问题

1、为什么周玲决定打的去天安门？

2、为什么修建了好几条环城公路以后，北京的交通还是非常拥挤？

3、出租汽车可分为哪三种？价钱怎么算？

4、打"夏利"有哪些好处？

5、张师傅觉得跑出租赚钱容易吗？为什么他喜欢当出租汽车司机？

二、完成对话

1、A：在美国，孩子什么时候离开家开始自己生活？

　　B：

　　　　（靠……吃饭；管……叫……）

2、A：你想了解一些什么情况？

　　B：

　　　　（一方面……一方面……；了解……的动态）

3、A：你家在郊区还是在市里？退休以后还做点儿什么？

　　B：

　　　　（来自……；给……出路）

三、听录音回答问题

1、小林平常出门的交通工具是什么?

2、小林为什么要到新华书店去?

3、他决定怎么去?为什么?

4、李师傅是哪里人?

5、李师傅对纽约的印象怎么样?

6、小林喜欢纽约吗?你是怎么知道的?

7、李师傅为什么要换条路开?

8、最后,李师傅找了小林多少钱?为什么?

四、阅读回答问题

我是从外地来北京打工的,北京人管我们这种人叫"打工仔"。刚到北京的时候我非常兴奋,觉得我很快就能找到工作,赚很多很多的钱,可以靠自己的本事吃饭了。可是,一个月过去了,我什么工作都没有找到,带来的钱也很快就花光了。正在我不知道该怎么办才好的时候,我碰到了一个老家(hometown)来的人。他介绍我进了他们的公司。这家公司是专门为人送东西的。如果你有一些很紧急的材料或者东西,需要很快送到北京市的一个地方,那你就可以来我们公司。我们会用最快的速度帮你把东西送到你要送的地方。一到公司,他们就给了我一辆自行车。你可别以为这车就白给我了,我得用我每天的收入来还自行车的本钱。还完本钱,我才能有我自己的收入,而且这辆自行车也就是我的了。这听起来很合理,可是其中的辛苦真是说也说不完呀!首先是竞争激烈,北京市像我们这样的公司有几十家,你不送,还有别人可以送。所以老板把价钱压得特别低。这样,我们一天辛辛苦苦送十来份活儿也赚不了几块钱。其次是交通问题。北京三环,四环的修了不少大马路,可是就是没考虑我们这些骑车的人。自行车道都既小又窄,我们常常得在汽车中钻来钻去,非常危险。前天就有一个同事被汽车撞了,一歇就是三个礼拜。别说赚钱了,光医药费就欠了一大笔,真是倒霉!最后,再看看我们公司的规定。说是还完了自行车的本钱以后,自行车就是自己的了。每次按照我自己的算法,觉得本钱已经还完了。可是到公司一看,还是不够。我总觉得不对,可是由于没上过学,我怎么也弄不明白是怎么回事。有的时候真想回家算了,可是已经出来了,怎么可能一分钱不赚就回去呢?那我可怎么回家见我的父母呢?

问题:

    1、为什么北京人管"我"叫"打工仔"?

    2、请你介绍一下"我"的工作。

    3、用两个例子说明为什么说"我"的工作很辛苦?

    4、为什么"我"不能回家?

五、 翻译

1. (In the taxi)

    A: Excuse me, Master. Do you know how to get to this place from the Third Ring Road?

    B: Yes. I know this place. It is right off the Third Ring Road.

    A: Do you know how long it takes to get there?

    B: It depends on the traffic today. If there are no traffic jams and it is not rush hour, I think it will take us about fifteen minutes.

2. The development in the city is very rapid. Quite a few highways were constructed (by the city) in order to solve (解决) the problems of city traffic.

3. If you want to know what is going on economically in the city, the most convenient way is to chat with a cab driver.

4. In just the last few years, more and more people have become private entrepreneurs and the competition is getting more and more fierce.

北京的月票 (monthly buspass) 发售站

语言使用练习
Tasks on Language Use

一、真实情景活动 🎥

（一）在北京的汽车站你常常会看见下面这样的牌子。从这个牌子上你可以知道很多信息：

1、你可以不可以用月票坐这路车？

2、这路车最早的一班是早上几点？

3、这路车的一般票价是多少？要是超过三十公里是多少钱？

（二）北京有各种不同的交通工具，请说出下面图中不同的交通工具的名称：

（三）在北京的每一辆出租车上，你都会看见这个牌子。牌子很清楚地告诉你出租汽车的价钱，只要你看懂了就不会上当受骗。

警告乘客

1、本车每公里租价1.60元，基价公里为5公里，起价10.00元。

2、单程行驶15公里以上部分加收50%空驶费。

3、时速低于12公里时，每分钟加收1公里租价的费用。

4、等候乘客每5分钟加收1公里租价的费用。

5、晚23时（含）至次日5时（不含），每公里租价加收20%。

6、不同顾主合乘按合乘里程各支付60%的车费。

7、打电话临时租车，每次加收电话租车费三元。

8、出北京客运业务应由双方议定。

9、过路、过桥费由乘客支付。

根据上边的牌子回答下面的问题

1、要是从天安门坐出租车去西单，差不多4公里，你应该付多少钱？

2、要是你跟你的朋友白萌一块儿去，你们每个人得付多少钱？

3、要是你晚上11点30坐车去西单，你应该付多少钱？

4、要是你觉得在外边叫车很麻烦，你要打电话叫出租车去西单，你应该付多少钱？

5、要是今天早上的交通堵塞很严重，你的车只能以每小时10公里的速度往前走，你得多交钱还是交一样的钱？

二、讨论

1、你觉得北京的交通怎么样？什么时间常塞车？

2、谈一次你打"的"的经验。（从哪儿到哪儿？花了多少钱？经过哪些地方？有没有塞车？等等。）

3、跟一个出租汽车司机聊天。问问他为什么当出租汽车司机？以前是做什么的？车是自己的吗？喜不喜欢这个工作等等。

4、在美国坐出租汽车跟在北京有什么相同和不同的地方？

5、中国的改革开放对中国的个体户有什么好处？

6、在中国的国营单位 (work unit) 工作和当个体户有什么不同？

三、语言实践

1、采访一个个体出租汽车司机，了解一下他们现在的情况：收入怎么样？竞争激烈吗？为什么？

2、采访三个北京人，请他们谈谈对北京市交通的看法。

四、作文

《个体出租汽车司机ＸＸＸ》

《北京人看北京的交通》

五、看图说话

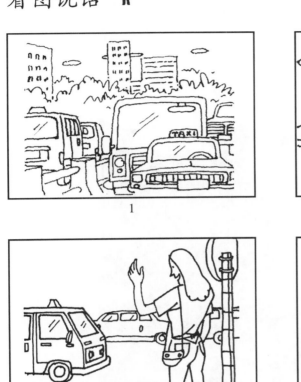

1

2

3

4

5

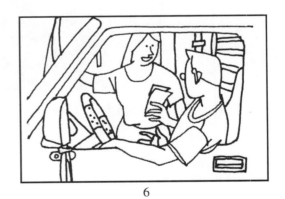

6

汉车、出租汽车等都在马路上行驶，人多车多，交通常常阻塞

Crossing Paths: Living and Learning in China

An Intermediate Chinese Course

岁月总是愈来愈短
友情总是愈来愈浓
生日总是愈来愈快
我的祝福也是愈来愈深

Happy Birthday

第十课　给朋友过生日 (1)

来，切蛋糕

✏️ <u>Notes</u> (1) "过生日"：This is a set phrase meaning "to celebrate one's birthday" or "to have one's birthday". When one wants to say "today is my birthday" in Chinese, one can of course say "今天是我的生日", but a more idiomatic way of saying it is "今天我过生日". For a sentence like "We will celebrate his birthday next week", the appropriate translation would be "我们下个礼拜给他过生日"。

课文

　　王小平是我在北京认识的朋友，他非常热情，经常带着我上各处[2]去参观，而且总是不让我付钱，这使我非常不好意思。上个星期天是他的生日，我想让他高兴高兴，所以我请了几个他认识的朋友一块儿给他过生日。这在美国很常见。可是据我的中国朋友说，给朋友办 surprise party 并不是中国人的习惯。中国人常给小孩儿和老人过生日，过生日的时候要吃面条，叫寿面。现在受了西方文化的影响，也改吃生日蛋糕了。小孩子们最喜欢在麦当劳过生日，在那儿有吃的还有玩的，孩子们觉得有意思。我觉得这种现象非常有趣。自从中国推行一家一个孩子的政策以来，孩子的生日反而变得比大人的还重要了。

　　我想选一样礼物送给小王，可是想来想去还是想不出到底送什么好。送吃的，不知道他喜欢不喜欢；送穿的，又不知道对他合适不合适，真难办。最后我决定送他一本书。

———◆———

（在客厅）

学生：小平，这是我送你的生日礼物，祝你生日快乐。

✎ **Notes** [2] "各处" vs. "到处"："各处" and "到处" (see Lesson 7 Vocabulary) both have the meaning of "everywhere". But "各处" may also mean "various places", which is less all-inclusive than "everywhere". Also, unlike "到处" which is always positioned before a verb, "各处" may either precede or follows a verb. Compare the following sentences: "他到处都参观过了"。(He visited everywhere.) "他们参观了各处就离开了"。(After visiting the various places, they took off.) "他喜欢骑自行车到处看看"。(He likes to ride around on a bike and look everywhere.) "在北京的时候，他常常骑自行车去各处看看"。(When he was in Beijing, he often rode his bike to various places.)

王： 哎呀，谢谢，真不好意思。

学生：没什么，希望你喜欢，这本书的内容是关于美国的节日的。你看，在美国，感恩节是每年十一月的第四个星期四，学校放两天假[3]，让学生们回家过节。感恩节那天我们吃火鸡。

王： 太棒了[4]，太棒了。我从来不知道美国有这么多有意思的节日，而且每个节日都那么有特色。

学生：其实我也对中国的节日很感兴趣，你可不可以给我介绍一下？

王： 好啊，让我想一想。

李： 我看[5]，先切蛋糕吧，边吃边说不是更好吗[6]？

学生：对，对，对，我差点儿忘了。小李，谢谢你提醒我。蛋糕还在冰箱里呢，是在万惠商场买的冰淇淋蛋糕。小李，请你帮忙把蜡烛跟火柴拿来。啊，小王，我还没问你，你多大了？

王： 虚岁三十，周岁二十九[7]，可是还是王老五[8]。（大家笑）

Notes [3] "放假"："放假" is a V-O meaning "to have a break or a holiday", and is often modified by a word designating the specific holiday (e.g. 放暑假). It is often used with the holidays, breaks, and vacations set or given by a government, an institution, a company, or one's supervisor or boss, e.g. "在美国七月四号全国放假一天"。 (In the US, the entire country has the day off on July fourth.) "学校什么时候放春假"？ (When does the school let out for spring break?) "今天我们不上班，因为公司放假"。 (We are not working today because our company is on a break.) "老板决定明天放我们一天假"。 (Our boss decided to let us off for a day.) When referring to "ask for a personal leave", or "go on a vacation", one would say "请假" and "度假".

[4] "太棒了"：This is an exclamatory expression used in casual colloquial speech to mean "great", "terrific", or "cool". It is hardly ever used in written or formal language.

[5] "我看"：This expression means "I'd say...", "in my opinion", "may I suggest...". While these meanings are derived from the literal meaning of "as I see it", one should avoid the direct translation "I see".

[6] "不是…吗"：This functions as a rhetorical question rather than a true question, e.g. "你不是今天去吗"？ (Aren't you going today?)

[7] "虚岁" and "周岁"：These two expressions refer to the two different ways in which the Chinese reckon their age. "虚岁" is reckoned by the traditional method, i.e. considering a person one year old at birth and adding a year each lunar new year. "周岁" is one's age as calculated by the Western system (zero at birth, add one year with each birthday).

[8] "王老五"：This is the name of a character in a movie who spent most of his lifetime being a bachelor until he was rather old.

生词

1. 过生日	guò shēng rì	*VO.*	to celebrate a birthday
2. 热情	rè qíng	*Adj/N.*	warm; enthusiasm
3. 经常	jīng cháng	*Adv.*	often
4. 各处	gè chù	*N.*	every place, various places
5. 参观	cān guān	*V.*	to visit (a place)
6. 付钱	fù qián	*VO.*	to pay
7. 常见	cháng jiàn	*Adj.*	common
8. 据	jù	*Prep.*	according to
9. 办	bàn	*V.*	to hold (a party), to manage, to arrange, to handle
10. 习惯	xí guàn	*N/V.*	habit; to be used to
11. 寿面	shòu miàn	*N.*	birthday noodles, longevity noodles
12. 西方	xī fāng	*N/Adj.*	the west; western
13. 影响	yǐng xiǎng	*N/V.*	influence; to influence
14. 改	gǎi	*V.*	to change, to switch over to
15. 蛋糕	dàn gāo	*N.*	cake
16. 麦当劳	mài dāng láo	*Place N.*	McDonald's
17. 有趣	yǒu qù	*Adj.*	interesting
18. 自从……以来	zì cóng...yǐ lái	*Prep.*	since
19. 推行	tuī xíng	*V.*	to promote, to carry out
20. 反而	fǎn ér	*Adv.*	on the contrary, instead
21. 想不出	xiǎng bù chū	*VP.*	cannot figure out
22. 难办	nán bàn	*Adj.*	hard to do, difficult
23. 祝	zhù	*V.*	to wish (someone...)
24. 快乐	kuài lè	*Adj/N.*	happy; happiness
25. 节日	jié rì	*N.*	holiday
26. 感恩节	gǎn ēn jié	*N.*	Thanksgiving
27. 放假	fàng jià	*VO.*	to have a holiday or vacation, to have a day off (cf. 放暑假, Lesson 1)
28. 过节	guò jié	*VO.*	to celebrate a holiday, to

			spend a holiday
29. 火鸡	huǒ jī	N.	turkey
30. 棒	bàng	Adj.	(colloquial) wonderful, great
31. 特色	tè sè	N.	characteristic
32. 感兴趣	gǎn xìng qù	VP.	to be interested
33. 切	qiē	V.	to cut
34. 边吃边说	biān chī biān shuō	VP.	to eat and chat at the same time (cf. 一边……一边 ……, Lesson 5)
35. 差点儿	chà diǎnr	Adv.	almost, nearly
36. 提醒	tí xǐng	V.	to remind
37. 万惠商场	wàn huì shāng chǎng	Place N.	Wanhui Shopping Center
38. 蜡烛	là zhú	N.	candle
39. 火柴	huǒ chái	N.	match
40. 多大	duō dà	QW.	how old
41. 虚岁	xū suì	N.	nominal age (reckoned by the traditional method, i.e. considering a person one year old at birth and adding a year each lunar new year.)
42. 周岁	zhōu suì	N.	actual age (reckoned by the Western method, i.e. consider the person one year older with each birthday)
43. 王老五	wáng lǎo wǔ	N.	an old bachelor (a character in a famous movie)

———◆◆— 补充词汇 —◆◆———

44. 庆祝	qìng zhù	V.	to celebrate
45. 寿星	shòu xīng	N.	birthday person
46. 长寿	cháng shòu	N.	long life, longevity
47. 许愿	xǔ yuàn	VO.	to make a wish, to grant a wish, to make a promise to someone

48. 十二生肖	shí èr shēng xiào	NP.	the twelve Chinese zodiac signs
49. 属	shǔ	V.	to belong to..., to be born in the year of (one of the twelve animals)
50. 鼠	shǔ	N.	mouse, rat
51. 牛	niú	N.	ox
52. 虎	hǔ	N.	tiger
53. 兔	tù	N.	rabbit
54. 龙	lóng	N.	dragon
55. 蛇	shé	N.	snake
56. 马	mǎ	N.	horse
57. 羊	yáng	N.	sheep, goat
58. 猴	hóu	N.	monkey
59. 鸡	jī	N.	rooster
60. 狗	gǒu	N.	dog
61. 猪	zhū	N.	pig
62. 国庆节	guó qìng jié	N.	National Day
63. 复活节	fù huó jié	N.	Easter
64. 圣诞节	shèng dàn jié	N.	Christmas
65. 圣诞树	shèng dàn shù	N.	Christmas tree

最后我决定送他一本书

句型

一、 据……(according to)

> ✍ "据" meaning "according to", is a synonymous with 根据 (cf. Lesson 9, Sentence Pattern 5), but 据", and not "根据", is usually coupled with a verb such as "说" or "看". "据……说" means "according to someone's words"; "据……看" means "according to someone's view".

☞ 据我的中国朋友说……

1、 据看过那个电影的人说，那个电影并不好。
Actually that movie is not very good according to the people who saw it.

2、 据我看，你大概是感冒了，休息休息就好了。
As I can see, you probably have a cold. (Looks like you've got a cold.) Rest a little bit then you will be fine.

二、 受（了/到）……的影响 (to be influenced by)

> ✍ In "受（了/到）……的影响 (to be influenced by)," "受", "to receive", is a transitive verb which is coupled with only certain objects, such as "影响" (influence), "批评" (criticism), "注意" (attention). "受……的 Obj." can be translated into either a passive or an active sentence in English depending on the context, e.g. "受到老师的批评", "to be criticized by the teacher"; "受西方人的注意", "to receive the attention of Westerners".

☞ 现在受了西方文化的影响，也改吃生日蛋糕了。

1、 你那么喜欢吃辣的东西，是受了谁的影响？
You really like to eat spicy things, whose influence was this?

2、 他受了父母的影响，也很喜欢上各处参观。
Due to his parent's influence, he also likes to visit various places.

三、 改 V (to change to V)

> ✍ "改" meaning "to change to" is used with a verb to describe the change from doing one activity to another, e.g. "我本来学日文，现在改学中文了"。 (I used to study Japanese. Now I have changed to studying Chinese.)

☞ 也改吃生日蛋糕了。

1、 因为有事，我改坐明天的飞机回家。
Because something came up, I changed my flight back home to tomorrow.

2、 他们家改装了国际直拨电话，现在打电话方便多了。
Since their family changed to the international direct dialing system, it is more convenient to make phone calls now.

四、 自从……以来 (ever since)

> ✍ "自从……以来" refers to a time period from a specific past time or event up to and including the present moment.

☞ 自从中国推行一家一个孩子的政策以来，孩子的生日反而变得比大人的还重要了。

1、 自从七月份以来，我已经认识了好几个中国朋友了。
Since July, I've already made quite a few Chinese friends.

2、 自从改革开放以来，很多人都改当个体户了。
Ever since the onset of economic reform and the "open door" policy, many people have become private entrepreneurs.

五、 反而 (on the contrary)

> ✍ "反而" is an adverb used in a compound sentence to indicate a situation that runs contrary to reason or expectation. "不但不 / 没" is often in the first clause of the sentence that includes "反而" to highlight the unexpected reality in the second clause.

☞ 孩子的生日反而变得比大人的还重要了。

1、老师不但没批评他，反而表扬了他。

The teacher did not criticize him. On the contrary, she gave praise to him.

2、我来中国以后，因为不上课，说中文的机会反而比在美国的时候还少。

Ever since coming to China, I've actually had even fewer opportunities to speak Chinese than in America because I often skip classes.

3、我没想到，北京的麦当劳的东西反而比纽约的贵。

I did not expect that McDonald's in Beijing would actually be more expensive than the ones in New York.

4、那本书写得并不好，可是看的人反而很多。

There are actually a lot of people who read that book even though it was not well-written.

六、比……还……(even more... than...)

> "比……还……" is a comparative structure meaning "A is even more Adj. than B". "还" here is an adverb normally placed before a comparative adjective meaning "even more". It can be replaced by "更", e.g. "现在北京的交通比三年前还拥挤"，"现在北京的交通比三年前更拥挤"。 (The traffic in Beijing nowadays is even worse than that of three years ago.) "还", however, sounds less formal than "更"。

☞ 孩子的生日反而变得比大人的还重要了。

1、我的屋子比你的还大一半。

My room is even larger than yours by half.

2、他看起来很老，其实他比我还小五岁。

He looks old, but he is actually five years younger than me.

七、V什么好 (what would be the best thing to V)

> This expression means "what would be the best thing to V". It indicates that the speaker is having some trouble deciding what to do.

☞ 想不出到底送什么好。

1、这个饭馆的菜真难吃，我真不知道吃什么好。

This restaurant's food is really bad. I do not know what to eat.

2、你觉得我买什么好，买旧车呢，还是新车？

What do you think is the best thing to buy? An old bike or a new one?

八、对……感兴趣 (to be interested in)

✍ "对……感兴趣" is a sentence pattern meaning "to be interested in". The preposition "对" must precede the verb phrase "感兴趣". Unlike most of the Chinese preverbal prepositional phrases, the negation of this structure places the "不" before the verb phrase and not before the preposition, e.g. "对……不感兴趣".

☞ 其实我也对中国的节日很感兴趣。

1、你对看电影感不感兴趣？

Are you interested in watching movies?

2、我对中国的独生子女问题很感兴趣。

I'm intrigued by China's problem of the single-child generation.

3、他对鲁迅的小说不感兴趣。

He is not interested in Lu Xun's novels.

九、边V边V (to V and V at the same time)

✍ This expression is similar to "一边……一边……" (cf. Lesson 5 Vocabulary). However, "边 V 边 V" is often used with monosyllabic verbs. Therefore, the sentence "我边喝咖啡边看报" does not sound as good as "我一边喝咖啡一边看报"。

☞ 边吃边说不是更好吗？

1、边走边看，边做边学。

To walk and read at the same time, to do and learn at the same time.

十、差点儿 V (almost)

> ✍ "差点儿" is an adverb meaning "almost did". It is used to indicate that something unfortunate almost happened, but did not happen in the end. If the meaning of the verb describes an undesirable situation, both the positive and the negative form of the same sentence have the same meaning, e.g. both "我差点儿没死". and "我差点儿死了". mean "I almost died". "我差点儿没死" can be interpreted to mean literally, "I missed by a tiny bit, (but) didn't die".

☞ 我差点儿忘了。

1、 因为交通很挤，我差点儿迟到了。

Because traffic was congested, I was almost late.

2、 我的护照在机场的时候找不到了，差点儿没坐上飞机。

I could not find my passport when I was at the airport, I almost couldn't get on my flight.

现在受了西方文化的影响，中国人过生日也改吃生日蛋糕了

语言形式练习
Tasks on Language Forms

一、读课文回答问题 📖

1、这位美国学生怎么给王小平过生日？

2、中国人过生日的时候怎么庆祝？

3、为什么现在中国孩子的生日比大人的还重要？

4、这位美国学生送王小平什么礼物？他为什么选这个礼物？

5、感恩节是什么时候？这一天美国人做什么特别的事情？

6、王小平今年多大了？

二、完成对话 👫

1、A：他为什么现在也爱吃饺子了？

B：

（受..影响；好几）

2、A：你为什么不看黑白电视了？

B：

（改V）

3、A：他是什么时候对中国历史感兴趣的？

B：

（自从……以来；比方说）

4、A：你为什么不打"的"去买东西？

188

B：

（正好；反而）

5、A： 明天我们要请老师来吃饭。

B：

（V什么好，VV看）

6、A： 你记得买冰淇淋了吗？

B：

（差点儿……了）

三、听录音回答问题

1、小张和小林是怎么成为好朋友的？

2、小张常常帮小林什么忙？

3、小林为什么送小张月饼？

4、小林为什么迟到了？

5、中秋节是每年的什么时候？

6、为什么离开家在外地工作或学习的中国人在春节、中秋节的时候特别想家？

四、阅读回答问题

中国最传统的节日是春节。但是随着社会的发展，人们观念的改变，老百姓过春节的方式已经在很多方面发生了变化，不那么传统了。以前，过春节的时候，也是家庭团聚的时候。无论一个人在那里工作，他都会尽量回家来跟家人在一起过春节。不能回家过年被看成是最大的不幸。可是现在，由于工作、学习的关系而选择在外地过年的人越来越多。小张说，他年底要考研究生，打算利用春节这个假期好好看看书，所以决定不回家了。王女士说，每次回家不但要花很多时间看亲戚朋友，还得拿出一大笔钱买礼物发"红包"（red envelope），这对她来说是一个沉重的负担。所以今年她也决定不回家了，而是选择和丈夫孩子一起去南方旅行，以后有机会再回家看父母。第二个变化是

"除夕"（一年的最后一天）晚餐（又叫"年夜饭"）。以前，除夕夜的这顿大餐是春节庆祝活动中最重要的一项。一般来说是一定要在家里吃，饭菜由全家人花差不多一个星期的时间精心准备。而且，全家人还要坐在一起包饺子，聊天，气氛非常轻松愉快。可是现在，城里人越来越忙，工作越来越紧张。他们觉得以前吃"年夜饭"的办法太麻烦，从准备到制作要花太多的时间。现代人工作那么忙，哪有时间买菜做饭呢？所以，现在越来越多的家庭选择在饭馆吃这顿特别的"年夜饭"。第三个变化是不再放鞭炮 (fire works) 了。以前放鞭炮是为了赶走坏的东西，迎接新的一年。可是从环境来看，鞭炮使空气污染变得更加严重。想象一下，如果在"除夕"夜，每个北京人放一个鞭炮，对这个有着一千多万人口的城市来说会是多么大的污染啊！所以，从1996年起，北京市政府规定，春节期间，不可以放鞭炮了。虽然没有了以往的热闹，但是为了能有一个更干净的城市，每个北京人都高高兴兴地接受了这个变化。

问题:

1、"春节"的传统是什么？

2、"春节"的传统都有那些变化？

3、请你为你的老师或者中国朋友介绍"圣诞节"的传统和变化。

4、除了"春节"以外，跟你的老师或者你的中国朋友再了解一下中国其它的传统节日。用你的话写出三个中国传统节日的特点，庆祝活动和意义。

五、翻译

1. My Chinese family is very friendly and warmhearted. When they celebrated my birthday, they prepared a tableful of dishes.

2. When Chinese people celebrate birthdays, they eat both noodles and birthday cake; moreover, they sing "Happy Birthday".

3. Having been influenced by Western culture, the living habits of the Chinese people have undergone many changes.

4. I am interested in both economics and history. Before I decided my major, I thought about it over and over, but I still could not decide what to choose. In the end, I chose to major in economics.

5. Tomorrow is my mother's birthday. Please remember to remind me to buy a birthday cake in the shopping center to help my mother celebrate her birthday.

语言使用练习
Tasks on Language Use

一、真实情景活动 🎥

生日蛋糕

（一）上面这个生日蛋糕上有两个字，应该从左往右念还是从右往左念？查字典看看蛋糕
上的字有什么意思。

（二）根据右边这张明信片回
答问题：

1、东玉的生日大概在几
月？

2、明远送给东玉两样什么
东西？东玉觉得怎么
样？（用东玉的话来回
答）

3、问问你的中国朋友，
"棒"是年轻人常用的
词还是老人常用的词？
还有一些什么词是中国
的年轻人喜欢用的？

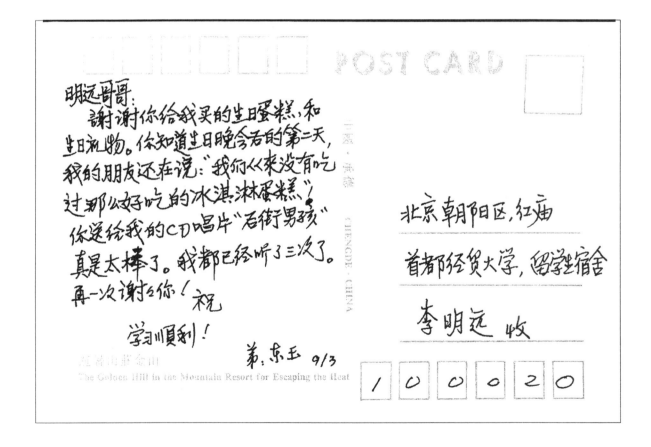

明远哥哥：
　　谢谢你给我买的生日蛋糕，和
生日礼物。你知道生日晚会后的第二天，
我的朋友还在说："我们从来没有吃
过那么好吃的冰淇淋蛋糕"。
你送给我的CD唱片"右街男孩"
真是太棒了。我都已经听了三次了。
再一次谢谢你！　祝

　　学习顺利！

　　　　　　弟：东玉　9/3

北京朝阳区，红庙

首都经贸大学，留学宿舍

李明远　收

1 0 0 0 2 0

红庙的新金山
The Golden Hill in the Mountain Resort for Escaping the Heat

（三）现在，很多中国孩子不但把麦当劳看成是每星期必去的地方，而且还在那里开生日晚会。下面的照片就是麦当劳做的给孩子们过生日的广告。请你写一封信给中国的孩子们谈谈你对在麦当劳吃饭以及在麦当劳过生日的看法。

麦当劳的生日晚会

（四）你的同学魏爱玲和你从一年级起就在一块儿学中文，到现在已经学了两年了。明天是爱玲的生日，你打算买一张生日卡送给她。请你用中文给她写一张生日卡，一方面祝她生日快乐，一方面也写一写这两年你跟她一块儿学习中文的一些有意思的经历。

爱玲同学：

给爱玲的生日卡

二、讨论

1、你的生日是什么时候？去年你的生日是怎么过的？
2、你看过中国小孩在麦当劳过生日吗？他们在那儿做些什么事情？
3、在美国，你给朋友送什么生日礼物？在中国呢？中国人的习惯是什么？
4、要是中国朋友请你介绍美国的节日，你会介绍那些？怎么介绍？
5、你知道不知道中国有些什么节日？在这些节日中国人做什么？

三、语言实践

1、请你访问你的中国朋友，问问他们听谈谈一谈中国的节日。
2、中国人觉得孩子的生日重要吗？请你访问几位在麦当劳带孩子吃饭的父母？问他们为什么带孩子到那儿去？

四、作文

《我最喜欢的一个美国节日》

五、看图说话

1

2

An Intermediate Chinese Course

第十一课　秀水市场

秀水市场的小摊

课文

　　秀水市场位于北京市的东城区，是由北京市的个体户组成的，专门为外国人出售服装和各种用品的市场。由于秀水街离使馆区比较近，所以是外国人常常去的地方。那里卖的东西从穿的到用的，从丝织品、纺织品到工艺品应有尽有。别看秀水市场小贩的文化水平都不算高，可是他们对经济信息却非常了解。国际上流行什么，外国人喜欢什么，他们都知道得一清二楚。在秀水市场上你不但可以找到地道的中国丝绸服装、传统手工制品，而且可以找到世界上所有的名牌产品，比方说，鳄鱼牌的T恤衫、奈克的球鞋、苹果牌的牛仔裤，还有世界上最抢手、最流行的毛衣、皮衣和大衣。

　　在秀水市场买东西可不是一件简单的事情，不会中文没关系，可是不了解商品价格，不会讨价还价就要吃亏了。一般衣服的要价都比实际价格高几倍，所以买东西的时候一定得照[1]一半砍价。比方说，一件衬衣要价是140元，可是你用七、八十块钱就可以就买下来。另外，当你看到一件好的东西时，一定不要表现出特别喜欢那件东西的样子，否则卖主就会死不降价。还有，要是你多买几件你要买的那种商品，你也可以要求卖主降价。在这种情况下价钱最容易降下来。

　　同学们都非常喜欢逛秀水市场，去那儿一方面可以买到一些既流行又便宜的东西，另一方面也可以跟那儿的小贩聊聊，就在这一条拥

Notes [1] "照"：　"照" (literally "to shine, to reflect"), when used as a preposition, can be translated variously as "according to, on the basis of, by the principle or model of" depending on the context. "照一半砍价" is an idiomatic expression meaning "to bargain by the half price rule-of-thumb" or simply "bargain down to half price". Other examples include "照三分之一切" (to cut out one third of it); "照百分之十付小费" (to tip 10% of the total cost).

挤的小街上你可以了解到很多中国的经济发展情况和商业变化。

———◆———

（高平和王义逛秀水街）

高：　喂，老板，这件衣服怎么卖？

老板：哪件？这件吗？800块。这件衣服是纯丝的，样式又是最流行的。要吗？要可以便宜点儿？

高：　800块？太贵了。可惜我没有那么多钱。这件衣服好倒是好，可是我就是不喜欢这种扣子。300块怎么样？

老板：300块？你看看，这是名牌产品，又是纯丝的，300块可买不下来。这样吧，500块怎么样？

高：　500块还是太贵。你知道我是一个穷学生，根本就没有收入。太贵了，我买不起。

老板：你从美国来，这点儿钱算什么？就500块了！

高：　不行！不行！别看我是从美国来的，可是我真的没有钱，到现在我还是靠父母生活呢！500块太贵了，350块怎么样？

老板：350……您知道，这衣服我进货就是400，要是350卖给你，我一分钱都不赚，还赔了呢，400块吧！

高：　好吧，就400块吧，给你钱。

老板：要不要一个塑料袋装你的衣服？

高：　不用了。谢谢[2]！

✏️ **Notes** [2]Spoken vs. written language: By this time, you have encountered many different words which share the same meaning but are used in different contexts or modes. Some are appropriate for spoken or informal settings, others are for written or formal settings. As a learner of Chinese language, developing a sensitivity to the usages in different contexts is not only crucial for conveying one's meaning, but also for avoiding sounding like an odd-ball foreigner. In lesson 11, "位于"，"出售"，and "服装" are normally used in formal or written situations. For example, while "出售" and "卖" both mean "to sell", one CANNOT go to a fruit stand and ask * "你出售苹果吗？" One also CANNOT comment on a friend's clothes by saying * "今天你的服装好漂亮"。 The oddity of these two sentences lies in mismatching formal vocabulary with informal daily-life settings.

———— ◆◆◆ ———— 生词 ———— ◆◆◆ ————

1. 秀水	xiù shuǐ	*Place N.*	(lit. "beautiful water") Silk Alley (usually followed by 街 or 市场)
2. 位于	wèi yú	*V.*	to be located in/at
3. 东城区	dōng chéng qū	*Place N.*	Eastern City District
4. 由……组成	yóu...zǔ chéng	*Prep...VP.*	to be composed of
5. 出售	chū shòu	*V.*	to sell
6. 服装	fú zhuāng	*N.*	clothing
7. 各种	gè zhǒng	*N.*	all kinds of
8. 用品	yòng pǐn	*N.*	articles for use
9. 由于	yóu yú	*Prep.*	because of, due to
10. 街	jiē	*N.*	street
11. 使馆区	shǐ guǎn qū	*N.*	embassy area
12. 丝织品	sī zhī pǐn	*N.*	silk products
13. 纺织品	fǎng zhī pǐn	*N.*	textile products
14. 工艺品	gōng yì pǐn	*N.*	handicrafts
15. 应有尽有	yīng yǒu jìn yǒu	*Idiom.*	have everything that one expects
16. 别看	bié kàn	*VP.*	do not see as... (cf. Sentence Pattern 5)
17. 小贩	xiǎo fàn	*V.*	peddler, street vendor
18. 信息	xìn xī	*N.*	information
19. 流行	liú xíng	*V/Adj.*	to become popular; popular
20. 一清二楚	yì qīng èr chǔ	*Idiom.*	very clear (清楚: clear)
21. 丝绸	sī chóu	*N.*	silk cloth
22. 传统	chuán tǒng	*Adj.*	traditional
23. 手工制品	shǒu gōng zhì pǐn	*NP.*	hand-made products
24. 所有的	suǒ yǒu de	*Adj.*	all, every
25. 名牌	míng pái	*N.*	name brand
26. 鳄鱼牌	è yú pái	*N.*	Crocodile, Izod Lacoste Brand
27. T恤衫	tī xù shān	*N.*	T-shirt

28. 奈克	nài kè	*N.*	Nike
29. 球鞋	qiú xié	*N.*	sneakers
30. 牛仔裤	niú zǎi kù	*N.*	jeans
31. 抢手	qiǎng shǒu	*Adj.*	(lit. "grab by the hand") popular (with buyers), fast-selling
32. 毛衣	máo yī	*N.*	sweater
33. 皮衣	pí yī	*N.*	leather or fur garments
34. 大衣	dà yī	*N.*	coat
35. 讨价还价	tǎo jià huán jià	*Idiom.*	to bargain, to haggle
36. 吃亏	chī kuī	*VO.*	to suffer losses, to get the short end of the stick
37. 要价	yào jià	*VO/N.*	to ask a price; asking price
38. 实际	shí jì	*Adj/N.*	actual, practical; reality, practicality
39. 倍	bèi	*N/Classifier*	times, -fold
40. 照	zhào	*Prep.*	based upon, according to
41. 一半	yí bàn	*N.*	half
42. 砍价	kǎn jià	*VO.*	to chop price
43. 衬衣	chèn yī	*N.*	shirt
44. 否则	fǒu zé	*Adv.*	otherwise
45. 卖主	mài zhǔ	*N.*	seller
46. 降价	jiàng jià	*VO.*	to reduce the price
47. 商品	shāng pǐn	*N.*	commodity, goods
48. 商业	shāng yè	*N.*	commerce, trade, business
49. 纯丝	chún sī	*N.*	pure silk
50. 样式	yàng shì	*N.*	style
51. 扣子	kòu zi	*N.*	button
52. 穷	qióng	*Adj.*	poor
53. 进货	jìn huò	*VO.*	to replenish one's stock, to stock (one's shop) with goods
54. 赔	péi	*V.*	to suffer a loss (selling below cost)
55. 塑料袋	sù liào dài	*N.*	plastic bag

| 56. 装 | zhuāng | *V.* | to pack, to load |

———————— 补充词汇 ————————

57. 肥	féi	*Adj.*	loose-fitting, large, fat (only refers to meats, not people)
58. 瘦	shòu	*Adj.*	thin, tight
59. 羊毛	yáng máo	*N.*	wool
60. 棉	mián	*N.*	cotton
61. 短袖	duǎn xiù	*N.*	short sleeves
62. 长袖	cháng xiù	*N.*	long sleeves
63. 上衣	shàng yī	*N.*	top
64. 睡衣	shuì yī	*N.*	pajamas
65. 风衣	fēng yī	*N.*	windbreaker
66. 衬衫	chèn shān	*N.*	shirt
67. 夹克	jiá kè	*N.*	jacket
68. 短裤	duǎn kù	*N.*	shorts
69. 长裤	cháng kù	*N.*	pants, trousers
70. 裙子	qún zi	*N.*	skirt
71. 袜子	wà zi	*N.*	sock
72. 拖鞋	tuō xié	*N.*	slippers
73. 凉鞋	liáng xié	*N.*	sandals
74. 运动鞋	yùn dòng xié	*N.*	sneakers
75. 皮鞋	pí xié	*N.*	leather shoes
76. 皮带	pí dài	*N.*	belt
77. 皮包	pí bāo	*N.*	purse
78. 化妆品	huà zhuāng pǐn	*N.*	cosmetics
79. 项链	xiàng liànr	*N.*	necklace
80. 耳环	ěr huán	*N.*	earrings
81. 减价	jiǎn jià	*VO.*	to reduce the price, to mark down
82. 讲价	jiǎng jià	*VO.*	to bargain over price
83. 打折	dǎ zhé	*VO.*	to sell at a discount, to give a discount

句型

一、 位于 (to be located at)

> ✍ "位于", which means "to be located at", is a verb. An expression of location must be used after the word "位于", e.g. "学校位于北京市". (The school is located in the city of Beijing.) As with most words that contain the classical Chinese particle "于", this expression is rather formal, and it often refers to a geographical area rather than a specific location. Therefore, one would NOT say: * "我的书位于桌子上". but rather "我的书在桌子上".

☞ 秀水市场位于北京市的东城区。

1、 他们的出租汽车公司位于市中心。
   Their taxi company is located in the heart of the city.
2、 使馆区位于北京市的东城区。
   The embassy area is located in the Eastern District of Beijing.

二、 由……组成 (to consist of)

> ✍ "组成", meaning "to compose", becomes a passive structure meaning "is composed of" when used with the preposition "由". "由" introduces the elements or the components which make up the composite entity, e.g. "我们的代表由老师和学生组成". (Our representatives are made up of teachers and students.)

☞ 是由北京市的个体户组成的。

1、 我们的老师是由两种类型的人组成的。一种是专业的老师；一种是在学校的研究生。
   Our teachers consist of two types of people: one type is specialized teachers and the other is graduate students at the school.
2、 我们的中文课是由四种不同的课型组成的。
   Our Chinese classes consist of four different types.

203

三、 由于 (due to)

> ✍ "由于" is a formal way to indicate a reason, and is rarely heard in spoken Chinese. It is usually a prepositional phrase in front of the main clause. It may also occur in the form of "是由于" in the latter part of the sentence, stating the cause for the situation described in the first clause.

☞ 由于秀水街离使馆区比较近，所以是外国人常常去的地方。

1、由于改革开放，中国的经济发展得很快。
Due to China's reform and open up policy, the economy has developed very quickly.

2、由于退休工人越来越多，生活的出路也越来越少。
Due to workers being laid off in increasing numbers, opportunities to make a living have become more and more scarce.

3、北京的交通越来越拥挤是由于人口、汽车都越来越多。
The traffic in Beijing is becoming more and more congested, and that's due to the increase in population and automobiles.

四、 从……到…… (from ... to)

> ✍ "从……到" is a prepositional phrase originally indicating location and time. But its usage has expanded to nouns, in which case it is used to indicate inclusiveness or a wide range. In this case, the adverb "都" should be used.

☞ 那里卖的东西从穿的到用的，从丝织品、纺织品到工艺品应有尽有。

1、这个市场什么都买得到，从吃的到穿的，要什么有什么。
From things to eat to things to wear, you can buy anything at this market. Whatever you want, they've got it.

2、要是你想了解中国就要去中国，在那里从社会到家庭都可以为你提供很多信息。
If you wish to understand China, you should go to China, where you will be able to get a great deal of information on everything, from society to family.

五、 别看 …… (do not see as...)

> ✎ "别看" (literally "don't look at") means "don't just look at (the surface) (and be misled)", and indicates that one should not be misled by an apparent situation or draw an erroneous conclusion from a given fact, e.g. "别看他才三岁，已经会写字了"！(Don't be misled because he is only three. He can already write!) The statement that he is three years old is true, as is the statement that he can already write.

☞ 别看秀水市场的小贩的文化水平都不算高，可是他们对经济信息却非常了解。

1、别看修自行车的工作赚钱不多，这样的工作还不那么容易找呢。

Don't be fooled by the fact that bike repairmen do not earn a lot of money. Even this type of job is not easy to find.

2、别看大使馆离学校近，可是你走路也要三十分钟。

The embassy may seem to be very close to the school, but it will still take thirty minutes to walk there.

六、 对 …… 了解 (to have an understanding of..., to be informed about)

> ✎ The preposition "对" is used with the verb "了解" to indicate the topic or area about which one has a good understanding. For example, "老师对学生非常了解"。(The teachers have a thorough understanding of their students.) The negative form is "对……不了解" and the question form is "对……了解不了解"？

☞ 可是他们对经济信息却非常了解。

1、学习中国文化一定要对中国历史十分了解。

When studying Chinese culture one must be fully informed about Chinese history.

2、别看他是一个外国人，他对中国的情况却非常了解。

Do not look at him as a foreigner; he is extremely well-informed about the situation in China.

七、否则 (otherwise)

> ✍ "否则" is an adverb used at the beginning of the second clause of a two-clause sentence to indicate an opposite scenario from the one presented in the first clause. The subject in the second clause is often implicit and therefore omitted.

☞ 另外，当你看到一件好的东西时，一定不要表现出特别喜欢那件东西的样子，否则卖主就会死不降价。

1、在小摊儿上买东西一定要看清楚，否则会上当受骗。

When buying things at a stall, one must check them thoroughly, otherwise, one can be tricked.

2、我想他一定是去了秀水街，否则早应该回来了。

I think he must have gone to the Silk Alley, otherwise he would have been back long ago.

八、在……（的）情况下 (under the condition of, under the circumstances of)

> ✍ "在……（的）情况下" is an adverbial phrase indicating the condition under which an action is carried out. It is often placed at the beginning of a sentence.

☞ 在这种情况下价钱最容易降下来。

1、他连一点收入都没有，也没有奖学金，在这种情况下，只好停学了。

He does not have any income, nor any scholarship. Under such a condition, he has to quit school.

2、在竞争很激烈的情况下，很多人决定放弃这个机会。

Under the circumstances of fierce competition, many people decided to give up this opportunity.

九、 V得下来/V不下来 (successfully finish doing something)

> ✍ "下来" is a directional complement. Here it is used in a figurative sense meaning "successfully finish doing something". "三百块钱买不下来" is the same as "三百块钱买不到" (300 RMB is not enough to purchase it.) When "下来" is used as a directional complement, it means "down." When the direction is away from the speaker, the word "去" is used; when the direction is toward the speaker, then the word "来" must be used. For example, "拿得下来" (be able to take down); "跳不下去" (not able to jump down); "你拿得下来拿不下来？" (Are you able to take it down?)

☞ 这是名牌产品，又是纯丝的，300块可买不下来。

1、 别看他好象很能干，可是连一个钟头的工作都干不下来。
  Do not mistake him as capable; he cannot even finish a one-hour job.

2、 那儿的东西太贵了，一百块钱连一件衣服都买不下来。
  The things there are too expensive; a hundred dollars cannot even buy a single piece of clothing.

十、 V得起/V不起 (able/unable to afford)

> ✍ "V 得起", like the preceding "V 得下来" and the "V得着" in Lesson 8, is another complement structure. "起", originally meaning "up" indicates the affordability (of money, time, energy, etc.). When used as a verb complement, it always appears in either the positive or negative potential complement form （"V 得/不起"）, never in the actual form "V 起了".

☞ 太贵了，我买不起。

1、 你花得起花不起这么多钱？
  Can you afford to spend that much money?

2、 我打不起"的"，只好坐公共汽车。
  I cannot afford to take a taxi, so I have to take the bus.

语言形式练习
Tasks on Language Forms

一、读课文回答问题 📖

1、秀水市场在什么地方？专门卖什么东西？

2、秀水市场的小贩怎么知道外国人喜欢什么？

3、为什么在秀水市场买东西不会讨价还价就要吃亏？

4、为什么同学们喜欢逛秀水市场？

5、高平买的那件衣服原来多少钱？后来高平付了多少钱？高平是怎么讨价还价的？

二、完成对话 👫

1、A：请你给我介绍一下ACC的情况。
　　B：好吧。
　　（位于；由……组成；专门为……）

2、A：秀水市场为什么会有这么多外国人来买东西？
　　B：
　　　　（由于；从……到）

3、A：这儿的个体户怎么会有这么多的国际经济信息？
　　B：
　　　　（别看；对……了解）

4、A：我很喜欢这条苹果牌的牛仔裤，50块行不行？
　　B：不行。
　　　　（V不下来）

5、A：这件 T 恤衫真漂亮，你要吗？

　　B：

　　　（可惜；V 不起）

三、听录音回答问题

1、小张为什么要买礼物送小李？

2、小张为什么决定买鳄鱼牌的衣服？

3、小张为什么没买红色的T恤衫？

4、为什么老板要小张买大号的T恤衫？

4、你想小李喜欢什么颜色？

5、小张最后选了什么样的衣服？什么颜色？

6、小张看上的衬衫原来多少钱？讨价还价以后，是多少钱？

7、最后小张买了什么东西？为什么？

这件 T 恤衫真漂亮

四、阅读回答问题

　　在北京，除了"秀水市场"以外，还有一个"雅秀市场"也很有名。"雅秀市场"位于朝阳区工体路，就在三里屯酒吧街的附近。和"秀水市场"相比，"雅秀市场"有下面几个特点。一是品种多，从服装、鞋帽，到丝绸、工艺品应有尽有。二是价钱比秀水市场便宜，因为"雅秀市场"在一片很大的居民区里，附近的老百姓都很喜欢到这里来逛逛，所以这里小贩的要价不敢太高。三是"雅秀市场"的小贩对经济信息和流行趋势非常熟悉。要想知道这个季节北京流行什么，去"雅秀"看看就知道得差不多了。那里是时髦的男孩女孩常常光顾的地方。

　　但是，如果你只是一个普普通通，赚钱不多的北京人，那么雅秀就不是一个最好的选择了。老百姓常去的是小商品批发市场和超市。在北京有几个很有名的小商品批发市场，比如"万通新世界"、"官园"小商品批发市场、"动物园"批发市场、"莲花池"批发市场等。那儿卖的东西虽然没有那么时髦，但都是很实用的和老百姓生活有密切关系的日常用品和必需品。价钱一般来说很公道，因为这些市场面对的顾客是收入中等以下的城市人口，所以只能以价钱便宜来吸引顾客。这些小商品批发市场总是非常热闹，特别是在周末的时候，这里更是人挨人，人挤人。就拿我最喜欢的"万通新世界"来说吧，那儿的商品从吃的到穿的，从玩儿的到用的，真是应有尽有。一层是卖化妆品和卫生用品的，二层是卖服装的，三层有各种各样的礼品、装饰品。四层则是一个电脑广场，卖各种电脑硬件，软件。要是你逛累了，旁边就有麦当劳，肯德基和很多小吃摊儿，冷饮摊儿，尽可以吃东西，喝饮料，坐下休息休息。所以周末和家人朋友逛逛小商品批发市场已经慢慢成为北京人的休闲方式了。

问题：

1、"雅秀市场"在哪儿？有什么特点？

2、从课文的上下文你知道光顾的意思是什么？

3、普通北京人喜欢去哪儿买东西？为什么？

4、"万通新世界"有什么特点？

5、请你给你的中国家庭或者朋友介绍几种美国人的休闲方式。

6、请你介绍一个美国的购物中心（在什么地方；有什么特点；为什么受到欢迎等等）。

五、翻译

1. The U.S. embassy is located in the east of Beijing. It provides services to American citizens in China.

2. If you want to be a good taxi driver, you must be well-informed about traffic conditions and very clear about the streets and alleys (胡同) in the city.

3. It is not an easy matter to bargain with the vendors in Beijing. Most things are marked higher than the actual price. You'd better bargain it down to half price.

4. A: I want to buy pajamas (睡衣) made of pure silk. Do you have anything like that?

   B: Yes. I do. Here is a set in the most popular style with Chinese style buttons.

   A: How much is it?

   B: 300.

   A: 300. That is too expensive! If you go down a little bit, maybe I can afford it.

   B: OK. How about 250? That is the lowest [cheapest] I can go.

语言使用练习
Tasks on Language Use

一、真实情景活动

雅秀服装市场的商品

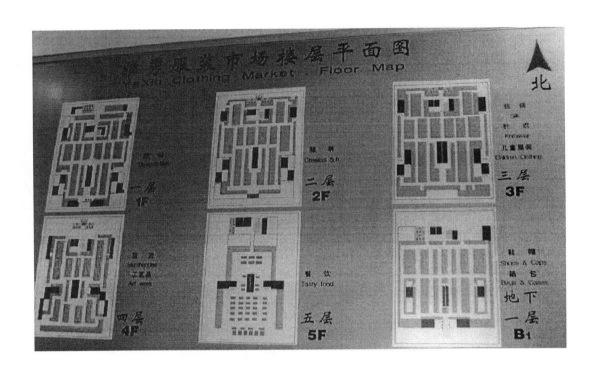

（一）从名字上看，雅秀服装市场是一个卖服装的地方，其实那里的商品应有尽有。请根据上面的介绍和下面的照片回答下面的问题：

1、雅秀服装市场共分几层 (floor)？

2、雅秀服装市场都出售些什么商品？

3、那里的环境和服务看起来怎么样？

雅秀服装市场的商品

（二）根据万惠商场的牌子查字典，然后回答下面的问题：

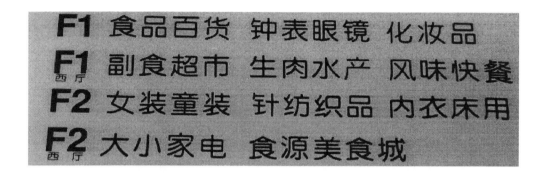

问题：

　1、万惠商场共分几层？

　2、买水果和牛奶去几层？

　3、要是你肚子饿了去几层可以买到一点小吃？去几层可以坐下来点菜吃饭？

　4、要是你想买一个录音机听中文得去几层？

　5、你要买T恤衫得去几层？

（三）北京有一个地方叫潘家园旧货市场，这个市场只有星期六和星期天才开。到过北京的人都喜欢去这个市场买东西。下面的几张照片就是介绍潘家园旧货市场的。请你根据这些照片回答下面的问题：

潘家园旧货市场

问题：

    1、这个市场由什么人组成？

    2、这个市场出售什么东西？

    3、这个市场的商品都放在哪里出售？卖的商品有什么特点？

    4、市场的气氛和环境都怎么样？

二、讨论

    1、谈谈你到市场买东西的经验。（买了什么东西？怎么跟老板讨价还价？）

    2、谈谈你跟市场的小贩聊天的经验，他们是怎么知道国际上流行什么的？

    3、你喜欢讨价还价吗？为什么？

    4、你觉得在中国买东西方便不方便？有没有什么你想买可是买不到的东西？

5、谈谈北京市个体户小贩的工作和生活。

6、中国的市场和美国的市场有什么不同？

三、语言实践

去北京的新疆街、文化街、或者浙江村看看，采访三个在那儿工作的个体户。了解一下这些人是从那儿来的，以前做什么，为什么要来北京，他们对自己的将来有什么看法。

四、作文

《中国的个体市场和经济发展》

五、看图说话

太贵了！再便宜一点儿吧！

第十二课　游览长城

从长城烽火台的窗口望出去

课文

长城可以说是北京附近最有名的旅游景点之一，凡是到北京来的观光客都会去游览长城。我们暑期班第一个周末的旅游活动就是去长城。出发以前，老师特地给我们介绍了一下长城的历史。秦始皇统一中国以后修了长城，修长城的主要目的是为了防止北边的敌人进入中国。为了修长城，成千上万的老百姓流血流汗，甚至牺牲了生命。孟姜女的故事就是其中最有名的，她为了寻找她的丈夫而哭倒了长城。我们去参观的八达岭长城是明代修筑的，到现在已经有六百多年了。

一大早我们就出发了，坐了两个多小时的车才到长城。排队买门票的人多极了，真是人山人海。老师告诉我们从前外宾[1]的门票比中国人的贵一些，连参观博物馆，公园的门票也分外宾和内宾两种。在我看来，这真不合理。现在中国人、外国人的门票都是一个价钱了。走到入口让查票员查过了门票，我和几位同学就比赛看谁爬得快，不一会儿[2]，我们就爬到了第六个烽火台。这儿游客比较少，我们站在烽火台上休息，看着青山和顺着山峰修筑的长城，凉凉的风吹过来，真是舒服极了。

Notes [1] "外宾": This term refers to "foreign guest" or "guest from outside". "宾" means "客人," but it is a "bound form" and is used only in combination with a preceding modifier. It is mostly used in formal or written settings. It is a polite but distant way of referring to the guests from foreign countries.

[2] "不一会儿": "不一会儿" is synonymous with "一会儿", but its use is limited to events in the past, whereas "一会儿" may apply to the future as well as the past, e.g. one can say "一会儿我就来" (I'll be there in a jiffy), but NOT * "不一会儿我就来". Another difference between the two is that "不一会儿" has an idiomatic flavor comparable to the English expression "in no time at all", which is not shared by "一会儿". Both may be used before or after the subject, e.g. "他一会儿就爬到山峰了"，"一会儿他就爬到山峰了"，"他不一会儿就爬到山峰了"，and "不一会儿他就爬到山峰了"，all mean "In just a short time, he climbed to the mountain peak".

学生甲： 你看那个人穿的T恤衫上有几个字……

学生乙： 让我看看，"不-到-长-城-非-好-汉"。哈哈，现在我们都
是"好汉"了。今天的旅游活动真值得参加，那些没来的同
学一定很后悔。

学生丙： 那是一定的。本来我一直不明白，长城在军事上和国防上已
经没有什么地位了，但是为什么中国人还以长城为荣呢？上
了长城以后才知道长城的确是世界上最伟大的建筑之一。

学生乙： 是啊，我想就是现在要修长城都非常困难，更别说两千年前
了。

　　时间过得很快，一会儿就到集合回学校的时间了，我们赶紧往回
走。在走回停车场的路上有许多卖纪念品的小贩想卖东西给我们。看
样子长城已经变得非常商业化了(3)。这是让我觉得最可惜的地方(4)。

生词

1. **长城**	cháng chéng	*Place N.*	the Great Wall
2. **凡是**	fán shì	*Adj.*	every, any

✎ **Notes** (3) "化" : The suffix "化" can be combined with many different nouns to add the suffixes "-ize" or "-ization", e.g. "商业化" (commercialize; commercialization), "现代化" (modernize; modernization), "西化" (westernize; westernization), "美国化" (Americanize; Americanization), "工业化" (industrialize; industrialization).

(4)Idiomatic expressions: The following are some of the most important idiomatic and fixed expressions we have seen so far in this textbook: "两室一厅" (two bedroom apartment); "大吃一惊" (a big surprise); "独生子女" (single child); "一般来说" (generally speaking); "应有尽有" (to have everything that one expects to find); "一清二楚" (crystal clear about); "讨价还价" (to bargain or haggle); "成千上万" (tens of thousands); "人山人海" (huge crowds of people, a sea of people); "在我看来" (in my opinion). Four-character idiomatic expressions are a distinctive characteristic of native Chinese speakers' speech, and mastery of them is a gauge of the student's proficiency in the language. Therefore, it behooves the student to remember them and use them correctly and idiomatically, especially those with high frequency in the spoken language.

3. 观光客	guān guāng kè	N.	tourist
4. 旅游	lǚ yóu	V/N.	to tour; tour
5. 景点	jǐng diǎn	N.	scenic spot
6. …之一	zhī yī	NP.	one of...
7. 暑期班	shǔ qī bān	N.	summer school
8. 活动	huó dòng	N/Adj/V.	activity; active; to have an activity
9. 出发	chū fā	V.	to take off, to depart
10. 特地	tè dì	Adv.	especially, for a special purpose
11. 秦始皇	qín shǐ huáng	Title.	the 1st Emperor of the Qin Dynasty
12. 统一	tǒng yī	V/N.	to unify; unification
13. 主要	zhǔ yào	Adj.	main
14. 防止	fáng zhǐ	V.	to prevent, to guard against
15. 北边	běi biān	N.	the north side
16. 敌人	dí rén	N.	enemy
17. 进入	jìn rù	V.	to enter
18. 成千上万	chéng qiān shàng wàn	Idiom.	tens of thousands, in considerable numbers
19. 流血流汗	liú xiě liú hàn	Idiom.	to shed blood and sweat, to pay a high human cost
20. 甚至	shèn zhì	Adv.	even to the extent of...
21. 牺牲	xī shēng	V/N.	to sacrifice; sacrifice
22. 生命	shēng mìng	N.	life
23. 孟姜女	mèng jiāng nǚ	Personal N.	a woman named Meng Jiang
24. 故事	gù shi	N.	story
25. 寻找	xún zhǎo	V.	to look for, to search for
26. 丈夫	zhàng fu	N.	husband
27. 而	ér	Conj.	and, but, thereby

28. 哭	kū	V.	to weep, to cry
29. 倒	dǎo	V.	to fall, to collapse
30. 八达岭	bā dá lǐng	Place N.	name of mountain ridge, a famous Great Wall site
31. 明代	míng dài	N.	the Ming Dynasty (1368-1644)
32. 修筑	xiū zhù	V.	to build, to construct
33. 排队	pái duì	VO.	to line up
34. 门票	mén piào	N.	entrance ticket
35. 人山人海	rén shān rén hǎi	Idiom.	"human mountain human sea," huge crowds of people
36. 外宾	wài bīn	N.	foreign guests/visitors
37. 博物馆	bó wù guǎn	N.	museum
38. 公园	gōng yuán	N.	park
39. 内宾	nèi bīn	N.	domestic guests/visitors
40. 在我看来	zài wǒ kàn lái	Idiom.	in my view, in my opinion
41. 合理	hé lǐ	Adj.	reasonable
42. 入口	rù kǒu	N.	entrance
43. 查票员	chá piào yuán	N.	ticket checker
44. 比赛	bǐ sài	V/N.	to race, to compete; race, competition
45. 爬	pá	V.	to climb
46. 不一会儿	bú yì huìr	Adv.	in no time at all, in a very short time
47. 烽火台	fēng huǒ tái	N.	beacon tower
48. 游客	yóu kè	N.	tourist
49. 青山	qīng shān	N.	green mountain
50. 顺	shùn	V.	to follow the path of, along
51. 山峰	shān fēng	N.	peak of the mountain
52. 凉	liáng	Adj.	cool
53. 风	fēng	N.	wind

54. 吹	chuī	*V.*	to blow
55. 不到长城非好汉	bú dào cháng chéng fēi hǎo hàn	*Idiom.*	If one does not go to the Great Wall, one is not a real man.
56. 值得	zhí de	*V.*	to be worthy of..., to deserve
57. 参加	cān jiā	*V.*	to participate in, to join
58. 后悔	hòu huǐ	*V.*	to regret
59. 一定	yí dìng	*Adv.*	certainly, surely
60. 本来	běn lái	*Adv.*	originally
61. 一直	yì zhí	*Adv.*	all along, along a straight path, continuously
62. 明白	míng bai	*V/Adj.*	to understand, to be clear about; clear
63. 军事	jūn shì	*N.*	military (affairs)
64. 国防	guó fáng	*N.*	national defense
65. 地位	dì wèi	*N.*	status
66. 以…为荣	yǐ... wéi róng	*VP.*	to be proud of
67. 的确	dí què	*Adv.*	indeed, really
68. 伟大	wěi dà	*Adj.*	great
69. 建筑	jiàn zhù	*N.*	building, architectural structure
70. 更	gèng	*Adv.*	even more
71. 别说	bié shuō	*VP.*	not to mention
72. 集合	jí hé	*V.*	to gather, to congregate
73. 赶紧	gǎn jǐn	*Adv.*	quickly, hurriedly
74. 往回走	wǎng huí zǒu	*VP.*	to go in the returning direction
75. 停车场	tíng chē chǎng	*N.*	parking lot
76. (在)路上	lù shang	*PrepP.*	on the way
77. 纪念品	jì niàn pǐn	*N.*	souvenir
78. 看样子	kàn yàng zi	*VO.*	it seems, it looks as

			if
79. 变得	biàn de	V.	to become, to change into
80. 商业化	shāng yè huà	Adj/V.	commercialized; to commercialize

—◆—— 补充词汇 ——◆—

81. 名胜古迹	míng shèng gǔ jì	NP.	scenic spots and historical sites
82. 唐代 (朝)	táng dài (cháo)	N.	the Tang Dynasty (618-907)
83. 宋代 (朝)	sòng dài (cháo)	N.	the Song Dynasty (960-1297)
84. 元代 (朝)	yuán dài (cháo)	N.	the Yuan Dynasty (1271-1368)
85. 清代 (朝)	qīng dài (cháo)	N.	the Qing Dynasty (1644-1911)
86. 游览车	yóu lǎn chē	N.	tourist bus
87. 观光团	guān guāng tuán	N.	tourist group
88. 导游	dǎo yóu	N.	tour guide
89. 故宫	gù gōng	Place N.	the Forbidden City
90. 天坛	tiān tán	Place N.	the Temple of Heaven
91. 颐和园	yí hé yuán	Place N.	the Summer Palace
92. 香山	xiāng shān	Place N.	Fragrant Mountain
93. 北海公园	běi hǎi gōng yuán	Place N.	The North Sea Park (or the Beihai Park)
94. 长江	cháng jiāng	N.	the Yangtze River
95. 黄河	huáng hé	N.	the Yellow River
96. 湖	hú	N.	lake
97. 海	hǎi	N.	sea

句型

一、凡是……都…… (anyone/thing who/that...)

> ✍ "凡是" is a collective modifier meaning "every," "any", or "all". Like the usage of "所有的", "凡是" is normally combined with a noun or a noun-phrase functioning as a topic and reinforced by "都" before the verb. In addition, a phrase that begins with "凡是" or "所有的" must be placed at the beginning of a sentence whether it be the logical subject or object of the sentence, e.g. "凡是去过秀水市场的人都知道那儿的东西不便宜". (Anyone who has been to Silk Alley knows that the things there are not cheap.) "凡是关于长城的讨论他都有兴趣". (He is interested in any discussion on the Great Wall.)

☞ 凡是到北京来的观光客都会去游览长城。

1、凡是学过中文的人都同意中文是很难的语言。
Anyone who has studied Chinese agrees that Chinese is a very difficult language.

2、凡是在中国留学的外国学生都必须办学生证。
Any foreign student studying in China needs to get a student ID.

二、……之一 (one of...)

> ✍ "……之一" means "one of……" "之" is a word from classical Chinese equivalent to the present-day "的", so "……之一" means "……的一个" in Modern Chinese. It is often used in formal and written settings. In Chinese, since a part of the whole must follow the whole, "……之一" must FOLLOW a noun denoting the whole group or whole category.

☞ 长城是北京附近最有名的旅游景点之一。

1、秀水市场是我最爱去的地方之一。
The Silk Alley is one of my favorite places to go to.

2、他是我们学校水平最高的学生之一。
He is one of the best students in our school.

三、 特地 V (especially V)

✍ "特地" is an adverb meaning "especially". It is used to indicate that an action has been taken for a special purpose. For example, "我知道你喜欢花，特地买了很多送给你"。 (I know that you like flowers, so I bought a bunch as a gift for you.)

☞ 老师特地给我们介绍了一下长城的历史。

1、 听说他病了，我特地去看他。
I heard that he was sick, so I made a special trip to see him.

2、 我这次到中国来，特地去吃了北京烤鸭。
On my trip to China this time, I made a special point of having Beijing Roast Duck.

四、 甚至 (even to the point of...)

✍ "甚至", "even to the point of...", is a conjunction functioning as an intensifier. It introduces an extreme case of the preceding statement. The structure "连……都" may be used with "甚至" to further reinforce the emphasis.

☞ 老百姓流血流汗，甚至牺牲了生命。

1、 他非常努力，甚至连周末的时候都在图书馆念书。
He is extremely diligent. He is at the library studying even during weekends.

2、 中国人很喜欢喝雪碧，甚至老人也喜欢喝。
Chinese people really like to drink Sprite; even old people like to drink it.

五、 为了……而…… (because of/in order to.., ...)

✍ "为了" is used to introduce the purpose of taking an action. "而" is the pivot linking the purpose with the action taken, but it is sometimes omitted. "为了……而……" is usually used in a written context, whereas "为了……，……" is used in the spoken medium. (cf. Lesson 4, Sentence Pattern 3)

☞ 她为了寻找她的丈夫而哭倒了长城。

1、他为了赚钱而在餐馆打工。

Because he wants to earn money he works at a restaurant.

2、我们为了学习中国的语言文化而到中国来。or 为了学习中国的语言文化，我们到中国来了。

We came to China in order to learn the Chinese language and culture.

六、一大早就V了 (to do something early in the morning)

> ✍ "一大早"，"early in the morning", is normally coupled with the adverb "就"，which conveys the nuance of "early, soon, fast", e.g. "我一大早就起床了"。(I got up very early.) (cf. Lesson 8, Sentence Pattern 8)

☞ 一大早我们就出发了。

1、今天我一大早就起来了，准备去参观故宫。

Today I got up early in the morning to get ready to go visit the Forbidden City.

2、他一大早就走了，不知道上哪儿去了。

He left early this morning. I do not know where he went.

七、才 (only then, later/slower than expected)

> ✍ "才" is an adverb indicating that something happened later or took longer than expected. In those sentences which use "才"，"了" is never used, even for a completed action. The adverb "就"，the opposite of "才"，indicates that an event occurred sooner or faster than expected. With the adverb "就"，it is necessary to use "了" when referring to a completed action. "才" can also be used to indicate a necessary condition, e.g. "只有这样，作文才能写好"。(This is the only way to write your essay well.). The English translation of a "才" sentence often takes the convoluted form of "Subj. ...not VP until..". (as in example 2).

☞ 坐了两个多小时的车才到长城。

1、那篇报告我写了一个多星期才写完。

It took me more than a week to finish writing that report.

2、这辆面包车的本钱我到上个月才还完。

I didn't finish paying off the loan on the mini-van until last month.

八、 在……看来 (in so-and-so's opinion)

> ✍ "在……看来" is used at the beginning of a sentence to introduce a person's opinion. A pronoun or person-noun should be put after "在". The possessive form cannot be used, e.g. one CANNOT say * "在他的看来" but one CAN say "在他看来".

☞ 在我看来……

1、 在中国人看来，长城是最伟大的建筑。

In Chinese people's opinion, the Great Wall is the greatest architectural feat.

2、 在学生看来，每天学五十个生字、十五个句型不算多。

To students, studying fifty new characters and fifteen new sentence patterns every day is not considered very much.

九、 在……上 (in the respect of, in, on)

> ✍ "在……上" is a prepositional phrase which is often combined with either an abstract or concrete noun to mean "concerning", "with respect to", "regarding", "on", "at", etc. The phrase is always placed either at the beginning of the sentence or immediately after the subject, e.g. "在经济上这个地区还不够独立". (This area is not quite independent with respect to economics.) "在这件事上，我有我的看法". (I have my own opinions regarding this matter.) "这儿的学生在学习上的态度跟别的学校不一样". (Here students' attitudes toward their studies are different from those of other schools.)

☞ 长城在军事上和国防上已经没有什么地位了。

1、 在历史上，秦始皇很有名。

Historically, the First Qin Emperor is very well-known.

2、 在学习上他非常努力，可是在生活上，他却不太注意。

With respect to studying he is very diligent, but in regards to his life he does not pay too much attention.

227

十、以……为荣 (to be proud of/about)

> ✎ "以" is a literary word meaning "拿" or "用", and its object may be either a concrete or an abstract noun. "为", pronounced in the second tone here, is also a literary word meaning "是". "以……为" can be translated as "to regard...as..." This expression is rarely used in spoken Chinese.

☞ 中国人还以长城为荣。

1、校长以这个学校的学生为荣。
   The principal is very proud of the school's students.
2、他的父母以他为荣，他的老师也以他为荣。
   His parents and teachers are proud of him.

十一、就是……都／也……，更别说……了 (even (if)..., not to mention...)

> ✎ "就是……都／也……，更别说……了" is a two-clause sentence structure in which the first clause "就是……也/都……" means "even (if)...", and the second clause "更别说……" means "not to mention that...". The two clauses are juxtaposed to intensify an extreme case... It can be used in both the positive and negative sense. However, the first sentence and the second sentence should be parallel in meaning. For example, "这本中文书就是中国人也看不懂，更别说外国人了". (This Chinese book is so difficult, even a Chinese person would have trouble reading it, not to mention a foreigner.) "他很有钱。就是最贵的汽车都买得起，更别说自行车了". (He is very rich. He could afford to buy even the most expensive car, not to mention a bike.) "就是" in this pattern may be translated either as "even" or "even if" depending on the context. "连" can be used instead of "就是" in this pattern, but only in the sense of "even" (not in the sense of "even if".) (cf. example 2)

☞ 就是现在要修长城都非常困难，更别说两千年前了。

1、那个地方就是坐汽车去也得三个小时，更别说骑车了。
   It will take three hours to get there even if one goes by car, not to mention riding a bike.
2、就是大人都爱吃冰淇淋，更别说小孩子了。
   Even adults enjoy ice cream, not to mention children.

228

十二、看样子 (it seems)

> ✍ "看样子", "it seems, judging from the way things look", is used at the beginning of a sentence to indicate the speaker is drawing a conclusion based on the situation given. For example, if someone was supposed to come at 5 p.m., but it's already 5:30 and he still hasn't shown up, one may say "看样子他今天不会来了". (It looks as if he won't be coming today.)

☞ 看样子长城已经变得非常商业化了。

1、看样子今天不能买纪念品了。

It seems one will not be able to buy souvenirs today.

2、看样子你好像还不明白这个句型的用法。

It seems you are still not clear on how to use this sentence pattern.

冬天的慕田峪长城

语言形式练习
Tasks on Language Forms

一、读课文回答问题

1、为什么凡是来北京的旅客都会去游览长城？
2、秦始皇修长城主要的目的是什么？
3、从前游览长城的门票分哪两种？有什么不同？现在呢？
4、"不到长城非好汉"是什么意思？
5、为什么中国人以游长城为荣？
6、这次游览长城，学生们觉得最可惜的地方是什么？

二、完成对话

1、A：谁都知道北京是中国的首都吗？
　　B：
　　（凡是；甚至）

2、A：他昨天为什么回家了？
　　B：
　　（特地；可惜）

3、A：这家饭馆的菜是不是学校附近最好的？
　　B：
　　（之一；不但……而且）

4、A：你为什么这几天看起来这么累？
　　B：
　　（为了……而……）

5、A: 你是哪所高中毕业的，你觉得你的学校怎么样？

B:

（以……为荣）

6、A: 他是什么时候发现自行车坏了的？

B:

（一大早就V了；看样子）

7、A: 在中国冬天用得着热水瓶吗？

B:

（就是……更别说……了）

三、听录音回答问题

1、为什么今天故宫的游客特别多？

2、故宫有多长时间的历史了？

3、故宫里面有多少间房子？

4、故宫里面为什么没有大树？

5、一般人怎么参观故宫？

6、今天小林除了故宫以外，还想到哪些地方去游览？

7、参观故宫以后，小林想做什么？

四、阅读回答问题

几年以前，北京旅游景点的门票是分外宾和内宾的，也就是说门票的价钱会根据内宾和外宾的不同而不同，外宾的门票比内宾的门票贵一些。就拿故宫来说，中国人付10元人民币就行了，而外国人则要付30元人民币。很多外国人认为这是对他们的歧视　(discrimination)。但有意思的是，很多中国人也认为这是中国人对自己的歧视。因为外国观光客付得钱比较多，就可以享受到一些特殊的待遇，很多中国人认为这是一种明显的不平等。比方说，在故宫，因为参观的人比较多，在进门时要排队，可是如果你是外宾，你就不必排队，走一个

231

外宾专用通道进入。再比方说，在颐和园，一些美丽的花园是普通中国游客所不能进入的。"外宾专用休息室"这样的牌子会把中国观光客挡在门外。随着改革开放的深入，政府也意识到这种老办法已经不能适应现代社会的发展了，老百姓收入的增加也允许他们接受高票价，享有和外国人同样的待遇。从前年开始，北京的旅游景点开始一个一个地实行统一票价，取消内宾外宾票价有别的制度。从今年开始，北京的一些有名的景点又开始试用一种全新的"季节性票价"制度。就是说，根据旅游季节的不同来决定门票的价钱。比方说，第一批使用这种制度的雍和宫 (the Yonghe Lama Temple)，在旅游旺季，也就是每年的7月、8月、9月和10月，票价是30元。而在旅游淡季，如1月、12月票价则是15元。还很难说这些新的制度是不是非常合理和有效，但是跟以往不平等的门票制度相比要好得多了。

问题：

1、以前，北京旅游景点的门票有什么特点？外国游客和中国游客的态度是什么？

2、外宾门票和普通门票有什么不同？

3、从课文的上下文来看，你知道"旺季"和"淡季"的意思是什么吗？

3、现在北京旅游景点新的门票制度是什么？

4、你怎么看北京门票制度的变化？如果你是门票制度的决定者，你会用什么办法？

五、翻译

1. The main purpose of building the Great Wall was to prevent enemies from entering China from the North. Therefore, in terms of national defense and military affairs, the Great Wall had a crucial position.

2. The Great Wall is one of the world's greatest architectural constructions. Not only do Chinese people feel proud of it, foreign tourists also want to visit the Great Wall.

3. I don't like to visit historical sites during weekends. There are too many visitors, and souvenir vendors are all over the place.

4. It seems that we will not be able to visit the museum today. Look, the line for tickets is too long. There are hordes of people (there are "people mountain, people sea".)

5. The First Qin Emperor made thousands of people sweat and bleed (shed blood and sweat) in order to build the Great Wall. Many people even lost their lives.

语言使用练习
Tasks on Language Use

一、真实情景活动 🎥

（一）这件T恤衫上写的是什么？要是你是小贩，你会想出一句什么样的话来吸引美国的
　　　游客买你的T恤衫？

这件T恤衫上的句子:

你写在T恤衫上的句子:

233

（二）这是一张挂在一家博物馆外面的牌子。根据上面的字，你知道现在还有内宾和外宾票吗？回答下面的问题：

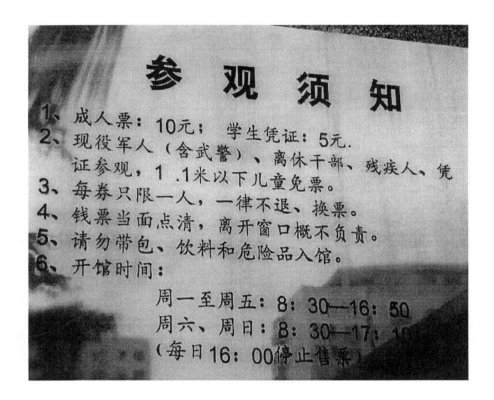

问题:

1、要是你去参观，你得付多少钱？

2、什么人不用买票？

3、这家博物馆什么时候闭馆 (close)？

4、要是你去参观，最晚什么时候应该到博物馆？为什么？

（三）把下面的日记翻译成英文。

二〇〇〇年九月十五日　　星期日　　天气：晴

　　　　昨天学校组织我们去了一趟慕田峪长城。从学校出发坐车坐了差不多两个多钟头就到了。那天的天气非常好，也不太热。我一口气就爬上了最高的地方。不知道为什么，跟八达岭长城比，我更喜欢慕田峪长城。

　　　　慕田峪长城跟八达岭长城一样，是中国明代长城的一部分。过去几千年来，它在军事上和国防上都起过重要的作用。慕田峪长城位于北京北郊区的怀柔县（Huairou county），最早是秦始皇修建的，后来到了明代初年，又有人把长城重修了一次，就成了现在的明长城。据说，我们多数看到的长城大多都是明代留下来的，现在很难看到最早的长城。我认为每一个来中国的观光客都应该去慕田峪长城参观游览，这是因为：一是慕田峪长城的修筑风格十分独特，光是正关台和烽火台就值得好好看看；二是长城都修建在险要的高山上，差不多海拔一千多米，所以风景比八达岭长城美得多；三是这里的游人毕竟没有八达岭长城那么多，所以商业化的程度也没有八达岭长城那么高。

一个留学生的日记 (diary)

235

二、讨论

1、谈谈你游览长城的经验。（什么时候去的，怎么去的，做了什么事情，买了什么东西？）

2、为什么从前参观博物馆、公园等，外国人的门票跟中国人的不同？你觉得这样合理吗？为什么？

3、你知道孟姜女的故事吗？请你说一说。

4、长城在历史上有什么地位？

5、你觉得中国人应该以长城为荣吗？为什么？

6、长城是不是变得很商业化了？请你用例子说明你看到的情形。你觉得可惜吗？

幕田峪长城位于北京的北郊区

三、语言实践

1、请你访问一个中国人，问问他（她）对长城的看法。
2、请你访问一下中国人，问问他们对门票分内宾、外宾两种票的看法，他们觉得这样公平吗？
3、跟你的中国朋友打听一下，秦始皇在中国人的心里是一个什么样的人？

四、作文

《一次最倒霉的旅游经历》

五、看图说话

1

2

3

4

5

6

我们暑期班第一个周末的旅游活动就是去长城

句型索引

A

A 离 B 不远/近 (Place A is not far from/near to Place B), *L1* （五）
A 也好，B 也好…… (either A or B, or...), *L7* （二）
Adj. + 得要命 (extremely + Adj.), *L2* （九）

B

把……用到……中 (to put something in use in...), *L5* （八）
比……还…… (even more... than...), *L10* （六）
比方说 (for example), *L5* （七）
比较 Adj. (relatively + Adj.), *L1* （六）
边 V 边 V (to V and V at the same time), *L10* （九）
别看…… (do not see as...), *L11* （五）
不但……而且 (not only...but also...), *L2* （五）
不到……就 (in less than...), *L6* （一）
不然 or 要不然 (otherwise), *L7* （六）
不至于 (cannot go as far as, not reach the point of), *L4* （六）

C

才 (only then, later/slower than expected), *L12* （七）
才……年（天、个月、个星期）的时间 (only for as short as...[year, month, day]), *L9* （三）
差点儿V (almost), *L10* （十）
除了……以外，……还/也... (besides; in addition to) and 除了……以外，……都…… (except for), *L3* （五）
从……到…… (from ... to), *L11* （四）
从……来看 (looking from, from the perspective of, from the standpoint of), *L2* （六）
从……起 (starting from), *L1* （一）

D

倒 (on the contrary), *L1* （八）
到处都…… (to be everywhere), *L4* （一）
到底 (after all), *L2* （八）
对……感兴趣 (to be interested in), *L10* （八）
对……过敏 (to be allergic to), *L3* （十）

对……来说 (as for ..., from the point of view of...), *L5* （五）

对……了解 (to have an understanding of..., to be informed about), *L11* （六）

F

凡是……都…… (anyone/thing who/that...), *L12* （一）

反而 (on the contrary), *L10* （五）

分……（等）类 (to be categorized into), *L8* （六）

分……类型 (to be classified as/into ...types), *L5* （三）

否则 (otherwise), *L11* （七）

G

改 V (to change to), *L10* （三）

给……介绍 (to introduce someone/something to), *L2* （二）

给……试体温/开药 (to measure the temperature for/to prescribe medication for), *L6* （三）

根据 (according to), *L9* （五）

管……叫…… (to call someone/something as...), *L9* （六）

H

好几 + classifier (quite a few), *L9* （四）

J

结果 (as a result, consequently), *L6* （四）

尽管……但是…… (although..., even though...), *L1* （二）

就是……都／也……，更别说……了 (even (if)..., not to mention...), *L12* （十一）

据……(according to), *L10* （一）

K

看样子 (it seems), *L12* （十二）

靠……吃饭 (to rely on... "to eat"), *L9* （九）

可惜 (it is a pity that; it is too bad that), *L8* （五）

可以说 (one may say, you can say), *L3* （四）

L

来自…… (place) (to come from), *L9* （七）

离……还有 (there is/are still... before...), *L5* （一）

利用 (to make use of, to utilize), *L1* （三）

了解……的动态 (to know and understand the development of), *L9* （八）

(Localizers) ……（的）对面, ……（的）附近, ……（的）东边, *L3* （二）

M

没想到 (unexpectedly; did not expect), *L2* （四）

免得 (so as to avoid), *L4* （九）

Q

却 (on the contrary; however), *L8* （二）

R

任何 (any), *L4* （八）

S

甚至 (even to the point of...), *L12* （四）

使 (to make, to cause), *L4* （四）

……是关于…… (to be about), *L9* （一）

受……的欢迎 (to be welcomed by), *L3* （八）

受（了/到）……的影响 (to be influenced by), *L10* （二）

算（是）(to be considered as), *L4* （七）

T

特地 V (specially V), *L12* （三）

替 (for, in so-and-so's stead), *L8* （四）

听……介绍 (as is introduced by, according to), *L6* （五）

听……说 (I was told, it is said), *L8* （一）

听说 (it is said that, (I) heard that), *L1* （四）

V

V 什么好 (what would be the best thing to V), *L10* （七）

V 得着, *L8* （十）

V 起来 (when it comes to V, V+up/away, begin to V), *L8* （八）

VV 看 (to try to), *L5* （十）

V + 一下 (to do something briefly), *L2* （三）

V 遍 (everywhere), *L7* （五）

V 来 V 去 (to V back and forth), *L8* （七）

V 得起/V 不起 (able/unable to afford), *L11* （十）

V 得下来 \ V 不下来 (successfully finish doing something), *L11* （九）

241

W

往……走 (to go toward), *L3* （三）

为……安排 (to arrange something for), *L2* （一）

为……服务 (to provide service for), *L6* （七）

为了 (in order to), *L4* （三）

为了……而…… (because of/in order to.., ...), *L12* （五）

位于 (to be located at), *L11* （一）

无论……都（就）…… (no matter + question), *L7* （四）

Y

要看 (it depends on), *L1* （七）

一般来说 (generally speaking), *L7* （三）

一边……一边…… (while...; at the same time), *L5* （九）

一大早就 V 了 (to do something early in the morning), *L12* （六）

一点儿也／都不…… (not at all, not the least bit...), *L2* （七）

一方面……一方面…… (on the one hand...; on the other hand...), *L4* （二）

一会儿……一会儿…… (now..., now...), *L6* （二）

一句（classifier）N也（都）不V (not at all), *L5* （二）

一是……二是……三是…… (first...; second...; and third...), *L3* （七）

以……为荣 (to be proud of/about), *L12* （十）

以……为主 (to focus on, to be primarily), *L5* （四）

用……交流 (to communicate in/by), *L5* （六）

尤其 (especially), *L7* （一）

由 (by), *L8* （三）

由……组成 (to consist of), *L11* （二）

由于 (due to), *L11* （三）

有……的，有……的 (some are..., some are...), *L3* （一）

有……特点 (to have the characteristics of), *L3* （六）

约…… (to make an appointment, to agree to meet), *L3* （九）

Z

在……看来 (in so-and-so's opinion), *L12* （八）

在……期间 (during the period of), *L4* （五）

在……（的）情况下 (under the condition of, under the circumstances of), *L11* （八）

在……上 (in the respect of, in, on), *L12* （九）

(在)……之内 (within), *L8* （九）

正好 V (as it happens), *L9* （二）

……之一 (one of...), *L12* （二）

专门 V (to specialize in), *L6* （六）

自从……以来 (ever since), *L10* （四）

生词索引

A

阿姨	ā yí	*N.*	mother's sister, auntie, *L4*
唉	āi	*Intj.*	alas (expressing sorrow or regret), *L7*
安排	ān pái	*V/N*	to arrange; arrangement, *L2*
按时	àn shí	*Adv.*	on schedule, *L6*

B

八达岭	bā dá lǐng	*Place N.*	name of mountain ridge, a famous Great Wall site, *L12*
拔丝	bá sī	*VO/Adj.*	to "pull out floss"; caramel floss (a sweet dish), *L3*
拜访	bài fǎng	*V.*	to visit (someone), *L4*
班机	bānjī	*N.*	flight, *L1*
办	bàn	*V.*	to hold (a party), to manage, to arrange, to handle, *L10*
办法	bàn fǎ	*N.*	way, means, *L7*
办理	bàn lǐ	*V.*	to handle, to go process , *L2*
办事	bàn shì	*VO.*	to handle affairs, to run errands, *L7*
棒	bàng	*Adj.*	wonderful, great, *L10*
包	bāo	*V.*	to wrap, *L8*
包装纸	bāo zhuāng zhǐ	*N.*	wrapping paper, *L8*
包子	bāo zi	*N.*	steamed stuffed bun, *L3*
保管	bǎo guǎn	*V.*	to take care of, to keep safely, *L4*
保险柜	bǎo xiǎn guì	*N.*	safe, *L4*
保证	bǎo zhèng	*V/N.*	to guarantee; guarantee, *L7*
报告	bào gào	*N/V.*	report; to report, *L9*
北边	běi biān	*N.*	the north side, *L12*
北海公园	běi hǎi gōng yuán	*Place N.*	The North Sea Park (or the Beihai Park), *L12*
倍	bèi	*N/Classifier*	times, -fold, *L11*
被子	bèi zi	*N.*	quilt, *L2*
本地	běn dì	*N.*	local area, *L9*
本来	běn lái	*Adv.*	originally, *L12*
本钱	běn qián	*N.*	capital, *L9*

本事	běn shì	N.	capability, ability, L9
比方说	bǐ fāng shuō	Idiom.	for example, L5
比较	bǐ jiào	Adv/V.	relatively, quite; to compare, L1
比赛	bǐ sài	V/N.	to race, to compete; race, competition, L12
笔记本	bǐ jì běn	N.	notebook, L5
边吃边说	biān chī biān shuō	VP.	to eat and chat at the same time (cf. 一边……一边……, Lesson 5), L10
变得	biàn de	V.	to become, to change into, L12
变化	biàn huà	N.	change, L1
表	biǎo	N.	form, L6
别看	bié kàn	VP.	do not see as... (cf. Sentence Pattern 5), L11
别说	bié shuō	VP.	not to mention, L12
冰箱	bīng xiāng	N.	refrigerator, L3
冰淇淋	bīng qí lín	N.	ice cream, L2
病假	bìng jià	N.	sick leave, L6
拨	bō	V.	to dial, L2
博物馆	bó wù guǎn	N.	museum, L12
伯伯	bó bo	N.	father's older brother, L4
伯母	bó mǔ	N.	wife of father's older brother, L4
不必	bú bì	VP.	do not have to, no need, L8
不到长城非好汉	bú dào cháng chéng fēi hǎo hàn	Idiom.	If one does not go to the Great Wall, one is not a real man., L12
不断	bú duàn	Adj.	unceasing, continuous, constant, L7
不过	bú guò	Conj.	but, L7
不好意思	bù hǎo yì si	Adj.	embarrassed, L4
不一会儿	bú yì huìr	Adv.	in no time at all, in a very short time, L12
不至于	bú zhì yú	Adv.	cannot go so far as..., not reach the point of..., L4
步	bù	N.	step, L3
不管	bù guǎn	VP.	do not care, not pay attention, L7
不合	bù hé	VP.	do not meet/fit (requirement), L7
不然	bù rán	Conj.	otherwise, L7
部首	bù shǒu	N.	radicals, L5

C

财经	cái jīng	Abbrev.	finance and economy, L8
菜单	cài dān	N.	menu, L3
餐厅	cān tīng	N.	dining hall, restaurant, cafeteria, L2
参观	cān guān	V.	to visit (a place), L10

参加	cān jiā	V.	to participate in, to join, L12
查	chá	V.	to look up (in a dictionary), to examine, to investigate, L8
查票员	chá piào yuán	N.	ticket checker, L12
差点儿	chà diǎnr	Adv.	almost, nearly, L10
产品	chǎn pǐn	N.	product, L7
常见	cháng jiàn	Adj.	common, L10
长城	cháng chéng	Place N.	The Great Wall, L12
长城饭店	cháng chéng fàn diàn	Place N.	Great Wall Hotel (Sheraton Hotel in Beijing), L6
长江	cháng jiāng	N.	the Yangtze River, L12
长裤	cháng kù	N.	pants, trousers, L11
长寿	cháng shòu	N.	long life, longevity, L10
长途	cháng tú	Adj.	long distance (phone call), L2
长途区号	cháng tú qū hào	NP.	area code
长袖	cháng xiù	N.	long sleeves, L11
超过	chāo guò	V.	to exceed, L8
炒菜	chǎo cài	VO.	stir-fried dish/vegetable, L3
车把	chē bǎ	N.	handlebar (of a bicycle, motorcycle), L7
车牌	che pái	N.	license plate, L7
衬衫	chèn shān	N.	shirt, L11
衬衣	chèn yī	N.	shirt, L11
城	chéng	N.	city, L4
城市	chéng shì	N.	city, L4
成千上万	chéng qiān shàng wàn	Idiom.	tens of thousands, in considerable numbers, L12
乘客	chéng kè	N.	passenger, L9
吃惊	chī jīng	VO.	to be shocked, to be surprised, L2
吃亏	chī kuī	VO.	to suffer losses, to get the short end of the stick, L11
吃药	chī yào	VO.	to take medicine, L6
尺	chǐ	N.	ruler, L8
抽水马桶	chōu shuǐ mǎ tǒng	N.	flush toilet, L2
初中	chū zhōng	N.	junior high school, L4
出发	chū fā	V.	to take off, to depart, L12
出路	chū lù	N.	way out, outlet, L7
出钱	chū qián	VO.	to pay, L9
出售	chū shòu	V.	to sell, L11
出租汽车	chū zū qì chē	NP.	taxi, L1
除了……以外	chú le ...yǐ wài	Prep.	except for, in addition to , L3
处	chù	N.	(bound form) place, L8
传统	chuán tǒng	Adj.	traditional, L11
床	chuáng	N.	bed, L2

床单	chuáng dān	N.	bed sheet, L2
吹	chuī	V.	to blow, L12
春天	chūn tiān	N.	spring, L1
纯丝	chún sī	N.	pure silk, L11
磁卡	cí kǎ	N.	IC Card, L2
词典	cí diǎn	N.	dictionary, L8
词性	cí xìng	N.	part of speech, L5
存钱	cún qián	VO.	to deposit money, to save money, L9
寸	cùn	N/Classifier.	inch, L9
错误	cuò wù	N.	mistake, error, L5
打包	dǎ bāo	V.	to wrap, L8

D

打不通	dǎ bu tōng	VP.	cannot get through (on phone), L2
打开	dǎ kāi	VP.	to open, L2
打喷嚏	dǎ pēn tì	VO.	to sneeze, L6
打气	dǎ qì	VO.	to inflate, to pump up (a tire), L7
打算	dǎsuàn	V/N.	to plan; plan, L1
打听	dǎ tīng	V.	to check around, to find out, L2
打折	dǎ zhé	VO.	to sell at a discount, to give a discount, L11
打针	dǎ zhēn	VO.	to give or have an injection, L6
大便	dà biàn	V/N.	to have a bowel movement; feces, L6
大饼	dà bǐng	N.	a kind of large flat bread, L3
大吃一惊	dà chī yì jīng	VO.	to be greatly shocked or startled (cf. 吃惊, Lesson 1), L4
大葱	dà cōng	N.	scallion, L3
大量	dà liàng	Quan.	large (amount/quantity), L5
大陆	dà lù	PlaceN.	mainland China, L1
大使馆	dà shǐ guǎn	N.	embassy, L7
大厅	dà tīng	N.	lobby, hall, L2
大衣	dà yī	N.	coat, L11
大致	dà zhì	Adv.	roughly, approximately, L9
待	dāi	V.	to stay (等待 děng dài to wait, to await), L7
担心	dān xīn	V.	to worry, L6
单班课	dān bān kè	N.	one-on-one class, L5
单位	dān wèi	N.	work unit, L4
蛋糕	dàn gāo	N.	cake, L10
蛋花汤	dàn huā tāng	NP.	egg drop soup, L3
当	dāng	V.	to be, to become, L9
倒	dào	Adv.	on the contrary, L7
倒	dǎo	V.	to fall, to collapse, L12

导游	dǎo yóu	N.	tour guide, L12
到处	dào chù	Adv.	everywhere, L4
到底	dào dǐ	Adv.	after all, in the final analysis (conveys emphasis in questions), L2
到现在	dào xiàn zài	PrepP.	up till now, L5
登机	dēng jī	VO.	to board a plane, L1
登机门	dēng jī mén	NP.	boarding gate, L1
登机证	dēng jī zhèng	NP.	boarding pass, L1
登记	dēng jì	V.	to register, to check in, L2
等等	děng děng		and so on, etc., L3
等候	děng hòu	V.	to wait, L6
的确	dí què	Adv.	indeed, really, L12
敌人	dí rén	N.	enemy, L12
地理	dì lǐ	N.	geography, L5
地铁	dì tiě	N.	subway, L9
地图	dì tú	N.	map, L1
地位	dì wèi	N.	status, L12
地下室	dì xià shì	N.	basement, L4
点	diǎn	V.	to order (food), L3
电灯	diàn dēng	N.	light, lamp, L2
电话	diàn huà	N.	telephone, phone call, L2
电话亭	diàn huà tíng	N.	telephone booth, L2
电视	diàn shì	N.	TV, L2
东城区	dōng chéng qū	Place N.	Eastern City District, L11
冬天	dōng tiān	N.	winter, L1
动词	dòng cí	N.	verb, L5
动态	dòng tài	N.	trends, L9
独生子女	dú shēng zǐ nǚ	NP.	single child, L5
堵车	dǔ chē	VO/N.	to have a traffic jam; traffic jam, L9
肚子	dù zi	N.	belly, abdomen, L6
度	dù	N.	degree, L6
度假	dùjià	VO.	to spend a vacation, L1
短裤	duǎn kù	N.	shorts, L11
短袖	duǎn xiù	N.	short sleeves, L11
对话课	duì huà kè	N.	conversation class, L5
对面	duì miàn	N.	the place across from, L3
蹲	dūn	V.	to squat, L2
多大	duō dà	QW.	how old, L10

E

而	ér	Conj.	and, but, thereby, L12
儿子	ér zi	N.	son, L4
耳环	ěr huán	N.	earrings, L11

| 鳄鱼牌 | è yú pái | N. | Crocodile, Izod Lacoste Brand, *L11* |

F

发票	fā piào	*N.*	receipt, *L8*
发烧	fā shāo	*V.*	to have a fever, *L6*
发生	fā shēng	*V.*	to happen, to occur, *L4*
发现	fā xiàn	*V/N.*	to discover; discovery, *L6*
发展	fā zhǎn	*V/N.*	to develop; development, *L9*
翻看	fān kàn	*V.*	to browse, to look over (books), *L8*
翻译	fān yì	*N/V.*	translation; to translate, *L8*
繁体字	fán tǐ zì	*N.*	complex (traditional) character, *L5*
凡是	fán shì	*Adj.*	every, any, *L12*
反而	fǎn ér	*Adv.*	on the contrary, instead, *L10*
反应	fǎn yìng	*N.*	reaction, response, *L3*
犯罪	fàn zuì	*VO.*	to commit crimes, *L4*
饭厅	fàn tīng	*N.*	dining room, *L4*
方便	fāng biàn	*Adj.*	convenient, *L1*
方面	fāng miàn	*N.*	aspect, *L5*
防止	fáng zhǐ	*V.*	to prevent, to guard against, *L12*
纺织品	fǎng zhī pǐn	*N.*	textile products, *L11*
放假	fàng jià	*VO.*	to have a holiday or vacation, to have a day off (cf. 放暑假, Lesson 1), *L10*
放暑假	fàngshǔ jià	*VO.*	to have a summer vacation (放假: to have a vacation, 暑: summer), *L1*
肥	féi	*Adj.*	loose-fitting, large, fat (only re meats, not people), *L11*
费	fèi	*V/N.*	to waste; fee, *L8*
费城	fèi chéng	*Place N.*	Philadelphia, *L4*
分	fēn	*N.*	cent, *L1*
分	fēn	*V.*	to divide, to classify, *L5*
丰富	fēng fù	*Adj/V.*	rich, abundant; to enrich, *L8*
封	fēng	*Classifier.*	classifier for letter, *L5*
风	fēng	*N.*	wind, *L12*
风景	fēng jǐng	*N.*	scenery, *L4*
风味	fēng wèi	*N.*	special flavor (style or region of cuisine), *L3*
风衣	fēng yī	*N.*	windbreaker, *L11*
烽火台	fēng huǒ tái	*N.*	beacon tower, *L12*
否则	fǒu zé	*Adv.*	otherwise, *L11*
服务	fú wù	*V/N.*	to serve; service, *L6*
服务员	fú wù yuán	*N.*	attendant, service personnel, *L2*
服装	fú zhuāng	*N.*	clothing, *L11*
副词	fù cí	*N.*	adverb, *L5*

复活节	fù huó jié	N.	Easter, *L10*
付钱	fù qián	VO.	to pay, *L10*
负责	fù zé	VO.	to be responsible, to be in charge of, *L8*
附近	fù jìn	N/Adj.	vicinity; nearby, neighboring, *L3*
妇女	fù nǚ	N.	woman, *L5*

G

改	gǎi	V.	to change, to switch over to, *L10*
改革	gǎi gé	V/N.	to reform; reform, *L7*
改正	gǎi zhèng	V.	to correct, *L5*
干	gàn	V.	(colloquial) to work, to do, *L9*
干干净净	gān gān jìng jìng	Adj.	clean, *L2*
赶紧	gǎn jǐn	Adv.	quickly, hurriedly, *L12*
赶快	gǎn kuài	Adv.	quickly, at once, *L2*
感恩节	gǎn ēn jié	N.	Thanksgiving, *L10*
感冒	gǎn mào	V/N.	to catch a cold; cold, *L6*
感兴趣	gǎn xìng qù	VP.	to be interested, *L10*
高考	gāo kǎo	N.	college entrance examination, *L4*
高中	gāo zhōng	N.	senior high school, *L4*
告辞	gào cí	V.	to take leave (of one's host), *L4*
告诉	gào sù	V.	to tell, *L2*
个体户	gè tǐ hù	N.	self-employed people, independent entrepreneur, *L9*
各处	gè chù	N.	every place, various places, *L10*
各种	gè zhǒng	N.	all kinds of, *L11*
根本	gēn běn	Adv.	(used in negative sentences) simply, fundamentally, (not)...at all, *L3*
根据	gēn jù	Prep.	according to, *L9*
更	gèng	Adv.	even more, *L12*
工具	gōng jù	N.	tool, *L7*
工艺品	gōng yì pǐn	N.	handicrafts, *L11*
功课	gōng kè	N.	schoolwork, *L4*
供应	gōng yìng	V.	to supply, to furnish, *L2*
公道	gōng dào	Adj.	reasonable, *L3*
公分	gōng fēn	N/Classifier.	centimeter, *L9*
公共	gōng gòng	Adj.	public, *L9*
公共汽车	gōng gòng qì chē	NP.	public bus, *L9*
公里	gōng lǐ	N/Classifier.	kilometer, *L9*
公立	gōng lì	Adj.	public, established/operated by government, *L4*
公路	gōng lù	N.	highway, *L9*
公司	gōng sī	N.	company, *L9*

公园	gōng yuán	N.	park, L12
宫爆鸡丁	gōng bào jī dīng	NP.	Gong Bao chicken, L3
狗	gǒu	N.	dog, L10
估计	gū jì	V.	to estimate, to surmise, L6
故宫	gù gōng	Place N.	the Forbidden City, L12
故事	gù shi	N.	story, L12
挂号	guà hào	VO.	to register (at a hospital), L6
关税	guān shuì	NP.	customs duty, tariff, L1
关心	guān xīn	V.	to be concerned, to care about, L4
关于	guān yú	Prep.	regarding, concerning, L9
观光客	guān guāng kè	N.	tourist, L12
观光团	guān guāng tuán	N.	tourist group, L12
管⋯⋯叫	guǎn...jiào	VP.	to call something or somebody (by the name of...), L9
逛逛	guàng guang	V.	to roam around, L8
柜台	guì tái	N.	service counter, L8
柜子	guì zi	N.	cabinet, L8
贵重	guì zhòng	Adj.	precious, valuable, L4
国防	guó fáng	N.	national defense, L12
国际	guó jì	Adj.	international, L2
国际医疗中心	guó jì yī liáo zhōng xīn	Place N.	International Medical Center, L6
国家代码	guó jiā dài mǎ	N.	country code, L2
国庆节	guó qìng jié	N.	National Day, L10
国营	guó yíng	Adj.	government-operated, state-owned, L7
果汁	guǒ zhī	N.	fruit juice, L2
过节	guò jié	VO.	to celebrate a holiday, to spend a holiday, L10
过来	guò lai	V.	to come over, L2
过敏	guò mǐn	V.	to be allergic to, L3
过生日	guò shēng rì	VO.	to celebrate a birthday, L10

H

海	hǎi	N.	sea, L12
海淀图书城	hǎi diàn tú shū chéng	Place N.	Hai Dian Book City, L8
海关	hǎi guān	N.	customs, L1
汉英	hàn yīng	Adj.	Chinese-English, L8
汉语	hàn yǔ	N.	Mandarin Chinese, L4
航空公司	hángkōng gōng sī	NP.	airline company, L1
豪华型	háo huá xíng	N.	deluxe model, L9
好处	hǎo chù	N.	advantage, benefit, L5
好客	hào kè	Adj.	hospitable, sociable, L4
好象	hǎo xiàng	Aux/V.	it seems, L6
合理	hé lǐ	Adj.	reasonable, L12

合适	hé shì	Adj.	suitable, appropriate, L4
合资	hé zī	NP.	joint venture, L6
烘干机	hōng gān jī	N.	dryer, L2
红绿灯	hóng lǜ dēng	N.	traffic light, L9
猴	hóu	N.	monkey, L10
后悔	hòu huǐ	V.	to regret, L12
胡椒	hú jiāo	N.	pepper, L3
湖	hú	N.	lake, L12
虎	hǔ	N.	tiger, L10
护发素	hù fà sù	N.	hair conditioner, L2
护士	hù shì	N.	nurse , L6
护照	hù zhào	N.	passport, L4
花茶	huā chá	N.	jasmine tea (also called 香片 xiāng piàn), L3
花钱	huā qián	VO.	to spend money, L7
华盛顿	huá shèng dùn	Place N.	Washington, L4
华氏	huá shì	N.	Fahrenheit, L6
画报	huà bào	N.	pictorial magazine or newspaper, L8
化验	huà yàn	V.	to have a laboratory test, L6
化妆品	huà zhuāng pǐn	N.	cosmetics, L11
欢迎	huān yíng	N/V.	welcome, popularity; to welcome, L3
环城	huán chéng	VO/Adj.	to encircle the city; around the city, L9
环境	huán jìng	N.	environment, L3
还	huán	V.	to pay back, to return, L9
换	huàn	V.	to exchange, to change, L1
黄河	huáng hé	N.	the Yellow River, L12
回	huí	Classifier.	occurrence, times, L7
活	huó	Adj.	flexible, lively, active, L7
活动	huó dòng	N/Adj/V.	activity; active; to have an activity, L12
活儿	huór	N.	business, work, L9
火柴	huǒ chái	N.	match, L10
火车	huǒ chē	N.	train, L7
火鸡	huǒ jī	N.	turkey, L10

J

机场	jī chǎng	N.	airport, L1
机场大巴	jī chǎng dà bā	NP.	airport bus, L1
机会	jīhuì	N.	opportunity, L1
机票	jīpiào	N.	airplane ticket, L1
激烈	jī liè	Adj.	fierce, intense, L9
鸡	jī	N.	rooster, L10

鸡蛋	jī dàn	N.	egg, L3
鸡肉	jī ròu	N.	chicken, L3
集合	jí hé	V.	to gather, to congregate, L12
急性肠炎	jí xìng cháng yán	N.	acute enteritis, L6
寂寞	jì mò	Adj.	lonely, L4
计划	jìhuà	V/N.	to plan; plan, L1
计算机	jì suàn jī	N.	computer, L8
记	jì	V.	to write down, to record, L5
记事本	jì shì běn	N.	memo book, pocket calendar, L8
纪念品	jì niàn pǐn	N.	souvenir, L12
纪念品	jì niàn pǐn	N.	souvenir, L4
夹克	jiá kè	N.	jacket, L11
家庭	jiā tíng	N.	family, L4
价钱	jià qián	N.	price, L3
架子	jià zi	N.	shelf, L8
驾驶执照	jià shǐ zhí zhào	N.	driver's license, L7
尖椒	jiān jiāo	N.	elongated pepper or hot pepper, L3
间接	jiàn jiē	Adv/Adj.	indirectly, indirect, L5
煎饺	jiān jiǎo	N.	fried dumpling, L3
简单地	jiǎn dān de	Adv.	briefly, simply (简单: simple), L2
简体字	jiǎn tǐ zì	N.	simplified character, L5
简直	jiǎn zhí	Adv.	simply, L6
减价	jiǎn jià	VO.	to reduce the price, to mark down, L11
健康保险	jiàn kāng bǎo xiǎn	NP.	health insurance, L6
建议	jiàn yì	N/V.	suggestion; to suggest, L4
建筑	jiàn zhù	N.	building, architectural structure, L12
讲	jiǎng	V.	to lecture, to tell (about), L5
讲价	jiǎng jià	VO.	to bargain over price, L11
酱油	jiàng yóu	N.	soy sauce, L3
降价	jiàng jià	VO.	to reduce the price, L11
降落	jiàng luò	V.	to descend, to land, L1
交	jiāo	V.	to turn in, to hand over, L4
交款单	jiāo kuǎn dān	N.	payment slip, L8
交流	jiāo liú	V/N.	to exchange; interchange, L5
交朋友	jiāo péng you	VO.	to make friends, L4
交通	jiāo tōng	N.	transportation, traffic, L7
郊区	jiāo qū	N.	suburb, L9
饺子馆	jiǎo zi guǎn	N.	dumpling restaurant, L3
教授	jiào shòu	N.	professor, L4
教育	jiào yù	N.	education, L8
轿车	jiào chē	N.	sedan, L9
接	jiē	V.	to pick up (someone), to receive, L1
街	jiē	N.	street, L11
节日	jié rì	N.	holiday, L10

结果	jié guǒ	Conj/N.	as a result; result, L6
结账	jié zhàng	VO.	to settle up, to pay the bill, L3
解决	jiě jué	V.	to solve, to resolve, L4
解释	jiě shì	N/V.	explanation; to explain, L8
借钱	jiè qián	VO.	to borrow money, L9
介绍	jiè shào	V/N.	to introduce; introduction, L2
紧	jǐn	V/Adj.	to tighten; tight, L7
紧张	jǐnzhāng	Adj.	nervous, L1
进步	jìnbù	N/V.	progress; to make progress, L1
进货	jìn huò	VO.	to replenish one's stock, to stock (one's shop) with goods, L11
进入	jìn rù	V.	to enter, L12
尽管	jǐnguǎn	Conj.	though, even though, L1
经常	jīng cháng	Adv.	often, L10
经济	jīng jì	Adj/N.	economical; economy, L3
经历	jīng lì	N/V.	experience; to experience, L7
景点	jǐng diǎn	N.	scenic spot, L12
竞争	jìng zhēng	N/V.	competition; to compete, L9
救护车	jiù hù chē	N.	ambulance, L6
旧车市场	jiù chē shì chǎng	NP.	used bike market, L7
旧金山	jiù jīn shān	Place N.	San Francisco, L4
舅舅	jiù jiu	N.	mother's brother, L4
据	jù	Prep.	according to, L10
句型	jù xíng	N.	sentence pattern, L5
决定	jué dìng	V/N.	to decide; decision, L2
军事	jūn shì	N.	military (affairs), L12

K

咖啡厅	kā fēi tīng	N.	coffee shop, L2
开	kāi	V.	to make out, to write, L8
开放	kāi fàng	V/Adj.	to open up; open, L7
开关	kāi guān	N.	switch, L2
开始	kāi shǐ	V.	to start, L6
开药	kāi yào	VO.	to prescribe medicine, to give prescription, L6
砍价	kǎn jià	VO.	to chop price, L11
看病	kàn bìng	VO.	to see a doctor, L6
看样子	kàn yàng zi	VO.	it seems, it looks as if, L12
靠	kào	V.	to rely on, L9
咳嗽	ké sòu	VO/N.	to cough; cough, L6
可乐	kě lè	N.	Coca-Cola, L2
可怕	kě pà	Adj.	terrible, terrifying, L4
可惜	kě xī	Adv.	it's a pity, it's too bad, L8

渴	kě	Adj.	thirsty, L2
客厅	kè tīng	N.	living room, L4
课文	kè wén	N.	text, L5
空调	kōng tiáo	N.	air conditioning, L2
口语	kǒu yǔ	N.	spoken language, L9
扣子	kòu zi	N.	button, L11
哭	kū	V.	to weep, to cry, L12
苦	kǔ	Adj.	bitter, L3
快乐	kuài lè	Adj/N.	happy; happiness, L10
矿泉水	kuàng quán shuǐ	N.	mineral water, L2
困难	kùn nan	N/Adj.	difficulty; difficult, L3

L

垃圾桶	lā jī tǒng	N.	trash can, L2
拉	lā	V.	to draw in, to pull, L9
拉肚子	lā dù zi	VO.	to suffer from diarrhea, L6
蜡烛	là zhú	N.	candle, L10
辣	là	Adj.	spicy, hot, L3
辣椒酱	là jiāo jiàng	NP.	hot sauce, L3
来自	lái zì	V.	to come from, L9
老百姓	lǎo bǎi xìng	N.	common people, the general public, L7
老爷	lǎo ye	N.	maternal grandfather, L4
姥姥	lǎo lao	N.	maternal grandmother, L4
类型	lèi xíng	N.	type, L5
冷饮	lěng yǐn	N.	cold drink, L2
离开	lí kāi	V.	to leave, L4
理解	lǐ jiě	V/N.	to comprehend, to understand; comprehension, L5
理想	lǐxiǎng	N/Adj.	ideal; ideal dream, L1
里头	lǐ tou	N.	inside, L7
礼拜	lǐ bài	N.	week (星期), L1
礼物	lǐ wù	N.	present, gift, L4
历史	lì shǐ	N.	history, L5
利用	lìyòng	V.	to use, to utilize, L1
例句	lì jù	N.	example sentences, L8
例外	lì wài	Adj/N.	exceptional; exception, L4
力气	lì qi	N.	strength, energy, L6
联合航空公司	lián hé háng kōng gōng sī	NP.	United Airlines, UA, L1
练习	liàn´xí	N.	exercise, L5
凉	liáng	Adj.	cool, L12
凉鞋	liáng xié	N.	sandals, L11
两室一厅	liǎng shì yì tīng	Abbrev.	two rooms and one living room, L4

辆	liàng	Classifier.	classifier for vehicle, L7
聊天	liáo tiān	VO.	to chat, L4
了解	liǎo jiě	V/N.	to understand; understanding, L2
零的	líng de	N.	small change, L8
灵活	líng huó	Adj.	flexible, agile, L9
另外	lìng wài	Adv/Adj.	besides; another, L7
留学	liúxué	VO.	to study abroad, L1
留学生	liú xué shēng	NP.	student studying abroad, foreign students, L1
流鼻涕	liú bí tì	VO.	to have a runny nose, L6
流行	liú xíng	V/Adj.	to become popular; popular, L11
流血流汗	liú xiě liú hàn	Idiom.	to shed blood and sweat, to pay a high human cost, L12
龙	lóng	N.	dragon, L10
楼	lóu	N.	building, stairs, floor, L2
鲁迅	lǔ xùn	Personal N.	Lu Xun, a famous writer, L8
(在)路上	lù shang	PrepP.	on the way, L12
录像带	lù xiàng dài	N.	video tape, L5
录音带	lù yīn dài	N.	audio tape, L5
旅游	lǔ yóu	V/N.	to tour; tour, L12
轮胎	lún tāi	N.	tire, L7
落后	luò hòu	Adj.	backward, underdeveloped, L2
洛山矶	luò shān jī	Place N.	Los Angeles, L4

M

麻烦	má fan	N/Adj.	trouble; troublesome, L7
麻婆豆腐	má pó dòu fu	NP.	a spicy tofu dish, L3
马	mǎ	N.	horse, L10
马路	mǎ lù	N.	road, street, L9
麦当劳	mài dāng láo	Place N.	McDonald's, L10
卖主	mài zhǔ	N.	seller, L11
馒头	mán tou	N.	steamed bun, L3
慢性	màn xìng	Adj.	chronic, L6
毛	máo	N.	ten cents, dime, L1
毛笔	máo bǐ	N.	writing brush, L8
毛病	máo bìng	N.	defect, L8
毛巾	máo jīn	N.	towel, L2
毛衣	máo yī	N.	sweater, L11
没法	méi fǎ	VO.	there is no way , L7
没想到	méi xiǎng dào	VP.	didn't expect, L2
美国航空公司	měi guó háng kōng gōng sī	NP.	American Airlines, AA, L1
美元	měi yuán	NP.	American dollar, L1
门票	mén piào	N.	entrance ticket, L12

孟姜女	mèng jiāng nǚ	*Personal N.*	a woman named Meng Jiang, *L12*
米	mǐ	*N/Classifier.*	meter, *L9*
米饭	mǐ fàn	*N.*	cooked rice, *L6*
棉	mián	*N.*	cotton, *L11*
免得	miǎn dé	*Adv.*	so as not to, so as to avoid, *L4*
免费	miǎn fèi	*Adj.*	free (of charge), *L6*
面条	miàn tiáo	*N.*	noodle, *L3*
明白	míng bai	*V/Adj.*	to understand, to be clear about; clear, *L12*
明代	míng dài	*N.*	the Ming Dynasty (1368-1644), *L12*
明信片	míng xìn piàn	*N.*	postcard, *L4*
明信片	míng xìn piàn	*N.*	postcard, *L8*
名词	míng cí	*N.*	noun, *L5*
名牌	míng pái	*N.*	name brand, *L11*
名胜古迹	míng shèng gǔ jì	*NP.*	scenic spots and historical sites, *L12*
摩托车	mó tuō chē	*N.*	motorcycle, *L7*

N

哪里	nǎ lǐ	*Adv.*	"nah" (used to negate what the other just said), *L9*
奶奶	nǎi nai	*N.*	paternal grandmother, *L4*
奈克	nài kè	*N.*	Nike, *L11*
难办	nán bàn	*Adj.*	hard to do, difficult, *L10*
难受	nán shòu	*V.*	to feel unhappy, to feel unwell, *L7*
内宾	nèi bīn	*N.*	domestic guests/visitors, *L12*
内容	nèi róng	*N.*	content, *L5*
牛	niú	*N.*	ox, *L10*
牛仔裤	niú zǎi kù	*N.*	jeans, *L11*
纽约	niǔ yuē	*Place N.*	New York, *L4*
女儿	nǚ ér	*N.*	daughter, *L4*

P

爬	pá	*V.*	to climb, *L12*
排队	pái duì	*VO.*	to line up, *L12*
牌子	pái zi	*N.*	brand, *L7*
跑遍	pǎo biàn	*VP.*	to go everywhere, *L7*
赔	péi	*V.*	to suffer a loss (selling below cost), *L11*
碰到	pèngdào	*VP.*	to encounter, *L1*
啤酒	pí jiǔ	*N.*	beer, *L2*
皮包	pí bāo	*N.*	purse, *L11*
皮带	pí dài	*N.*	belt, *L11*

皮鞋	pí xié	N.	leather shoes, L11
皮衣	pí yī	N.	leather or fur garments, L11
偏旁	piān páng	N.	character component, L5
便宜	pián yi	Adj.	cheap, inexpensive, L3
票	piào	N.	receipt (abbreviated form for 票, cf. Lesson 8), ticket, L9
拼音	pīn yīn	N.	Pinyin, Romanization, L5
拼音	pīn yīn	N/VO.	Pinyin; to combine sounds into syllables, L8
平安	píng ān	Adj.	safe and sound, L2
瓶	píng	Classifier.	bottle, L2

Q

期间	qī jiān	N.	time period, duration, L4
其实	qí shí	Adv.	actually, L4
其他	qí tā	Adj.	other, else, L4
其中	qí zhōng	PrepP.	among which, L9
骑车	qí chē	VO.	to ride a bike (or a motor cycle), L7
气氛	qì fēn	N.	atmosphere, ambience, L3
汽车厂	qì chē chǎng	N.	automobile factory, L7
铅笔	qiān bǐ	N.	pencil, L8
签证	qiānzhèng	N.	visa, L1
前台	qián tái	N.	front desk, L2
抢劫	qiǎng jié	N/V.	robbery; to rob, L4
抢手	qiǎng shǒu	Adj.	(lit. "grab by the hand") popular (with buyers), fast-selling, L11
切	qiē	V.	to cut, L10
秦始皇	qín shǐ huáng	Title.	the 1st Emperor of the Qin Dynasty, L12
青椒	qīng jiāo	N.	green pepper, L3
青山	qīng shān	N.	green mountain, L12
轻松	qīng sōng	Adj.	relaxing, relaxed, L3
清代 (朝)	qīng dài (cháo)	N.	the Qing Dynasty (1644-1911), L12
情况	qíng kuàng	N.	condition, L2
请假	qǐng jià	VO.	to ask for leave of absence, to request to be absent, L6
庆祝	qìng zhù	V.	to celebrate, L10
穷	qióng	Adj.	poor, L11
秋天	qiūtiān	N.	autumn, L1
球鞋	qiú xié	N.	sneakers, L11
全集	quán jí	N.	complete works, L8
全身	quán shēn	N.	the whole body, L6
却	què	Adv.	on the contrary, L8

| 裙子 | qún zi | N. | skirt, L11 |

R

然后	rán hòu	Adv.	then, L6
让	ràng	V.	to let, to cause, L4
绕路	rào lù	VO.	to make a detour, to take the long route, L9
热情	rè qíng	Adj/N.	warm; enthusiasm, L10
热水瓶	rè shuǐ píng	N.	thermos bottle, L2
热水澡	rè shuǐ zǎo	NP.	hot bath or shower, L2
热饮	rè yǐn	N.	hot drink, L2
人口	rén kǒu	N.	the number of people in a family, population, L4
人民币	rén mín bì	N.	renminbi (RMB) (Chinese currency), L1
人山人海	rén shān rén hǎi	Idiom.	"human mountain human sea," huge crowds of people, L12
任何	rèn hé	Adj.	any, L4
日记本	rì jì běn	N.	diary (volume), L8
入口	rù kǒu	N.	entrance, L12

S

三环	sān huán	Abbrev.	The Third Ring Road (三环路), L9
三联书店	sān lián shū diàn	Place N.	San Lian Bookstore, L8
杀人	shā rén	VO.	to kill people, L4
刹不住	shā bú zhù	VP.	cannot brake, L7
山峰	shān fēng	N.	peak of the mountain, L12
商场	shāng chǎng	N.	shopping center, L3
商品	shāng pǐn	N.	commodity, goods, L11
商业	shāng yè	N.	commerce, trade, business, L11
商业化	shāng yè huà	Adj/V.	commercialized; to commercialize, L12
上	shàng	V.	to serve (food), to bring on (a dish), L3
上班	shàng bān	VO.	to go to work, L7
上当	shàng dàng	VO.	to be cheated, L7
上下班	shàng xià bān	VO.	to go to and get off work, L9
上下班时间	shàng xià bān shí jiān	NP.	rush hour, L9
上衣	shàng yī	N.	top, L11
稍等	shāo děng	V.	to wait a moment, L6
烧到	shāo dào	VP.	(fever) reach to (a certain degree), L6

烧茄子	shāo qié zi	NP.	stewed eggplant, L3
蛇	shé	N.	snake, L10
摄氏	shè shì	N.	Celsius, L6
社会	shè huì	N.	society, L4
社会学	shè huì xué	N.	sociology, L5
设备	shè bèi	N.	facilities, equipment, L2
申报单	shēn bào dān	NP.	declaration form, L1
甚至	shèn zhì	Adv.	even to the extent of..., L12
声音	shēng yīn	N.	sound, L9
生词	shēng cí	N.	vocabulary, L5
生命	shēng mìng	N.	life, L12
圣诞节	shèng dàn jié	N.	Christmas, L10
圣诞树	shèng dàn shù	N.	Christmas tree, L10
师傅	shī fu	N.	chef, master worker, general term of address for service personnel, L3
十二生肖	shí èr shēng xiào	NP.	the twelve Chinese zodiac signs, L10
十字路口	shí zì lù kǒu	N.	intersection, L3
实惠	shí huì	Adj.	substantial, solid, L3
实际	shí jì	Adj/N.	actual, practical; reality, practicality, L11
实践	shí jiàn	N/V.	practicum, practice; to put into practice, L9
实现	shíxiàn	V.	to realize, to become reality, L1
使	shǐ	V.	to let, to cause, L4
使馆区	shǐ guǎn qū	N.	embassy area, L11
世界贸易中心	shì jiè mào yì zhōng xīn	Place N.	World Trade Center, L4
市场	shì chǎng	N.	marketplace, market, L7
市内	shì nèi	N.	inside the city, L7
市中心	shì zhōng xīn	N.	downtown, city center, L1
试	shì	V.	to test, to measure, L6
收	shōu	V.	to store, to put away, to collect, L4
收费	shōu fèi	VO/N.	to charge a fee; fee, L6
手工制品	shǒu gōng zhì pǐn	NP.	hand-made products, L11
手续	shǒu xù	N.	procedure, L2
手续费	shǒu xù fèi	NP.	service charge, processing fee, L1
首都	shǒu dū	N.	capital, L1
首都经贸大学	shǒu dū jīng mào dà xué	NP.	Capital University of Business and Economics, L1
寿面	shòu miàn	N.	birthday noodles, longevity noodles, L10
寿星	shòu xīng	N.	birthday person, L10
售货员	shòu huò yuán	N.	shop attendant, salesclerk, L8
受	shòu	V.	to receive (used in passive voice), L3
受骗	shòu piàn	VO.	to be fooled, to be deceived, to be

			cheated, *L7*
瘦	shòu	*Adj.*	thin, tight, *L11*
叔叔	shū shu	*N.*	father's younger brother, *L4*
暑期班	shǔ qī bān	*N.*	summer school, *L12*
鼠	shǔ	*N.*	mouse, rat, *L10*
属	shǔ	*V.*	to belong to..., to be born in the year of (one of the twelve animals), *L10*
水平	shuǐ píng	*N.*	proficiency, standard, *L4*
睡衣	shuì yī	*N.*	pajamas, *L11*
顺	shùn	*V.*	to follow the path of, along, *L12*
顺便	shùn biàn	*Adv.*	conveniently, to do something along the way, *L9*
司机	sī jī	*N.*	driver, *L9*
丝绸	sī chóu	*N.*	silk cloth, *L11*
丝织品	sī zhī pǐn	*N.*	silk products, *L11*
四声	sì shēng	*N.*	the four tones (in Chinese), *L5*
松	sōng	*V/Adj.*	to loosen; loose, *L7*
松仁	sōng rén	*N.*	pine nut, *L3*
送	sòng	*V.*	to give something as a gift, *L4*
宋代 (朝)	sòng dài (cháo)	*N.*	the Song Dynasty (960-1297), *L12*
素菜	sù cài	*N.*	vegetable dish, *L3*
素馅	sù xiàn	*NP.*	vegetable filling, *L3*
速度	sù dù	*N.*	speed, *L9*
塑料袋	sù liào dài	*N.*	plastic bag, *L11*
酸	suān	*Adj.*	sour, *L3*
酸辣汤	suān là tāng	*NP.*	hot and sour soup, *L3*
算	suàn	*V.*	to regard as, to be considered, *L4*
随便	suí biàn	*Adv/Adj.*	do as one pleases; casual, *L8*
孙子	sūn zi	*N.*	grandson, *L4*
索引	suǒ yǐn	*N.*	index, *L8*
锁	suǒ	*N/V.*	lock, to lock, *L7*
锁门	suǒ mén	*VO.*	to lock door, *L4*
所	suǒ	*Classifier.*	classifier for schools and other institutions, *L4*
所有的	suǒ yǒu de	*Adj.*	all, every, *L11*

T

台灯	tái dēng	*N.*	desk lamp, *L2*
堂	táng	*Classifier.*	classifier for class period, *L5*
唐代 (朝)	táng dài (cháo)	*N.*	the Tang Dynasty (618-907), *L12*
躺	tǎng	*V.*	to lie (down) on one's back, *L6*
讨价还价	tǎo jià huán jià	*Idiom.*	to bargain, to haggle, *L11*

讨论	tǎo lùn	*N/V.*	discussion; to discuss, *L5*
套	tào	*Classifier.*	set, *L8*
特地	tè dì	*Adv.*	especially, for a special purpose, *L12*
特点	tè diǎn	*N.*	characteristic, distinguishing feature, *L3*
特色	tè sè	*N.*	characteristic, *L10*
疼	téng	*V.*	to hurt, *L6*
T恤衫	tī xù shān	*N.*	T-shirt, *L11*
提高	tí gāo	*V.*	to raise, *L8*
提醒	tí xǐng	*V.*	to remind, *L10*
体温	tǐ wēn	*N.*	(body) temperature, *L6*
替	tì	*Prep.*	for, *L8*
天安门	tiān ān mén	*Place N.*	Tiananmen, *L9*
天坛	tiān tán	*Place N.*	the Temple of Heaven, *L12*
填	tián	*V.*	to fill out, *L6*
甜	tián	*Adj.*	sweet, *L3*
甜酸肉	tián suān ròu	*NP.*	sweet and sour pork, *L3*
挑	tiāo	*V.*	to select, *L7*
条	tiáo	*Classifier.*	classifier for road, river, rope, etc., *L7*
条件	tiáo jiàn	*N.*	(living) conditions, *L2*
铁板牛肉	tiě bǎn niú ròu	*NP.*	beef on an iron plate, *L3*
听力	tīng lì	*N.*	listening ability, *L5*
听说	tīng shuō	*VP.*	it is said that, (I) heard that, *L1*
停	tíng	*V.*	to stop, *L7*
停车场	tíng chē chǎng	*N.*	parking lot, *L12*
婷婷	tíng ting	*Personal N.*	Tingting, *L4*
通常	tōng cháng	*Adv.*	generally, usually, *L5*
同时	tóng shí	*Adv.*	at the same time, *L8*
统一	tǒng yī	*V/N.*	to unify; unification, *L12*
偷窃	tōu qiè	*N/V.*	theft; to steal, *L4*
头昏	tóu hūn	*Adj.*	dizzy, *L6*
土豆丝	tǔ dòu sī	*N.*	shredded potato, *L3*
吐	tù	*V.*	to vomit, *L6*
兔	tù	*N.*	rabbit, *L10*
推行	tuī xíng	*V.*	to promote, to carry out, *L10*
退	tuì	*V.*	to return merchandise (and get refund), *L8*
退休	tuì xiū	*V.*	to retire, *L7*
拖鞋	tuō xié	*N.*	slippers, *L11*

W

| 袜子 | wà zi | *N.* | sock, *L11* |
| 外办 | wài bàn | *N.* | foreign affairs office, *L2* |

外宾	wài bīn	N.	foreign guests/visitors, L12
万惠商场	wàn huì shāng chǎng	Place N.	Wanhui Shopping Center, L10
王老五	wáng lǎo wǔ	N.	an old bachelor (a character in a famous movie), L10
王义	Wáng Yì	Personal N.	Wang Yi, L1
往	wǎng	Prep.	towards, L3
往回走	wǎng huí zǒu	VP.	to go in the returning direction, L12
为	wèi	Prep.	for, L4
为了	wèi le	Prep.	in order to, L4
伟大	wěi dà	Adj.	great, L12
味精	wèi jīng	N.	MSG, L3
胃疼	wèi téng	VP/N.	to have a stomach-ache; stomach ache, L6
位于	wèi yú	V.	to be located in/at, L11
卫生间	wèi shēng jiān	N.	bathroom (厕所 cè suǒ, restroom), L2
卫生纸	wèi shēng zhǐ	N.	toilet paper, L2
温度计	wēn dù jì	N.	thermometer, L6
文化	wén huà	N.	culture, L9
文具	wén jù	N.	stationery, L8
文史	wén shǐ	Abbrev.	literature and history, L8
文学家	wén xué jiā	N.	writer, man of letters, L8
无聊	wú liáo	Adj.	boring, bored, L4
无论	wú lùn	Adv.	no matter, L7

X

西单图书大厦	xī dān tú shū dà shà	Place N.	Xi Dan Book Center, L8
西方	xī fāng	N/Adj.	the west; western, L10
西红柿	xī hóng shì	N.	tomato, L3
吸毒	xī dú	VO.	to "inhale" drugs, to take drugs, L4
牺牲	xī shēng	V/N.	to sacrifice; sacrifice, L12
希望	xī wàng	V/N.	to hope; hope, L1
习惯	xí guàn	N/V.	habit; to be used to, L10
洗发水儿	xǐ fā shuǐr	N.	shampoo (also called 香波 xiāng bō), L2
洗碗	xǐ wǎn	VO.	to do dishes, L4
洗衣粉	xǐ yī fěn	N.	(powder) detergent, L2
洗澡	xǐ zǎo	VO.	to take a bath or shower, L2
洗澡间	xǐ zǎo jiān	N.	bathroom, L2
下岗	xià gǎng	VO	to be laid off, L7
下面	xià miàn	Adj.	following, next, L9
夏利	xià lì	N.	a brand of small sedan, L9
夏天	xià tiān	N.	summer, L1

咸	xián	*Adj.*	salty, *L3*
现代化	xiàn dài huà	*Adj.*	modernized, *L2*
现金	xiàn jīn	*N.*	cash, *L4*
现象	xiàn xiàng	*N.*	phenomenon, *L7*
馅儿	xiànr	*N.*	filling, stuffing, *L3*
馅儿饼	xiànr bǐng	*N.*	stuffed flat bread, *L3*
香蕉	xiāng jiāo	*N.*	banana, *L3*
香山	xiāng shān	*Place N.*	Fragrant Mountain, *L12*
详细	xiáng xì	*Adj.*	detailed, *L8*
想不出	xiǎng bù chū	*VP.*	cannot figure out, *L10*
想家	xiǎng jiā	*VO.*	to miss home, to be homesick, *L2*
项链	xiàng liànr	*N.*	necklace, *L11*
小便	xiǎo biàn	*V/N.*	to urinate; urine, *L6*
小菜	xiǎo cài	*N.*	appetizer, small side dish, *L3*
小吃	xiǎo chī	*N.*	snacks, light refreshment, *L3*
小贩	xiǎo fàn	*V.*	peddler, street vendor, *L11*
小费	xiǎo fèi	*N.*	tip, *L3*
小公共	xiǎo gōng gòng	*NP.*	mini bus (used for public transportation), *L9*
小说	xiǎo shuō	*N.*	novel, fiction, *L8*
小摊儿	xiǎo tānr	*N.*	street stall, *L7*
小型	xiǎo xíng	*N.*	small size, *L9*
校外	xiào wài	*N.*	off campus, *L3*
写作	xiě zuò	*N.*	writing, composition, *L5*
辛苦	xīn kǔ	*Adj.*	hard, laborious , *L9*
新华书店	xīn huá shū diàn	*Place N.*	New China Bookstore, *L8*
心脏	xīn zàng	*N.*	heart, *L6*
信得过	xìn de guò	*Adj.*	trustworthy, reliable, *L7*
信封	xìn fēng	*N.*	envelope, *L8*
信息	xìn xī	*N.*	information, *L11*
信用卡	xìn yòng kǎ	*N.*	credit card, *L2*
信纸	xìn zhǐ	*N.*	letter paper, *L8*
兴奋	xīngfèn	*Adj.*	excited, *L1*
形容词	xíng róng cí	*N.*	adjective, *L5*
行李	xíng li	*N.*	luggage, *L1*
行人	xíng rén	*N.*	pedestrian, *L9*
行驶	xíng shǐ	*V.*	(vehicles) to run along (roads), *L9*
休息	xiū xi	*V/N.*	to rest, rest, *L6*
修车	xiū chē	*VO.*	to fix the vehicle, *L7*
修建	xiū jiàn	*V.*	to build, to construct, *L9*
修筑	xiū zhù	*V.*	to build, to construct, *L12*
秀水	xiù shuǐ	*Place N.*	(literally "beautiful water") Silk Alley (usually followed by 街 or 市场), *L11*
需要	xū yào	*V/N.*	to need; need, *L1*

虚岁	xū suì	N.	nominal age (reckoned by the traditional method, i.e. considering a person one year old at birth and adding a year each lunar new year.), L10
许愿	xǔ yuàn	VO.	to make a wish, to grant a wish, to make a promise to someone, L10
选	xuǎn	V.	to choose, L5
选课	xuǎn kè	VO.	to select courses, L5
学分	xué fēn	N.	course credit, L5
学期	xuéqī	N.	semester, L1
学问	xué wèn	N.	learning, knowledge, L7
雪碧	xuě bì	N.	Sprite, L2
寻找	xún zhǎo	V.	to look for, to search for, L12

Y

牙膏	yá gāo	N.	toothpaste, L2
牙刷	yá shuā	N.	toothbrush, L2
盐	yán	N.	salt, L3
严	yán	Adj.	strict, L5
严重	yán zhòng	Adj.	serious, severe, L6
研究生	yán jiū shēng	N.	graduate student, L5
羊	yáng	N.	sheep, goat, L10
羊毛	yáng máo	N.	wool, L11
样式	yàng shì	N.	style, L11
邀请	yāo qǐng	V.	to invite, L4
腰果鸡丁	yāo guǒ jī dīng	NP.	cashew chicken, L3
药店	yào diàn	N.	drugstore, pharmacy, L6
药片	yào piàn	N.	tablet, L6
药水	yào shuǐ	N.	liquid medicine, L6
要不然	yào bu rán	Conj.	otherwise (cf. Lesson 7, Sentence Pattern 6), L9
要价	yào jià	VO/N.	to ask a price; asking price, L11
要看	yào kàn	VP.	it depends on..., L1
要命	yào mìng	Adv.	extremely, L2
要求	yāo qiú	N/V.	request; to demand, L5
爷爷	yé ye	N.	paternal grandfather, L4
医疗	yī liáo	N.	medical treatment, L6
医院	yī yuàn	N.	hospital, clinic, L6
一半	yí bàn	N.	half, L11
一大早	yí dà zǎo	NP.	very early in the morning, L6
一定	yí dìng	Adv.	certainly, surely, L12
一定的	yí dìng de	Adj.	fixed, certain, L9

颐和园	yí hé yuán	*Place N.*	the Summer Palace, *L12*
以……为荣	yǐ... wéi róng	*VP.*	to be proud of, *L12*
以……为主	yǐ...wéi zhǔ	*VP.*	to focus on, to be primarily, *L5*
一般	yì bān	*Adj.*	ordinary, general, *L6*
一般来说	yì bān lái shuō	*Idiom.*	generally speaking, *L7*
一边……一边	yì biān...yì biān	*Adv.*	while..., at the same time, *L5*
一方面	yì fāng miàn	*Adv.*	on one hand, *L4*
一会儿	yì huǐr	*NP.*	a little while, *L6*
一门课	yì mén kè	*NP.*	one course (门: classifier for courses), *L5*
一清二楚	yì qīng èr chǔ	*Idiom.*	very clear (清楚: clear), *L11*
意外	yì wài	*N/Adj.*	accident, mishap; unexpected, *L4*
一直	yì zhí	*Adv.*	all along, along a straight path, continuously, *L12*
一桌子	yì zhuō zi	*N.*	a tableful, *L4*
饮料	yǐn liào	*N.*	drink, beverage, *L2*
饮料	yǐn liào	*N.*	drink, beverage, *L3*
印刷	yìn shuā	*V/N.*	to print; printing, *L8*
印象	yìn xiàng	*N.*	impression, *L4*
英尺	yīng chǐ	*N/Classifier.*	foot, *L9*
英里	yīng lǐ	*N/Classifier.*	mile, *L9*
应有尽有	yīng yǒu jìn yǒu	*Idiom.*	have everything that one expects, *L11*
影响	yǐng xiǎng	*N/V.*	influence; to influence, *L10*
拥挤	yōng jǐ	*Adj.*	crowded, *L9*
用	yòng	*V.*	to use, *L5*
用得着	yòng de zháo	*VP.*	to have use for something, *L8*
用法	yòng fǎ	*N.*	usage, *L8*
用户	yòng hù	*N.*	customer, user, *L2*
用品	yòng pǐn	*N.*	articles for use, *L11*
尤其	yóu qí	*Adv.*	especially, *L7*
由	yóu	*Prep.*	by, from, *L8*
由……组成	yóu...zǔ chéng	*Prep...VP.*	to be composed of, *L11*
由于	yóu yú	*Prep.*	because of, due to, *L11*
游客	yóu kè	*N.*	tourist, *L12*
游览	yóu lǎn	*V.*	to tour, *L7*
游览车	yóu lǎn chē	*N.*	tourist bus, *L12*
有趣	yǒu qù	*Adj.*	interesting, *L10*
有效	yǒu xiào	*Adj.*	effective, *L5*
有意思	yǒu yì si	*Adj.*	interesting, *L9*
鱼	yú	*N.*	fish, *L3*
语法	yǔ fǎ	*N.*	grammar, *L5*
语言誓约	yǔ yán shì yuē	*NP.*	language pledge, *L5*
玉米	yù mǐ	*N.*	corn, *L3*
预备	yù bèi	*V.*	to prepare, *L4*

元代 (朝)	yuán dài (cháo)	N.	the Yuan Dynasty (1271-1368), L12
原文	yuán wén	N.	original text, L8
圆珠笔	yuán zhū bǐ	N.	ball-point pen, L8
愿意	yuàn yì	Aux/V.	to be willing to, L7
约	yuē	V.	to make an appointment or date, to agree to meet, L3
钥匙	yào shi	N.	key, L2
阅读	yuè dú	N/V.	reading; to read, L5
运动鞋	yùn dòng xié	N.	sneakers, L11

Z

杂志	zá zhì	N.	magazine, L8
在我看来	zài wǒ kàn lái	Idiom.	in my view, in my opinion, L12
糟糕	zāo gāo	Intj.	terrible, awful, L6
闸	zhá	N.	brake, L7
张开	zhāng kāi	VP.	to open (mouth, eye, etc.), L6
丈夫	zhàng fu	N.	husband, L12
账单	zhàng dān	N.	bill, check, L3
招手	zhāo shǒu	VO.	to wave, to beckon, L9
找	zhǎo	V.	to give change, to search for, L8
照	zhào	Prep.	based upon, according to, L11
照片	zhàopiàn	N.	photo, L1
这样吧	zhè yàng ba	Idiom.	Let's do this., L8
针灸	zhēn jiǔ	N.	acupuncture, L6
枕头	zhěn tou	N.	pillow, L2
枕头套	zhěn tou tào	N.	pillow case, L2
诊所	zhěn suǒ	N.	clinic, L6
蒸饺	zhēng jiǎo	N.	steamed dumpling, L3
整理	zhěng lǐ	V.	to tidy up, to put in order, L2
正好	zhèng hǎo	Adv.	as it happens, fortuitously, by coincidence, L9
政策	zhèng cè	N.	policy, L7
政治	zhèng zhì	N.	politics, L5
芝加哥	zhī jiā gē	Place N.	Chicago, L4
知识	zhī shi	N.	knowledge, L5
……之内	zhī nèi	Prep.	within..., L8
……之一	zhī yī	NP.	one of..., L12
职工	zhí gōng	Abbrev.	staff, employees, L4
直拨	zhí bō	VP.	to dial directly, L2
直飞	zhífēi	VP.	to fly directly to, L1
直接	zhí jiē	Adv/Adj.	directly; direct, L5
执行	zhí xíng	V.	to carry out, L5
值得	zhí de	V.	to be worthy of..., to deserve, L12

只	zhǐ	Adv.	only, L5
质量	zhì liàng	N.	quality, L7
治安	zhì ān	N.	safety, security, L4
中德诊所	zhōng dé zhěn suǒ	Place N.	Sino-German Clinic, L6
中国书店	zhōng guó shū diàn	Place N.	China Bookstore, L8
中外	zhōng wài	Adj/N.	Chinese and foreign; China and foreign countries, L6
终于	zhōngyú	Adv.	finally, L1
种	zhǒng	Classifier.	kind, L2
种类	zhǒng lèi	N.	kind, type, variety, L8
重要	zhòng yào	Adj.	important, L5
周玲	ZhōuLíng	PersonalN.	Zhou Ling, L1
周末	zhōu mò	N.	weekend, L8
周岁	zhōu suì	N.	actual age (reckoned by the Western method, i.e. consider the person one year older with each birthday), L10
猪	zhū	N.	pig, L10
猪肉	zhū ròu	N.	pork, L3
主要	zhǔ yào	Adj.	main, L12
住房	zhù fáng	N.	housing, lodging, L4
注意	zhù yì	V.	to pay attention, L6
祝	zhù	V.	to wish (someone...), L10
专卖	zhuān mài	VP.	to sell something exclusively, L3
专门	zhuān mén	Adj/Adv.	special, specialized; especially, L6
赚钱	zhuàn qián	VO.	to earn money, L7
装	zhuāng	V.	to pack, to load, L11
装订	zhuāng dìng	V/N.	to bind; binding, bookbinding, L8
准备	zhǔn bèi	V.	to prepare, L4
自从……以来	zì cóng...yǐ lái	Prep.	since, L10
自己	zì jǐ	N.	oneself, L6
自来水	zì lái shuǐ	N.	running water, L2
自行车	zì xíng chē	N.	bicycle, L7
自由	zì yóu	N/Adj.	freedom; free, L9
自由神像	zì yóu shén xiàng	N.	Statue of Liberty, L4
字典	zì diǎn	N.	dictionary, L5
总算	zǒng suàn	Adv.	at long last, finally, L8
阻塞	zǔ sè	V.	to block, to clog L9
最	zuì	Adv.	most, -est, L1
最好	zuì hǎo	Adv.	had better, L4
最后	zuì hòu	Adv.	at last, finally, L8
最近	zuì jìn	Adv.	recently, L4
遵守	zūn shǒu	V.	to obey, to abide by, L5
作笔记	zuò bǐ jì	VO.	to take notes, L5
坐车	zuò chē	VO.	to go by car, L6

缩略语表

Abbrev.	Abbreviation
Adj.	Adjective
AdjP.	Adjectival phrase
Adv.	Adverb
Aux.	Auxiliary verb
Classifier.	Classifier/measure word
Conj.	Conjunction
Idiom.	Idiomatic expression
Intj.	Interjection
Loc.	Localizer
N.	Noun
NP.	Noun phrase
Number.	Number word
Personal N.	Personal name
Place N.	Place name
Prep.	Preposition
PrepP.	Prepositional phrase
Pro.	Pronoun
Quan.	Quantifier
V.	Verb
VO.	Verb object construction
VP.	Verb phrase

ALSO BY HONG GANG JIN & DE BAO XU

Shifting Tides: Culture in Contemporary China
An Intermediate Chinese Course
By Hong Gang Jin and De Bao Xu
with Songren Cui, Yea-fen Chen, Yin Zhang
Photography by Laurie A. Wittlinger
Shifting Tides is designed to present intermediate students with the cultural context that will enable them to establish a solid foundation for interaction and communication with Chinese people. After working through *Shifting Tides'* authentic materials and task-based activities and exercises, students will better understand some of the important ideas and perspectives underlying Chinese society. The topics and settings are drawn from the actual experiences of hundreds of students who studied abroad in China; each text is accompanied by language notes that clearly explain how to incorporate new vocabulary, idioms, and grammar patterns into students' everyday speech. In simplified characters.
Paperback, 0-88727-372-6

China Scene: An Advanced Chinese Multimedia Course
By Hong Gang Jin, De Bao Xu and James Hargett
This course provides third and fourth year students with a rigorous but engaging presentation of modern Chinese based on new instructional theories and methods. Subjects are contemporary and diverse, with topics such as single-parent households, film and theater personalities, baby adoptions, China's gymnasts, and the market economy. In the text, students are introduced to new vocabulary and structures through original television texts. The accompanying audio and video materials provide authentic broadcast media reports from mainland China, allowing students to hear and see for themselves how the texts they are reading and translating appear in life. The text includes both traditional and simplified characters, and workbook sections.
Textbook & Workbook, Paperback, 0-88727-330-0
2 Audiocassettes, 0-88727-332-7
VHS Videocassette, 0-88727-333-5

Chinese Breakthrough: Learning Chinese through TV and Newspapers
By Hong Gang Jin, De Bao Xu and John Berninghausen
This audio-visual program targets students who are at the intermediate-to-advanced level, and emphasizes the comprehension of Mandarin Chinese television programs. In addition, the fully annotated ensemble (videotapes, audiotapes, textbook, workbook, and CD-ROM) provides authentic journalistic Chinese in printed form and in the rapidly spoken form of radio and TV news broadcasters. In traditional and simplified characters.
Textbook, Paperback, 0-88727-194-4
Workbook, Paperback, 0-88727-210-X
Mac CD-ROM, 0-88727-248-7
VHS Videocassette, 0-88727-195-2
4 Audiocassettes, 0-88727-211-8

Please visit our website at **www.cheng-tsui.com** for information
on these and many other books.

CHENG & TSUI PUBLICATIONS OF RELATED INTEREST

Cheng & Tsui Chinese-Pinyin-English Dictionary for Learners
Wang Huan, Editor-in-Chief
"What makes this dictionary stand out from most others is that it combines…learner features…with [the] sophistication of some of the better pinyin-English dictionaries."
—Journal of the Chinese Language Teachers Association
Paperback, 0-88727-316-5

Across the Straits: 22 Miniscripts for Developing Advanced Listening Skills
By Jianhua Bai, Juyu Sung and Hesheng Zhang
This thoughtfully developed Chinese language program aims to improve the listening skills of intermediate and advanced students. It utilizes recordings of unscripted conversations on a variety of topics, introducing students to social and cultural issues in Taiwan, mainland China, and the U.S. These engaging dialogues are designed specifically to facilitate learning and provoke discussion.
Student's Book (T), Paperback, 0-88727-305-X
Student's Book (S), Paperback, 0-88727-309-2
Transcript of audio portion (T & S), Paperback, 0-88727-307-6
3 Audiocassettes, 0-88727-306-8

Making Connections: Enhance Your Listening Comprehension in Chinese
By Madeline K. Spring
Listening comprehension is a vital part of language learning—but one that is frequently underemphasized in Chinese textbooks except at the advanced levels (see *Across the Straits*, above). *Making Connections* helps fill that gap for beginning and intermediate students. It offers students an early start to develop strategies that will improve their listening comprehension. This set includes 2 audio CDs, containing natural and unrehearsed conversations by native Mandarin Chinese speakers; the book includes extensive written exercises that guide students through the conversations, and focus on particular aspects of the language that surface in each dialogue.
Paperback with 2 Audio CDs (Traditional Char. Ed.), 0-88727-365-3
Paperback with 2 Audio CDs (Simplified Char. Ed.), 0-88727-366-1

Taiwan Today: An Intermediate Course—Revised Second Edition
By Shou-hsin Teng and Lo Sun Perry
This highly regarded intermediate level text brings the customs, traditions, and manners of present-day Taiwan to life. Interactive student participation is encouraged through the use of role-playing techniques, puzzles, and the presentation of stimulating topics for further discussion. In traditional and simplified characters, with pinyin.
Paperback, 0-88727-342-4
3 Audiocassettes, 0-88727-261-4

Please visit our website at **www.cheng-tsui.com** for information
on these and many other books.